W9-AER-828

SIR WILLIAM DAVENANT

Iv. Grenhill pinx.   W. Faithorne Sculp.

Sir William D'avenant Kt.

SIR WILLIAM
DAVENANT

Poet
Venturer
1606-1668

By
ALFRED HARBAGE

1971
OCTAGON BOOKS
New York

SALEM COLLEGE LIBRARY
WINSTON-SALEM, N. C.

PR
2476
H3
1971

Copyright 1935 by the University of Pennsylvania Press

Reprinted 1971

by special arrangement with the University of Pennsylvania Press

OCTAGON BOOKS

A DIVISION OF FARRAR, STRAUS & GIROUX, INC.

19 Union Square West

New York, N. Y. 10003

LIBRARY OF CONGRESS CATALOG CARD NUMBER: 75-120624

ISBN 0-374-93659-5

Printed in U.S.A. by

NOBLE OFFSET PRINTERS, INC.

NEW YORK 3, N. Y.

To

JOHN and ELIZABETH HARBAGE

94264

PREFACE

THIS book is designed as a companion study to the life and critical estimate of Thomas Killigrew published by the present author five years ago. In it I have attempted to supply the need for a research biography and critical reëvaluation of Sir William Davenant, the most conspicuous of the Cavalier poets, and the one who, with Killigrew, was entrusted by King Charles II with the management of the restored stage. Although practical considerations have delayed publication until the present time, this book was written not long after my book about Killigrew. Since completing it, I have been engaged in preparing a survey of the entire dramatic output of the years of Killigrew's and Davenant's activity—the Caroline, Commonwealth, and early Restoration era—and I have become more than ever impressed with Davenant's key position as chief link between the common and courtly schools of play-writing, and between the old seventeenth-century drama and the new. However, I have felt that to revise the present study in order to stress matters of historical interest would run counter to my original aim: to present *as an individual* a neglected or misunderstood figure—an engaging old writer whose life was always picturesque and whose poetry was sometimes inspired.

My chief debt to recent books is to Leslie Hotson's *Commonwealth and Restoration Stage,* in which are printed several Chancery cases of much biographical interest concerning Davenant. Recently I have read at Harvard his manuscript dissertation out of which Mr. Hotson's volume grew, and I found included there, though excluded from the larger study, allusions to

PREFACE

Davenant quoted from certain seventeenth-century news-letters which I had missed. These added no new episode to Davenant's life as I had reconstructed it, but in several instances they supplied interesting confirmations; and I have referred to them in the footnotes to Chapters IV and V, with the proper acknowledgment. To Mr. Hotson, also, and to Mr. Allardyce Nicoll, I am indebted for guidance through the perplexed early years of Restoration theatrical history. Although I have tried to illuminate the background of a prime mover in theatrical affairs, I have at no point pretended to write a history of the stage.

I wish to thank for their assistance several of my friends and colleagues: Professor Felix E. Schelling for his encouragement while he read parts of this book in manuscript; Professor Albert C. Baugh for sacrificing time from his own researches to lend me his aid at the English Public Record Office; and Dr. Ralph B. Allen, Dr. Edgar L. Potts, and Mr. Edward H. O'Neill for helping me to put the book through the press. I wish also to thank my wife, for her aid with the proof, and, above all, for her good-humored patience in putting up with all this.

A. H.

Philadelphia
January, 1935

CONTENTS

INTRODUCTION

I<small>T</small> appears like sacrilege in our day to couple the names of William Davenant and John Milton. But if the Cavaliers had been challenged to name their champion, they would have matched with easy confidence the author of *Gondibert* against the author of *Paradise Lost*. The two poets were almost exact contemporaries. Davenant was born two years before Milton, and wrote his first play two years before Milton wrote his ode "On the Morning of Christ's Nativity." In 1634, when *Comus* was performed at Ludlow Castle, *The Wits* brought Davenant his first success in the theatre. The literary careers of the two men suffered the same interruption of the Civil Wars while Milton served Parliament and Davenant served the King. Then both returned to Helicon, and Milton's great epic was damp from the press while Davenant's version of *The Tempest* was giving him his final taste of popular success. Within a few years of each other, Milton was buried humbly at St. Giles Cripplegate and Davenant was laid with pomp and ceremony in the poet's corner of Westminster Abbey. Of the two men Davenant had the larger public, the greater popularity in their day. The name Davenant would have spelled poet to more contemporaries than the name Milton, and as symbol of the fact Davenant, not Milton, was England's Poet Laureate.

We may smile at this, but we should not be surprised. Davenant was a professional author in a sense in which Milton was not: His livelihood, his social station, his experiences in life were direct results of the exercise of literary talent, while Milton's life, at least in external outline, would have been little changed had he written nothing but his political tracts. Davenant was recognized by his generation because he expressed his generation, adapting himself to its ideals, its moods, its capricious tastes. Milton's artistic purposes never swerved a degree through popular pressure. The critics may call him Hebraistic, Hellenistic, Medieval, Elizabethan, according to their point of view. Davenant was purely and simply a Carolinian. And that was a limitation! But though Davenant placed a debt upon his own generation, Milton upon posterity, posterity dare not ignore the lesser man. As leading Royalist poet, Davenant complements the picture of Milton, the leading Puritan poet; and the very fact that he expressed the ideals of those who were the traditional patrons of the arts makes him the truer historical index. He was in the main stream of development, and the school which he represents determined the course of literary history for a century and a half.

Davenant's very prominence raises a question which must be answered. How could he, without a fraction of Milton's genius, have achieved such a commanding position? Even among the Cavaliers themselves the initiate considered Waller and Cowley as the better poets. A few witty sophisticates such as Denham and Villiers considered Davenant no poet at all. Yet he won his place, was defended as often as attacked, and having succeeded to the laureateship, was no more disturbed in that position than Ben Jonson had been before him. Dryden, afterwards, looked upon this man with a degree of reverence. The explanation of this success lies partly in the fact that as a dramatist as well as a courtly poet Davenant brought pleasure to a large number of people. But chiefly his success was due to the sheer force of aspiration. He was, as his contemporaries recognized—and this is a matter quite apart from his artistic endowment—a poet in his heart. He brought to the shrine of the Muses a devotion of which the other Caroline writers were incapable. And this devotion was expressed in actual works, for Davenant possessed energy and initiative unparalleled in the enervated circle of which he formed a part.

Energy and initiative made Davenant the Poet Venturer. He was a venturer in the realm of life and of literature. At sixteen years of age he was sent to London with two suits of clothes and £40 to serve an apprenticeship in a city shop; instead of doing so, he penetrated as a page into noblemen's houses, into the society of the Inns of Court, and within a dozen years was a servant of the Queen. He accomplished this feat by skill in the art of the poet and the courtier; yet if asked his vocation he would have replied that he was a soldier. The drums never beat that he did not take the field. He served in Buckingham's last campaigns, in the Bishops Wars, and finally, during the Rebellion, as a general of ordnance and, by way of versatility, as commander of a barque running the Parliamentary blockade. Frequently he played a lone hand. As a youth he offered to coöperate with one other in blowing up Dunkirk. Just before the great upheaval he narrowly escaped execution for joining in a Royalist plot to bring down an army to overawe Parliament. Later he accepted a commission to seek out the imprisoned Charles I, and, as a political expedient, to convert him to Presbyterianism! When the cause of the Cavaliers was lost, he outfitted a ship in Jersey and actually set sail on an expedition to colonize in the American plantations. When past his prime, he recovered from a long Parliamentary imprisonment and absolute destitution by a succession of provident marriages and risky enterprises, so that a decade later he was an elderly London dignitary of whom Pepys eagerly sought information from his gossip, Shoemaker Wotton. There is a charming knight-errantry about all this which removes Davenant definitely from the category of the soft and fawning courtier to that of the man of action.

His literary activities were no less venturesome. His first play echoed belatedly the blood and passion of early Stuart tragedy. Then he suddenly shifted tactics and gave the Caroline audience exactly what it wanted. He had the hardihood to step into Jonson's shoes as the collaborator with Inigo Jones in supplying court masques. Essentially a dramatist, he selected to be his magnum opus a narrative poem in which he would ignore all precedent and institute a new mode of epic literature. Returning to drama, he produced works which have led to his being variously nominated the founder of English opera and the originator of the heroic plays. Finally he essayed to revise Shakespeare to make him palatable to a Restoration audience. His chief literary venture began with his historic duel with the Commonwealth, when he brought back theatrical entertainment to England in the face of express Parliamentary prohibitions and his own status as a recently discharged malignant Royalist. Continuing his playhouse managership into the Restoration, he more than any other one man proved the expediency of women actors and of scenery in the public theatre, and gave us our modern picture-frame stage.

There is certainly enough here to illustrate the interest of the man. Yet Davenant has received practically no attention as an individual. He has been accorded incidental treatment, has been used as a convenient peg upon which to hang a discussion of the decline of the drama, the traduction of Shakespeare, the development of neo-classicism, the heroic plays, the Restoration stage. Perhaps writers have been a little reluctant to appear in Davenant's company: He is one of the disreputables of literary history. In what way, may be illustrated by a few quotations from the many available. First, as to the man himself in his traditional aspect, witness this dialogue in Sir Walter Scott's *Woodstock*:

"Why we are said to have one of his [Shakespeare's] descendants among us—Sir William D'Avenant," said Louis Kerneguy; "and many think him as clever a fellow."

"What!" exclaimed Sir Henry—"Will D'Avenant, whom I knew in the North, an officer under Newcastle, when the Marquis lay before Hull? Why, he was an honest Cavalier, and wrote good doggerel enough; but how came he akin to Will Shakespeare, I trow?"

"Why," replied the young Scot, "by the surer side of the house, and after the old fashion, if D'Avenant speaks truth. It seems that his mother was a good-looking, laughing, buxom mistress of an inn between Stratford and London, at which Will Shakespeare often quartered as he went down to his native town; and that out of friendship and gossipred, as we say in Scotland, Will Shakespeare became godfather to Will D'Avenant; and not contented with this spiritual affinity, the younger Will is for establishing some claim to a natural one, alleging that his mother was a great admirer of wit, and there were no bounds to her complaisance for men of genius."

"Out upon the hound!" said Colonel Everard. "Would he purchase the reputation of descending from poet, or from prince, at the expense of his mother's good fame?—his nose ought to be split."

"That would be difficult," answered the disguised Prince, recollecting the peculiarity of the bard's countenance.

The "peculiarity of the bard's countenance," alas, we shall never escape. Before writing *Woodstock*, Scott had written his *Life of Dryden*, in which Davenant appears in a more dignified light, but Scott was not the man to let facts spoil a good story. But now as to the poet—from a metaphor in Edmund Gosse's *Shakespeare to Pope*:

The vast tree of his [Southey's] poetical works, with its spreading epic branches, its close foliage of tales and ballads, and its parasitical growths of laureate odes and hymns, is dead at the root, and the wind rustles in its dry leaves. It will stand there in the wood, a mere historic memorial, while every year its sisters of the forest put forth fresh foliage and renew their youth. So stands Davenant in that closer and more fantastic grove of the seventeenth century, one of the largest of the trees in girth and height, but the deadest of them all, with scarcely a cluster of green buds here and there when the sap rises in the woodland.

This arborous appraisal illustrates nothing so well as that critics, in practising their "art of praise," secrete by natural laws of compensation a quantity of bile that must be vented at intervals upon minor authors.

All of which leads to this confession. The present writer admires Davenant, and the present study is admittedly a vindication of Davenant as a man and an author. A sojourn among contemporary sources of biographical information and among his poetic and dramatic remains themselves has led to the belief that the traditional conception of the Cavalier laureate is fundamentally false. To what extent this conclusion is based upon anything but a proprietary fondness of the writer for his subject must be left to the charity of the reader to decide. One word of reassurance may be offered, lest anyone suspect that the impulse to whitewash may survive even in our generation—not one fact which the records have yielded up, and by no means all of them are creditable, has been suppressed.

Davenant, albeit he may sometimes have been weak both in the spirit and the flesh, was not a licentious cad, nor a conceited time-server. He was a quixote—courageous, loyal, sincere, rather naïve, but withal shrewd and resourceful. His literary works are not a vast heap of dust and dead artistic issues. Shallowness characterizes them certainly, and we find here neither the sublimity of great poetry nor the depth of great emotions, but they retain to this day a measure of color, charm, and vitality. The traditional conception of Milton as a totally unsympathetic figure, like that of Davenant as a tawdry one, is no doubt distorted and mechanical. Yet generous amiability was certainly not Milton's forte. We prefer to read Milton—true. Yet we should prefer to have made a journey with Sir William Davenant.

I

A TAVERNER'S SON

I

USUALLY a man's birth requires of his biographer no more than a date, a harmless whimsicality or two, and a rapid transition to his less irresponsible actions. But the birth of William Davenant is in a special category. The repute of that occasion has been embellished by the arabesques of anecdote and legend, thus to give us immediate pause. A rumor of illegitimacy is the lion in the path—a kind of aureate illegitimacy—foisted upon Davenant and the world by the ingenious mind of the minor Restoration rake, John Aubrey. The rumor itself, that Davenant was not the son of his father but the son of his father's friend, was not an excitingly novel creation for the late seventeenth century—except in one particular: Aubrey did things in a large way, and selected as Davenant's authentic parent, not any strolling citizen, but the greatest genius of Elizabethan England. The Restoration age was a gossiping one, but the age which followed, that frivolously known as the English Augustan, was even more (and more maliciously) gossiping, and it was at this time that the conception of Davenant and his life story crystallized into its historical form. And at this time men were holding his portrait beside Shakespeare's, and finding in the two a marked resemblance! The portrait in question was the one which (at the risk of prejudicing the reader) has been reproduced as frontispiece to the present volume, so no one need be informed that the resemblance claimed is not striking.

Descent from Shakespeare, on either the right or the left

hand, may be a thing to which neither a poet nor his biographer should object. In fact, Aubrey added spice to his ragout by hinting that Davenant flaunted his own bar sinister. At least one Augustan, Alexander Pope, had the grace to reject this part of the story, and when a friend asked him why, he explained with an elegance befitting the Earl of Oxford's table where they sat, that "There might be in the garden of mankind such plants as would seem to pride themselves more in a regular production of their own native fruits, than in having the repute of bearing a richer kind by grafting." [1]   In later days reputable scholars rejected all of Aubrey's story. But what are scholars? And what is chilling, unsensational truth?   This Restoration rumor, which within a generation had thrust down the deep roots of tradition, is a lusty plant to this day. The one thing which everyone knows about Davenant is that he might have been Shakespeare's son, and the one comment which everyone, with unconscious obliquity, makes upon the subject, is that the fact would be hard to *prove*. It might be gratifying to feel that we were about to trace the career of Shakespeare's son, but in the name of historical accuracy, if not of good manners, we must examine the evidence.

It is lucky, after all, that this old scandal invites a closer inspection of the home life of a certain Oxford family than might otherwise be made. It is not often that anything remains to allow us a glimpse into the obscure homes which produced the poets of three hundred years ago, and in this case it is a home which may actually have known Shakespeare on terms of friendly intimacy. Moreover, the Davenant household is a pleasant place to visit for its own sake—pleasant as any would be where there were domestic peace, sturdy self-respect, a devoted father and mother, and seven handsome and talented children. It is unlikely that in 1606, the year of William Davenant's birth, there was any family in England to which scandal would be less expected to attach.

[1] "Choyce Notes of William Oldys," *N. & Q.*, 2nd Series, XI, 183.

The ancestry of our poet's parents need not detain us long. Of his mother we know only that her maiden name was Jane Shepherd and that her family came from the northerly county of Durham.[2] Of his father's family we can discover much more. The Davenants were good stock. Tracing back to Sir John Davenant, knight of the thirteenth century, the family had established itself by the time of Henry VII as freeholders of the Davenant lands in the parish of Sible Headingham in Essex. In the sixteenth century that branch which was to produce a poet laureate, a bishop, a political economist, and many church and university incumbents, removed from Essex and established itself in London. Although the London Davenants went into trade and the Essex Davenants soon dwindled from existence, the family never lost its tradition of gentility nor forgot that it had once thrived in *worshipful degree*. They retained their arms (Gules, between nine cross-crosslets fitchee or, 3 escallops ermine), and when a Davenant entered a university, though his father might be a small shopkeeper or a taverner, he matriculated *generosi filius*.[3]

They are worth viewing in the large, members of this family, during the sixteenth and seventeenth centuries in their evolution from obscure country gentry, through prosperous tradesmen, to Anglican clergy. As soon as a Davenant made money, he educated his sons and cultivated the universities. However, it would be a mistake to suppose that Trade, the bridge from landed gentility to surpliced gentility, was a base one or was so considered by the Davenants. Even when the family kept shops on Watling Street in the shadow of St. Paul's, their estate was not contemptible. They were Merchant Taylors and were thus affiliated with one of the three most august groups of London burghers. Mem-

[2] *Registers of Westminster Abbey*, p. 168.
[3] A Davenant pedigree appears in Sir Richard Colt Hoare, *History of Modern Wiltshire*, V, ii, 85, 125; and comment on this pedigree in M. Fuller, *Life of John Davenant, D.D.*; their coat is given in trick by Aubrey, see below. For the Davenants at the universities, see *Alumni Oxonienses*, I, 375-76, and *Alumni Cantabrigienses*, II, 13. The conjectural pedigree made by K. Campbell, "Notes on D'Avenant's Life," *M. L. N.*, Vol. XVIII, 1903, proves inaccurate.

bers of the Merchant Taylors' Company, far from being, as the proverb has it, nine to a man, were often men of dignity and affluence, the founders of schools and hospitals.   The Davenants were of this order,[4] and our poet's father was a cousin of Edward Davenant, who was an opulent "merchant of Persia and Russia" and a Cambridge scholar as learned as his nephew, the famous divine, Thomas Fuller, or as his brother Doctor John Davenant, who, as incumbent of the See of Salisbury, became one of the Lords Spiritual.[5]

In forsaking London and the Merchant Taylors Guild to sell wine in Oxford, John Davenant renounced the custom of the Elizabethan Davenants, just as his son, in becoming a poet in-stead of a clergyman, renounced the custom of the Stuart Davenants.   This family produced just one taverner and one poet.   In other respects the Oxford branch ran true to form. Numerous children, usually boys and often appearing in pairs, were the rule wherever Davenants mated.   The poet himself was to have a half dozen sons after he had reached the age of fifty.   The Oxford branch too showed the family conservatism in the choice of Christian names: John, William, Robert—it is hard to find a generation in any line of this family which did not begin by distributing these names; Nicholas, Edward, Ralph, were the next choice, and it was only when families were ap-proaching a dozen that they resorted to such names as Hugh and Dennis.   The poet was to give the name William to two sons by different wives, the proper thing to do, but he was also to name a son Charles, and another Alexander—a symbol perhaps that in these later days the family was losing its old conservatism. The Oxford Davenants also ran true to form in their affiliation with the Church, for although one of them went questing after

[4] *Memorials of the Guild of Merchant Taylors,* pp. 93, 116–17.

[5] For family relationships not included in published pedigrees see the registers of All Hallows, Bread Street, and neighboring parishes (*Harleian Society Publications*), and the wills and other authorities cited by A. Acheson, *The Shakespeare Sonnet Story,* pp. 607–17. This book contains useful information, although it advances the chimerical theory that the Oxford vintner had a first wife who was the Dark Lady of Shakespeare's sonnets.

the Muses, his elder brother, two of his brothers-in-law, and his son-in-law all were to wear the cloth. The father had not descended in the social scale by exchanging the trade to which he had been born and apprenticed for that of a vintner, for vintners were in as high repute as in the days of Chaucer, and a license to sell wine was granted only to a "sufficient citizen."

It is in connection with the issuing of his wine license, and the baptism of his elder children, that we begin to hear of John Davenant in Oxford. By 1604 the names of a son and a daughter had been inscribed in the parish register of St. Martin's Church, and their father had been made free of the city, with the office of a bailiff and the privilege to sell wine in his own right. In the following decade, the vintner and his wife Jane continued to bring their family into the world and to establish themselves as substantial Oxford citizens. In 1612 John, now the father of seven children, became a burgess, and in the following year, a bailiff of the University of Oxford. A few years later the University and the City began to quarrel over which should have the right to license vintners, and John met this situation by the pacific if expensive method of paying both for his privilege. This was characteristic of the man, and until the end he lived in quiet amity with his fellow tavern-keepers, and with the officials of the University and the City Corporation. In 1622 he attained all the dignity which his estate permitted, and became Mayor of the City of Oxford.[6]

So much for the brief external history of this adopted family of the old university town. It is the wineshop itself and the personalities within it that really concern us. The Davenant tavern[7] was a twin-gabled building of two stories with a series

---

[6] For this information see 'Survey of the Antiquities of Oxford' composed in 1661–62 by Anthony Wood, Vol. III, passim, and especially the excellent monograph based on Oxford University records: E. Thurlow Leeds, The Crosse Inn and The Tavern at Oxford.

[7] E. Thurlow Leeds, op. cit. It was during the Restoration that this tavern became known as The Crown. The walls of one of the original rooms has recently been uncovered, and a picture of them with their pious ornamental inscriptions may be found in E. K. Chambers, William Shakespeare, Vol. II.

SALEM COLLEGE LIBRARY
WINSTON-SALEM, N. C.

of rambling additions and a garden to the rear. The site, 110 feet in length, was owned (as it has been ever since) by the warden and scholars of New College, Oxford. Known as Tattleton's House in the sixteenth century, in Davenant's time it was simply The Taverne, and displayed as its sign only the usual vintner's bush. It was situated opposite the Corn Market on High Street, and was thus convenient to anyone entering Oxford on a journey from Warwickshire to London. The Taverne itself was, like The Mermaid, a resort of polite entertainment, retailing wine, and offering neither lodging nor stabling; but neighboring it upon the north was the Crosse Inn which offered both these conveniences, so that a weary traveler from Stratford-upon-Avon might dismount at these twin tenements and find in the combination all that his heart desired.

Here the Davenant couple reared their children with the firm hand of intelligent devotion. The sons were given the best of schooling, but when the eldest of them had entered the University, he was made to know that any wine which he or his college chums should drink must be paid for; and the daughters, although generous marriage portions were reserved for them, were not to consider themselves above waiting behind the bar.[8] The children were: Jane, the eldest daughter, born in 1602 and developing at the time of her parents' death into a docile and thrifty young woman; Robert, the eldest son, born in 1603 and a youth apparently somewhat solemn and prematurely ecclesiastical; two younger daughters, Alice and Elizabeth, both beautiful girls who were to find waiting behind the bar no obstacle to making matches with substantial clergymen; and finally three younger sons, William, the future poet, and his brothers John and Nicholas, of whom we know only that Nicholas was to become an attorney while John was to be apprenticed to a tradesman and was to live and die in the town of his birth. The eldest of these children was twenty and the youngest eleven when

[8] John Davenant's will; see below.

their parents died.[9] If Shakespeare actually came among them, it was when they were all youngsters, and when the dramatist was approaching fifty and had become the Shakespeare of *Cymbeline, The Tempest,* and *The Winter's Tale*—plays with their clearest note a tender solicitude for the brief happiness of children and unstained youth.

That Shakespeare actually did come among them seems probable to all but the complacent agnostic. Although the information comes from John Aubrey, whose intimacy with Robert and William Davenant did not prevent him from playing antics with their mother's name, yet Aubrey, except when the filmy eye and unsteady hand of the morning after made him weak in matters of factual detail, or when his chronic love of scandal or his prejudice against particular persons governed his pen, wrote with honest care. In his words:

Mr William Shakespeare was wont to goe into Warwickshire once a yeare, and did commonly in his journey lye at this home in Oxon. where he was exceedingly respected. I have heard parson Robert [Davenant] say that Mr. W. Shakespeare haz given him a hundred kisses.[10]

This statement coming to us through his friend Aubrey from Dr. Robert Davenant (and let us remember that Shakespeare's kisses were not then so much the boastful distinction we might think them today) is more direct than most testimony concerning the great poet. Anthony à Wood, who leaned heavily on Aubrey's notes but who had his own sources of information (and was himself an excellent customer of the Oxford tavern by the time it had been named The Crown), concurs that the vintner

[9] Transcripts of their baptismal and burial records appear in *Wood's City of Oxford,* Vol. III, *passim;* E. Thurlow Leeds, *op. cit.;* and A. Acheson, *op. cit.* The marriages of the daughters are also indicated in Wood, and our scant insight into the character of these children derives from hints in Wood, Aubrey, their father's will, and their own subsequent careers.

[10] John Aubrey, *Brief Lives Chiefly of Contemporaries,* I, 204–08. Unless otherwise noted this is the reference for all citations of Aubrey in this chapter.

was "an admirer and lover of plays and play-makers, especially Shakespeare, who frequented his house in his journies between Warwickshire and London." [11]

John Davenant must have seen many of Shakespeare's plays on the stage when he lived in London during the great closing decade of the sixteenth century, and he must have been an eager spectator when in October 1606 Shakespeare's company visited Oxford and played before the mayor and the corporation. The taverner's admiration and friendship for the great Elizabethan "play-maker" may account for an interesting fact about his son: In the circle of Caroline and Restoration writers William Davenant was to become Shakespeare's most ardent advocate.

Aubrey's supplementary statement that Shakespeare played the amorous gallant in the home of his friend can be more justly evaluated after we take a parting glance at the taverner's family life. Until 1622 the Davenants lived in Oxford in increasing prosperity and good esteem. A contemporary concoctor of "biting satyres" raking up all the scandal he could about Oxford vintners was forced to omit the Davenant couple from his catalogue.[12] Then at the beginning of April 1622 the mother died. The vintner survived his wife only two weeks, and on the twenty-third of the month, in this the year of his mayoralty, he was borne to St. Martin's Church and laid beside her. This conjunction of deaths, and a recollection of the life the couple had led, appealed to the poetic impulse of Oxford contemporaries, and several elegies remain to commemorate the occasion:

> If to bee greate or good deserve the baies,
> What merits hee whom greate and good doth praise?
> What meritts hee? Why, a contented life,
> A happy yssue of a vertuous wife,
> The choyce of freinds, a quiet honour'd grave,

---

[11] Anthony à Wood, *Athenae Oxonienses*, III, 802–09. Unless otherwise noted this is the reference for all citations of Wood in this chapter.

[12] This interesting although purely negative evidence is offered by J. O. Halliwell-Phillips, *Outlines*, I, 217.

All these hee had; what more could Dav'nant have?
Reader, go home, and with a weeping eie,
For thy sinns past, learne thus to live and die.

A second tribute runs:

> . . . Why should hee dye?
> And yett why should he live, his mate being gone,
> And turtle-like sigh out an endlese moone?
> No, no, hee loved her better, and would not
> So easily lose what hee so hardly gott.
> Hee liv'd to pay the last rites to his bride;
> That done, hee pin'd out fourteene dayes and died.
> Thrice happy paire! Oh, could my simple verse
> Reare you a lasting trophee ore your hearse
> You should vie yeares with Time; had you your due,
> Eternety were short-liv'd as you.
> Farewell, and, in one grave, now you are deade,
> *Sleepe ondisturb'd as in your marriage-bed.*[13]

There is more in these quaint couplets than conventional dirge.

But since elegies, like funeral sermons, are notoriously charitable, it is fortunate that another kind of document remains to reveal the affinity between the vintner and his wife. This document, absorbingly intimate and human, is John Davenant's last will and testament, the sole literary remains of an excellent man.[14]

A few days after he had buried his wife, the vintner had set himself to his task. His mind had been upon his great loss, upon the welfare of his soul, and the future of his children; thinking of these last, he had striven to the utmost "to settle a future amity and love among them that there may be noe strife

---

[13] "On Mr. Davenantt, who died at Oxford in his Maioralty a fortnight after his wife," printed from contemporary MS by J. O. Halliwell-Phillips, *Outlines*, II, 48–49. The elegy first quoted is titled simply "On the Same."

[14] P. C. C., 113 Savile. This will was printed by J. O. Halliwell-Phillips in a twelve-copy edition, 1866; it also appears in his *Outlines*, II, 46–48, and in A. Acheson, *op. cit.*, pp. 658–63.

in the division of those blessings which god hath lent. . . ." One is tempted to linger too long over this will and its provisions. As Mayor of Oxford the vintner wished his funeral to be conducted "in comely manner neither affecting pompe nor too much sparing." He wished to have made, twenty-four hours after his death, an inventory of his household goods, of his pipes and butts of sweet wines, of his tuns of Gascogne. With a large impartiality he divided his estate among his seven children, and then, with singular minuteness, instructed his executors in the careers of these children "till it shall please god to order and direct them to other courses." Although he would not stoop to coercion, he expressed the hope that, provided "he and she can fancy one another," one of his daughters would marry his honest apprentice, Thomas Hallom,[15] in which case the tavern should be conducted by them and one portion of it with its chambers, gallery, kitchen, and "cockeloftes" should be reserved for the use of any of the other children, whenever they, in sickness or in health, should need the haven of their old home. There is an utter forgetfulness of self in this will which fixes for us the character of the man. That his wife was such as such a man deserved is also implicit in the will. We should see this woman as the man who knew her best saw her. He spoke of his estate as "of noe great value considering the many children I have and the mother dead which would guide them," and he made a provision, preceded only by the commission of his soul to God— "my body I committ to the earth to be buryed in the parish of St. Martin's in Oxford as nere my wife as the place will give leave where she lyeth."

Aubrey's blast is best seen in juxtaposition with the above.

His [William's] father was John Davenant, a vintner . . . , a very grave and discreet citzen: his mother a very beautifull woman, and of a very good witt, and of conversation extremely agreable. . . .

---

[15] His wish was granted. Within a year Jane, the eldest daughter, had married the apprentice. He died in 1636, but Jane remained at the tavern until Restoration times. See E. Thurlow Leeds, *op. cit.*

Now Sir William would sometimes, when he was pleasant overe a glasse of wine with his most intimate friends—e. g. Sam Butler (author of Hudibras), &c.—say, that it seemed to him that he writt with the very spirit that Shakespeare [did], and seemed contented enough to be thought his son. He would tell them the story as above, in which way his mother had a very light report.

Warming to his task, Aubrey struck out the last phrase, and applied to Madam Davenant one ugly monosyllable. He repented later and scored out this word very carefully, then the whole sentence; but whereas he had the grace to score out, indefatigable researchers have had the industry to uncover what lies beneath the scorings.

Some will already have formed the opinion that the crux of this whole matter is not a question of whether Davenant was Shakespeare's son, but of whether he claimed he was. The probability is that he did not. No contemporary other than John Aubrey seems to have known of such a claim; his enemies, as we shall see, at one time went to the trouble of preparing two complete publications by way of satirical attack, and they would have made much of such a tidbit. It is not necessary to assume that Aubrey lied. He may have mistaken Davenant. The poet may have claimed a poetical kinship—claimed that he was a "Son of Shakespeare" as others claimed they were "Sons of Ben." It is also possible that he made jests upon the likelihood of another kind of relationship with his parents' friend. How common such tasteless jests were, even between father and son, son and father, is testified by nearly every extant Elizabethan play. But a jest was one thing, a seriously intended allegation of infidelity another, for the integrity of a wife and mother was never more strenuously prized. Loyalty was William Davenant's one great virtue, and the action he is charged with, defaming his mother, is consonant with no other action of his life. One last argument for the cynical: In the eyes of the seventeenth century Shakespeare was a mere poet, a good poet but not a divinity, and no intelligent man of that day would have believed that he could gain prestige by sacrificing his legitimacy for such a kinship. Perhaps more space has been given this subject than it deserves, but the point must be settled if we are to decide what manner of man Davenant was.

It is not an extreme assumption to say that Aubrey was mistaken. He was mind and body of the Restoration, and was apt to see the domestic side of life in terms of a Restoration play. In his words are distinguishable the three main characters: *Dull Husband* ("John Davenant . . . , a very grave and discreet citizen), *Coquettish Wife* (Jane Davenant, "a very beautifull woman, and of a very good witt"), and *Rakish Wit* (Shakespeare!). This pattern is observable elsewhere in Aubrey, for he speaks of Sir John Suckling as getting his wit from his mother, his father "being but a dull fellow," [16] a statement demonstrably false, for the elder Sir John Suckling was in all things except a flair for scintillant verse an abler and brainier man than his dashing but sophomoric son. Aubrey will be useful in later chapters, and we have nothing to gain by discrediting him; we must repeat that he is substantially dependable *except* when personally biased or when writing about conjugal relationships. We may conclude with one more instance of the latter quirk: In noting that Ben Jonson, like the actor, Clun, had one eye larger and lower than the other, Aubrey made the startling deduction, ". . . perhaps he begott Clun"! [17]

Whether there is any foundation to Aubrey's contrast of the personalities of William's father and mother is hard to say. Anthony à Wood ignored the scandal of illegitimacy, but he may have been following Aubrey's notes when he wrote:

The poet's mother was a very beautiful woman, of a good wit and conversation, in which she was imitated by none of her children but by this William, while the father was of a melancholic disposition, and was seldom or never seen to laugh in which he was imitated by none of his children but by Robert his eldest son. . . .

[16] John Aubrey, *op. cit.*, I, 240.
[17] *Ibid.*, II, 14.

That there may have been some disparity in temperament in the poet and his father, that Langbaine's phrase the *Mercurial Son of a Saturnine Father* [18] may be fairly apt, is suggested by a hint in the vintner's will, the specific provisions of which for his most gifted son have not yet been cited.

2

William Davenant's parents, their antecedents, their life in the Oxford tavern, have occupied us thus long, not only because of the rumors about his birth, but because as a boy his life was their life and about him individually there is scanty evidence. Even the exact date of his birth eludes us; however, since the parish register of St. Martin's Church records that on March 3, 1606, was baptized "William Devenet, the sonne of John Devenet vintener," [19] it is certain that he was born late in February of this year. The spelling of the last name is not disturbing, for the name occurs in dozens of forms, from the debased "Dabnett" to the unjustified "D'Avenant" which the poet himself sometimes affected. The first name suggests the pleasant inference so often and so confidently made that William Shakespeare was his godfather and name-giver, but in the absence of any evidence and in the light of the ubiquity of Williams among the Davenants, we must admit of something more than a reasonable doubt.

The figure of Shakespeare confronts us again in connection

[18] Gerard Langbaine, *Account of the English Dramatick Poets*, p. 106.

[19] E. Thurlow Leeds, *op. cit.* The name became fixed as "Davenant" during the seventeenth century, and the poet himself used this form on ordinary occasions. The Frenchified "D'Avenant" he invented for his title-pages, a foible for which he was gibed by satirists:

> Thus Will intending D'Avenant to grace,
> Has made a Notch in's name like that in's face.

Certain Verses Written by Severall of the Author's Friends, p. 23 (see below, (p. 133). Further ridicule, this time concerning the derivation of the name, contains the line, "D'Avenant from Avon comes," (*The Incomparable Poem Gondibert Vindicated,* p. 29), and this has been taken as an allusion to the rumor of illegitimacy, *D. N. B.,* XIV, 101. Had the wits known of this rumor, however, they would never have confined themselves to innuendo. There is no reference to the story by them or by any contemporary other than John Aubrey.

with what may have been Davenant's literary baptism. In his first issue of non-dramatic poems appears an ode "In Remembrance of Master William Shakespeare"—

> Beware (delighted Poets!) when you sing
> To welcome Nature in the early Spring,
> Your num'rous Feet not tread
> The Banks of Avon, for each Flowre
> (As is nere knew a Sunne or Showre)
> Hangs there, the pensive head. . . .[20]

Since this effusion is elegiac and juvenile, it has been generally believed to have been composed shortly after Shakespeare's death, when the taverner's son was a child of ten or eleven. We are always inclined to suspect these proofs of infant prodigy, but it is certain, since he was to evolve as a full-fledged dramatist at twenty-one, that William's poetic development began early. This may be the reason why he was treated differently from his three brothers. This child, with his "beauty and phancy," [21] was evidently of that type, talented but erratic, which is kept at home under parental surveillance. His older brother and his younger brothers were all sent to London to Merchant Taylors' School,[22] but William remained in Oxford, and was destined to trudge each morning from the tavern to All Saints parish where Mr. Sylvester kept his day school.[23]

Schoolmasters are an important part of a man's life. Edward Sylvester was one of those unlucky scholars whose humble origin denied them the money and influence to poise their indubitable learning, and he had become the door mat (almost literally, since he prepared students for entrance) of St. Mary's College, which had bred him. The University condescended to use him at times, and when Metrophanes Critopylus visited Oxford and created there the embarrassing necessity of the University's find-

[20] *Madagascar, with other Poems*, 1638, p. 37.
[21] Aubrey's phrase.
[22] *Register of Merchant Taylors School, passim.*
[23] Anthony à Wood, *op. cit.*, III, 803.

ing someone who could converse in Greek, Edward Sylvester was called upon.[24] In the cogent sentence of a contemporary,

. . . he was the common drudge of the university either to make, correct or review the Latin sermons of certain dull theologists thereof before they were to be delivered at St. Mary's: as also the Greek or Latin verses of others (as dull as the former) that were to be put in, or before, books that occasionally were published.[25]

If William's schoolmaster proved irascible at times, he could hardly be blamed; or perhaps his temper was sweetened by his former students, who, after they had risen one by one to positions of dignity in the University, used to give their old master an occasional dinner, at which times "he would feed their minds with learned discourses and criticisms in grammar."

William gained a great deal at Sylvester's school. For all Aubrey's suggestion that his schooling ceased "before he was ripe enough," the works of his later years display in their allusiveness, and especially in their deep reverence for learning, the badge of an educated man. Several of the poet's schoolfellows later attained rank in the Church. William Chillingworth attended Sylvester's school, and although he was several years older than Davenant, the latter seems to have known this man who is claimed to have risen above his age simply by being reasonable.[26]

It was the custom of John Davenant to keep his sons in school until they were just fifteen. At this age William's elder brother entered St. John's College, which, founded by a member of the guild, granted occasional scholarships to Merchant Taylors' School. Two years later, William may also have entered Oxford, for according to Wood, he matriculated at Lincoln College under the tuition of Daniel Hough, making there "but a short stay." The antipathy of poets for logic is the somewhat stale explanation given for his discontinuing the academic life, Langbaine telling us that

24 *Ibid.*, II, 896.
25 Anthony à Wood, *Fasti Oxonienses*, II, 34.
26 Of one thing Chillingworth did, Davenant did not approve, see p. 51.

. . . his Genius rather inclin'd him to walk in the more flowry Fields of Poetry, in which he made a Prodigious discovery: advancing even without any Guide, but his own Wit and Ingenuity, as far as the Herculean Pillars.[27]

But the fact is that William missed a university career because his father so decreed.

The poet was sixteen when his father died, and the vintner's will, while providing for Robert to remain at St. John's, and Nicholas and John at Merchant Taylors' School, fixed a more disciplinary regimen for the poetic member of the family. William was to receive within a year £150, and at a later date one-seventh of the accrued profits of the wine business, just as his three brothers were, but it was expressly stated that he "being now arrived at 16 years of age shall be put to prentice to some good merchant of London or other tradesman." As a young man William was to prove erratic, and that at sixteen he had already proved rather restive, too mercurial to be trusted as his father's successor and too spirited to be content as anything else, is indicated not only by the fact that the vintner chose his apprentice to manage the tavern, but also by his final insistence that William, outfitted with "double apparrell" and £40 for his master, be sent to London "within the compasse of 3 monthes after my death for avoyding of Inconvenience in my house for mastership when I am gone." This decree put an end to the young poet's life in Oxford:

> City of weathered cloister and worn court;
> Gray city of strong towers and clustering spires:
> Where art's fresh loveliness would first resort;
> Where lingering art kindled her latest fires.

3

William Davenant did go to London, but not to let down the shutters or hold the tape for any of those worthies in the parish

[27] *Account of the English Dramatick Poets*, p. 106.

of All Hallows, Bread Street. In this taverner's son there was a strain of quixotism that drove him from the bourgeois class to which he belonged, and in which he might soon have found a great though unromantic cause, to the other camp, where bannerets fluttered more poetically and music beat to a gayer tempo. He was to become an acquaintance of peers, a servant of majesty, a soldier in the Royal cause, but he might well have lived and died a solid London merchant, perhaps boasting in his age of how he had withstood Prince Rupert's charges while carrying a musket in one of Cromwell's trained bands. There may be some, with fragile appetites appalled by anything but literary delicacies, who think it were just as well if he had gone into trade. The thought was to be suggested in 1668 in one of those satirical elegies with which it was once the unhappy custom to pursue the dead:

> Industrious to a Prodigie,
> Of yt nor the Important Bee,
> Nor ye Grave Ant had more than hee,
> As by his laboured lines ye see.
>
> .   .   .   .
>
> Had hee but some good trade began
> When into riming rage he ran,
> He had been Maire or Alderman,
> But still his Muse did him trepan.[28]

There is a measure of wisdom in this cruelty: Davenant with his boundless energy and shrewd venturousness might have added to golden numbers golden numbers until he carried his port at the head of the city corporation. Success he was finally to attain in his chosen way of life, but it was an unquiet success and won after years of daunting adversity. Misfortune, courted equally by his vices and virtues, was to descend upon him. Poverty and disease, the persecution of political foes, and, worse

---

[28] Written in a copy of Sir John Denham's *Poems and Translations, with the Sophy,* 1668; printed in *N. & Q.,* 4th Series, V, 576.

than either, the taunts and jeers of clever rivals—these he was to know. Within a few decades of his father's death he was himself to face death on three occasions, as familiarly as most men do but once, and in each case it was an ignominious death. John Davenant was a wise man, and by following that man's will, William Davenant would have lived a more contented life.

Yet it is fortunate he did not. After all, there can be much cheapening of all lives if we go in for *post mortem* bargaining. Davenant's life was to prove by no means uniformly unhappy, and it was never to prove drab. He was to have his fat years, and his moments of triumph. He was to taste the pleasure of brilliant companionships, to feel the warmth which kindles at the loyalty of friends, and to know the exuberance of artistic creation. Finally he was to achieve what he wanted most—some small place in the memory of posterity. From our own point of view too it is fortunate that William Davenant did not elect to become a Merchant Taylor. Had he done so, the stage, which is a small precious world in itself, would have missed one of its staunchest supports; and our English literature would have been the poorer for one of the threads which compose its multicolored skein.

FOOT-LOOSE IN LONDON

D AVENANT's first years in London began with an intoxi-
cating sip of high life, and ended with a long and crush-
ing illness. It is a vital period in his career, but a vex-
ing one with which to deal, for his name, that of a youth as yet
totally unimportant, rarely found its way into the correspondence
and official documents which furnish the materials of research.
Such is always the case with that interval in lives thus remote,
between the breaking of home ties and the beginning of a reputation in the world. This period in Shakespeare's life, his "lost
years in London," remains a blank to us. For this period in
Davenant's life all early commentators relied exclusively on the
statement of his contemporary, John Aubrey, that he was a page,
first in the household of Frances, first Duchess of Richmond, and
then in the household of Fulke Greville, Lord Brooke.

Yet this is by no means all that is discoverable. There are
facts available concerning a youthful marriage, an early military
venture, and most important, the auspices under which the poet
began his writing career and made the friends who were to shape
the course of his entire future. Although he is an elusive figure,
and many phases of his youth can be reconstructed only in dim
outline, yet most of the time we can see him. We see him, too,
moving about in a curiously restricted area—an area between
London proper and the royal precincts of Westminster, bounded
on the north by the suburban liberty of Clerkenwell, on the south
by the Thames bending past Temple Gardens, and including

within its narrow strip the region of Holborn, the Inns of Court, Fleet Street, and the Strand.

This was not the neighborhood of "good merchants or other tradesmen," and there is nothing definite to show how the taverner's son found his way here. Given three months to remain in Oxford after his father's death, he must have arrived in London with his double apparel and his £40 in the summer or early fall of 1622. At this time the London Davenants had broken away from the Merchant Taylors' Guild, but the Gore family, which had intermarried with them and had been intimate with the vintner's parents, was still active in the craft, and William's apprenticeship may have been entrusted to them.[1] The Gores were prosperous and influential, and would have had little difficulty if, seeing how his inclinations lay, they had decided to place young Davenant as a page in a nobleman's household. On the other hand, the particular nobleman who concerns us now himself had dealings with London burghers,[2] and may have taken the initiative in rescuing a bright and handsome youngster already left to pine in a City shop. However it was arranged, William was soon precipitated into the charged atmosphere of Ely House, Holborn, the town dwelling of King James's kinsman and Steward, Lodowick Stuart, Duke of Lennox and Richmond.

The year before Davenant's arrival in London, James had arranged a match for Lodowick with Frances, Countess of Hertford, and it was as a page to this rather elderly bride that William was initiated to courtly life. Frances Stuart was such a woman as that age occasionally produced. She was handsome and energetic, but quarrelsome, eccentric, and ludicrously proud. Grandchild of two great peers, the Dukes of Norfolk and Buckingham, and widow of Edward Seymour, son of the first Duke of Somerset, it had seemed to her no signal honor to espouse her sov-

---

[1] For the Gores and the Davenants see *Harleian Society Publications*, "Visitation of London," I, 326; and A. Acheson, *op. cit.*, pp. 607–12.

[2] Lodowick Stuart profited by a kind of partnership with the Merchant Adventurers Company because of his royal patent to export cloth; see *Calendar S. P. D.*, 1634–35, p. 601; *Ibid.*, 1639, p. 540.

ereign's cousin, and she had required the Stuarts to make the concessions. The arrogance of the Duchess was aggravated by the smarting of an old wound. In her youth, some queer quirk, possibly love, had impelled her to marry a citizen, a London vintner named Pranell, and the perpetual urge to live down this old disgrace shaped her later behavior into patterns of high comedy. She snubbed the new nobility created by King James, corresponded with Elizabeth of Bohemia expressly, it seems, to be able to distribute a queen's confidences about the court, and, after the marriage to Lennox, set up an establishment at Holborn which miniatured the royal household at Whitehall. It is this last phase of her foibles which concerns us, for Davenant probably owed his pageship to the augmented suite at Ely House during the years 1622-24 when the Duchess was at her height. One section of this spacious old ecclesiastical mansion was inhabited by Lady Hatton, and in order to humble this woman (who had refused to surrender her lease) the Duchess was wont to appear in state, preceded by four principal officers in velvet gowns and bearing white staves, and followed by a covey of gentlemen-ushers, ladies to carry her train, and "countesses walking in couples behind." [3]

As a page in this household William's duties would have consisted usually of carrying notes and running errands, but would have included anything from strewing fresh rushes about the halls to taking up an ornamental position in one of the processions just described. We know of only one specific service he performed. He told Aubrey that once the Duchess

. . . sent him to a famous apothecary for some Unicornes-horne, which he was resolved to try with a spider which he incircled in it, but without the expected success; the spider would goe over, and through and through, unconcerned. [4]

[3] For these facts concerning Frances, see *Calendar S. P. D.*, 1619-23, p. 554; *Ibid.*, 1623-25, pp. 86, 441; and the biographical notices of her husbands, *D. N. B.*, LI, 311, LV, 107.

[4] John Aubrey, *op. cit.*, I, 205.

Unicorn's horn, which dealers of the time found advisable to sell in powdered form and (naturally in view of its rarity) at a high price, was a specific against many ills, including poisoning, and the Duchess probably used it in her hobby of concocting drugs and potions. Once when the wife of George Villiers was ill, she administered her broths and "caudles" so efficaciously that they touched the gratitude of King James to the extent of £3500.[5] For all her contempt for the new nobility, Frances was shrewd enough to except from her disfavor such rising favorites as the Buckinghams. Her husband Lodowick was constantly receiving new offices and emoluments to counterpoise those heaped by King James upon his "Steenie," and apparently Ely House made it a point to cultivate the handsome young man who was soon to become England's virtual ruler.

The *entente cordiale* between the Richmonds and the Buckinghams is significant because it may account for the inception of the friendship between William Davenant and Endymion Porter. Endymion Porter, who as a beloved servant of Charles I and as a patron of the arts was to become Davenant's greatest friend and benefactor, had married in 1620 Buckingham's niece, Olivia Boteler, and during the period with which we are dealing he was in the household of the favorite as his master of the horse, and was soon to be his trusted agent in the Spanish match and other great matters of state.[6] No doubt he, as well as his master, was often entertained by Frances Stuart. Others besides Porter may have taken notice of the Duchess's page, for Ely House was a strategic position in which to be placed. For two years it was a social center of the first brilliance, and here was entertained everyone from royalty to Toby Mathews and Gondomar, ambassador from Spain.[7] This *milieu* and this magnificence must have been educational to the boy fresh from the drowsy lanes of Oxford, but they must also have been "unsettling." In either case, he was not exposed to them long. In

[5] *Calendar S. P. D.,* 1619–23, p. 380.

[6] D. Townshend, *Life and Letters of Endymion Porter.*

[7] *Calendar S. P. D.,* 1619–23, p. 390.

February 1624 Lodowick Stuart died, and his Duchess, after cutting off her hair and exhibiting a picturesque grief, rapidly subsided. One shrewd observer remarked that her grief was chiefly that her reign as prime courtier was over,[8] and it was rumored that she now had matrimonial ambitions aiming at the King himself. But the following year James died, and by 1627 Frances had retired to the country and was humbly petitioning the new government for a yearly pension of not one-fifth the sums formerly granted her as his Majesty's free gift.[9]

The alteration in the affairs of the Duchess after her husband's death is only one of the indications that William left her service early in 1624. At the time of the Duke's death, or shortly before, he came into the £150 provided him by his father's will, and we are startled to learn that, although he was only eighteen and had neither a settled occupation nor a future, he celebrated his influx of riches by getting married. Except that her name was Mary, that she bore her husband two children, and that she died before these children were fully reared, we can discover little about this early wife. About two later marriages of the poet we have fuller information, and since these were disturbingly like business ventures, we may hope that his youthful marriage was as idyllic as it was indiscreet. We are reminded of one of his lyrics which, departing as it does from the occasional nature of most of his non-dramatic verse, occurs in curious isolation among the poems in the folio "never before printed":

> The Lark now leaves his watry Nest
> And climbing, shakes his dewy Wings;
> He takes this Window for the East;
> And to implore your Light, he sings
> Awake, awake, the Morn will never rise,
> Till she can dress her Beauty at your Eies.
>
> The Merchant bowes unto the Seaman's Star,
> The Ploughman from the Sun his Season takes;

[8] *Ibid.*, 1623–25, p. 167.
[9] *Ibid.*, 1627–28, pp. 100, 110.

But still the Lover wonders what they are,
   Who look for day before his Mistress wakes.
Awake, awake, break through your Vailes of Lawne!
Then draw your Curtains, and begin the Dawne.[10]

These gracious lines, worth quoting for their own sake, would
have been appropriate had Mary been some gentle attendant
upon the Duchess of Richmond, but not so appropriate in the
more probable alternative that she was an apple-cheeked barmaid in one of the numerous Holborn taverns. However, they
may suggest to the sympathetic the emotions attending the love
affair of an eighteen-year-old poet—and must serve in lieu of
love letters, a sonnet sequence, or a tender epitaph, all of which,
unhappily, do not exist.

   Neighboring Holborn upon the north were the bowling greens
and vegetable gardens of the thinly settled suburb of Clerkenwell,
and it was in this district that the young couple began their
married life. On October 27, 1624, the baptism of William, son
of William and Mary Davenant, was recorded in the parish
register of St. James, Clerkenwell.[11] A daughter, Mary, was
born soon afterwards, but the date of her birth like the exact
date of her parents' nuptials entirely eludes us. These two children ultimately found their way to Oxford, probably to the old
tavern kept by their aunt, Jane Hallom, which their grandfather
had wisely decreed to be an asylum for his children. It was at
Oxford that the son was to die and that the daughter was to
find her husband, Thomas Swift, fellow of Balliol College.[12]
But this was not until the time of their father's thin years during
the Commonwealth, and they were first to share his foreign
exile and its disastrous conclusion. William's first wife and her
two children will confront us in future years, but until the end

[10] Folio, 1673, p. 320. This lyric has been selected for reprinting in the
Oxford Book of English Verse, and elsewhere.
[11] Harleian Soc. Publications, "Register of St. James, Clerkenwell," I, 99.
[12] Wood's City of Oxford, III, 172–73. The daughter is also mentioned in
a chancery case printed by Leslie Hotson; see below. Her husband, Thomas,
was a near kinsman of the father of Jonathan Swift.

they remain but shadowy figures in the background of his youth.

Within a few years of his marriage William was living a life indistinguishable from that of a bachelor. He entered a second nobleman's household, went abroad to the wars, and lived for a time in the man's paradise of the Inns of Court instead of in the Fleet Street household where he seems to have established his family after leaving Clerkenwell. All of this, let it be remembered, was not unusual for an amicably married man of the time. The adroitness with which husbands then evaded domestication must remain for men of today a thing of almost reverent awe. Of course if we knew more of Mary Davenant, we might find that she was not always pleased with her active young husband. One of the most interesting correspondences of the day is that between Davenant's friend, Endymion Porter, and his wife Olivia. Endymion was obliged by his duties as a courtier to spend most of his time from home, and one of his major activities was composing love letters to pacify his lonely and irate wife. A biographer can only regret the fact that Time has permitted the survival of no similar series of letters to reveal the intimate relations of William and Mary.

2

The friendship between Davenant and Porter does not emerge clearly until some years after the poet's marriage, but it may be that this courtly lover of music, painting, and poetry, having noticed Davenant in Richmond's household, was instrumental, after his service there had ended, in placing him in the neighboring Holborn mansion of Brooke House. Endymion was acquainted with Lord Brooke, for the old Elizabethan poet and statesman had been his father's friend. He had stood as godfather for one of Endymion's brothers, and his kinsman, Sir Edward Greville, had been a neighbor of the Porters at Aston-under-Hill upon the Cotswold downs.[13] Of course it is purest

13 D. Townshend, *op. cit.,* pp. 4, 134.

supposition that Porter secured Davenant his place with Fulke Greville, and it may even be that it was at Brooke House that they first became acquainted. Either alternative is unimportant compared with the salient fact that the poet was actually received into the home of the great Lord Brooke—*Servant to Queen Elizabeth, Councillor to King James, and Friend to Sir Philip Sidney.*[14]

Brooke House between 1624 and 1628 was the sanctuary of a man who had grown old in the service of a nation whose springtime he had outlived. With what emotions he watched Buckingham's overtures to the nation of the Catholic Armada, or sat through the fiascoes of the council board to which he was still called at times of national crisis, we can conjecture. It is to the credit of James that Greville was treated generously so that his declining years lacked neither private means nor public prestige. After 1625 when Charles I and Buckingham had ascended the throne, and when it is most likely that Davenant entered his service, Greville had retired almost completely from public life and was occupying himself with the poetry to which he had been devoted all his life. A garbled account of these twilight activities comes to us from John Aubrey:

. . . This Sir Fulke G. was a good witt, and had been a good poet in his youth. He wrote a poeme in folio which he printed not till he was old, and then, (as Sir W. said) with too much judgement and refining spoyled it, which was at first a delicate thing.[15]

None of Greville's work was printed until late in life and very little until after his death, and since all of it underwent constant revision, it is impossible to say what poem Davenant had mentioned to Aubrey. Still it is interesting to hear that he made this, indubitably just, stricture upon his master's literary efforts.

It is curious that Davenant's life should have touched the lives both of Shakespeare and Fulke Greville, for no two men

---

[14] His Epitaph, written by himself.
[15] John Aubrey, *op. cit.*, I, 205.

could have been better touchstones of the literary greatness of the preceding age. Greville had been of the Pembroke circle, an intimate not only of his idol, Philip Sidney, but also of the greatest of the non-dramatic poets, Edmund Spenser. His fidelity to letters had shown itself in patronage of the gifted, and Camden, Bacon, and others had known his kindness. Samuel Daniel wrote that Greville,

> Did first draw forth from close obscuritie
> My unpresuming verse into the light,
> And grac'd the same, and made me known thereby. . . .[16]

No similar lines have reached us from the pen of Davenant, and it is unlikely that Greville was ever his active teacher. Yet it is remarkable that Davenant was to become the outstanding one among the Royalist poets who advocated the doctrine, explicit in Sidney's *Apologie for Poetrie* and implicit in all of Greville's works, that poetry is, to use Walter Scott's phrase, "an auxiliary of religion, policy, law, and virtue." And just as his dramas often reflect his love of Shakespeare, so his non-dramatic poem, *Gondibert,* the work he prized most, often reminds us of the gnomic and preceptorial quality of the poems of Lord Brooke.

There is nothing to show in what capacity William served in Brooke House. Aubrey conjectured that it was again as a page, but this is unlikely since by now he was approaching his majority. He may have been a groom, or even, considering his particular talents, a kind of clerk or amanuensis. In September 1628 Lord Brooke was murdered by a malcontent servant, and Aubrey has preserved some intimate details of the event which Davenant had furnished him, among others that the tragedy "was at the time that the duke of Buckingham was stabbed by Felton, and the great noise and report of the duke's, Sir William told me, quite drowned this of his lord's." [17] This statement checks so well with the dates of the two assassinations that it lends some weight

---

[16] *Certain Small Works,* 1607; quoted in *D. N. B.,* XXIII, 159 ff.
[17] John Aubrey, *op. cit.,* I, 205.

to Aubrey's affirmation that Davenant served Greville until the latter's death.[18] But in that case it must have been an intermittent service, for by September 1628 certain passages in the checkered youth of the poet carried him not only away from Brooke House but even away from England.

3

The beginnings of Davenant's literary and military careers are so intertwined that it is impossible to treat of one without the other. The literary career began first, and, strange that so interesting a fact has been missed, it came partly under the ægis of that breeding place of lawyers, statesmen, poets, and gallants—the Inns of Court. On January 12, 1627, Davenant's first play, *The Cruel Brother,* was licensed for the stage and was thereupon acted by his Majesty's Servants at Blackfriars.[19] It was not a huge success, and when its author came forth with a second play, *Albovine, King of the Lombards,* the actors—"Copper-lac'd Christians" as they are called in verses commending the published version of the play—could not be persuaded to produce it. Yet both these plays contain fine things, and often remind the reader that the Shakespeare folio, published four years before, had put the greatest of all plays constantly within the young poet's reach. Davenant was just twenty-one, and these first plays—they are tragedies of course—bear the stamp of the literary neophyte: They are old-fashioned for their time. Both of them are dramas of blood and revenge such as had had their vogue in the first decade of the century. After a year's interruption, occasioned as we shall see by the call to arms, the aspiring dramatist produced two more plays, *The Siege* and *The Just Italian.* These, one a tragi-comedy and the other a serious comedy of

---

[18] Greville's assassin was himself an old man, and followed his act of violence with suicide. Davenant expressed some sympathy for him; and that he had not entirely lacked provocation is attested by a tract, "On Patronage and Dependency" (B. M. Add. MSS, 4839, 27), and by several contemporary poems (*Works of Fulke Greville, Lord Brooke,* I, xcv–c).

[19] *Dramatic Records of Sir Henry Herbert,* p. 31.

manners, were better keyed to the tastes of the day, and both were licensed and acted in 1629.[20]

So much for summary. The question now arises as to where and why these plays were written. It is commonly known that James Shirley, Fletcher's successor as most popular English dramatist, gave up school teaching after 1625 and lived for a time in Gray's Inn, where he found his literary vocation. It now appears that at about the same time, a second of the four Inns of Court (and the one, by the way, which had produced John Ford) was incubating the playwright who was to rival Shirley in popularity. We come to this conclusion by a somewhat circuitous route. Davenant first appeared in print in 1629 when *Albovine* was published, prefaced by no fewer than eight sets of commendatory verses. The first of these was contributed by the Lord Chief Justice's nephew, Edward Hyde, future Earl of Clarendon, historian of the Civil Wars, and virtual Prime Minister of England. In January 1626 Edward Hyde, having left Oxford, had entered the Middle Temple,[21] where, by his own confession, he showed less interest in reading law than in cultivating the wits and the social and literary amenities of his day.[22] In 1627, after a period of illness, he gave up his single room and acquired a suite of chambers including a kitchen, woodshed, and study on the fourth floor of the new wing.[23] A relative of Davenant, Gerard Gore, had been admitted to the Middle Temple in 1626,[24] and whether or not this gave William his entrance to the place, it is certain that by 1628 he had been welcomed into this circle of gentlemen's sons and was lodging with Edward Hyde in his commodious new apartments.[25] We are not surprised then to find that Roger Lorte, another contributor of verses to *Albovine*, had been admitted to the Middle Temple in

---

[20] *Ibid.*, p. 32.
[21] *Minutes of the Parliament of the Middle Temple*, II, 703.
[22] *Life of Edward Earl of Clarendon written by Himself*, I, *passim*.
[23] *Minutes of Parliament of the Middle Temple*, II, 725.
[24] *Ibid.*, II, 713.
[25] State Papers in the Public Record Office, 16: 126; item 42; see below.

May 1627,[26] nor that Davenant was befriended in later years by Bulstrode Whitelocke, since the latter was a Middle Templar at this time and a few years hence a colleague of Edward Hyde in organizing a magnificent Inns of Court masque to entertain royalty.[27] This masque, calculated to soothe the tender sensibilities of the King and Queen injured by the attack on court theatricals in Prynne's *Histriomastix,* was a coöperative effort on the part of the four Inns, and Shirley was selected to write it; but when the Middle Temple gave a masque individually a few years later, we shall see that William Davenant was selected as the author. There is no doubt that he was claimed by the Middle Temple as surely as Shirley was by Gray's Inn.

The names of those who commended *Albovine* have proved revealing even though most of these names are quite obscure. One which is not obscure is that of the poet William Habington, who also wrote verses for the Gray's Inn dramatist, James Shirley, commending his *Wedding* published in the same year as *Albovine.* It appears that Davenant had his circle of friends at Gray's Inn as well as at the Temple. Henry Blount, not unknown to students of literature, helped to herald *Albovine* although he was a member of the rival Inn.[28] This is true also of the brothers, Thomas and Robert Ellice, both of whom contributed their praise to the tragedy, and both of whom, one in February and one in August of 1627, had entered Gray's Inn.[29] In view of Davenant's family calling and his possible friendship with the Gores, it is worth noting that Thomas and Robert were the sons of Griffith Ellice, a Bow Lane Merchant Taylor.[30] Final evidence connecting Davenant with a Gray's Inn group, which must have included Shirley, is the fact that he now became a boon companion of the poet John Suckling, and John Suckling had

---

[26] *Minutes of Parliament of the Middle Temple,* II, 721.
[27] Sir Bulstrode Whitelocke, *History of England* . . ., 1713, p. 4.
[28] *Register of Admissions to Gray's Inn,* p. 160.
[29] *Ibid.,* pp. 181–82.
[30] *Memorials of the Guild of Merchant Taylors,* p. 593.

been admitted to Gray's Inn in the same year as the Ellice brothers.[31]

Davenant's association with the Inns of Court has been insisted upon for several reasons. It will interest the student of literature as one more example of the influence exerted upon the drama by these Inns ever since they had been instrumental in producing *Gorboduc*, the first English tragedy. It is interesting too as a shaping influence upon the poet's life. The Inns of Court furnished the nearest approach to a liberal education obtainable in England at the time. In contrast with the stilted curricula of the ecclesiastical institutions of Oxford and Cambridge, the Inns provided means to acquire such accomplishments as modern languages, elocution, and dancing. Organized ostensibly to train lawyers, they were actually much patronized by prospective heirs sketchily interested in how to manage their estates. Here William might have met scions of most of the leading families of England, a residence among whom would have divested him of any rusticity not already polished away by his training as a nobleman's servant. These young men had built up for themselves an equivalent to that sacred thing cherished by modern students as "College Life." They formed smart cliques, tasted the pleasures of London, and contracted debts. Their governors were often worried at the proportion of time spent in study to that spent at the playhouses or in mastering the new vice of "drinking" tobacco. But despite its streak of rakishness, this was an intelligent and cultivated society, and the weight of legal study never pressed hard upon a love of literature and a love of life. Davenant was only a guest at the Middle Temple, but this distinguished him little from many of the students regularly enrolled.

Unlike the regularly enrolled students, Davenant was free to leave the Temple at will, and right in the midst of his first period of play-making he answered a call to arms. In the year 1628,

[31] *Register of Admissions to Gray's Inn*, p. 180.

as the result of Buckingham's vagaries, war fever was in the air. A token of our poet's martial spirit has come down to us in a document recording his offer to wage single-handed warfare against the port of Dunkirk. Buckingham had wanted to seize this wasp's nest of privateers ever since hostilities had opened with Spain, and here we have our twenty-two-year-old dramatist, like a character in one of his own plays, coming blithely forth with the means:

The action I would preferr unto your Lo^{pp}, concernes the Store-howse, or Magazin of Dunkerck; and is to be effected, by a secrett illumination of Powder. The meanes to this performance, I arrive at, by the easinesse of a friend; whoe is now Officiall in the Magazin; and his assistance hath given me power to receave imploymente there. I have knowledg of a small Engine, that will inforce a usefull fire, at my owne limitte, or just when some assault upon the Towne shall apoint the distruction of the Powder. If ought in this certifi-cate give hope of advantage to his Matie, I shall performe the service, though with the losse of my life.
                    Endorsed m^r Dauenant lodging
                       in ye middle temple
                       with m^r Hide; sonne
                       to my Ld Chiefe Ius-
                       tice elder brother.[32]

The offer caused no flutter among the war lords, but let us hope that it received a smile of sympathy. It is characteristic of Davenant and the quioxtic enthusiasm which marked his whole life.

While William was not permitted to enforce his useful fire at Dunkirk, he was permitted to take part in a military project almost as foolish. The culminating blunder of Buckingham's career was his expedition to aid, whether it wished aid or not, the Protestant city of Rochelle threatened by Louis and the Cardinal. In June 1627, 6,000 foot and 100 horse left Portsmouth

[32] State Papers in the Public Record Office, 16: 126, item 42; written by Secretary Dorcaster and catalogued "abt. 1628."

under the Duke's personal leadership, and laid siege to St. Martin's on the Isle of Rhe near Rochelle. This army (of "rogues and vagabonds") was so ill trained and mutinous that Buckingham had to flog his men to attack, and neither his gallantry nor the courage of a sprinkling of faithful followers could avert a terrific defeat. In November of the same year the army, or the remaining half of it, returned sick and starved to England. Nevertheless the following spring saw the Duke raising levies for a second expedition, and that William Davenant had gone on the first and planned to return on the second appears from the following letter:

Mr Nicholas, this young gentleman, Mr William Davenant, has heertofore been imployed in ye warrs abroad in forrain countries. Hee is my neer kinsman, & one whome I wish well; in regard whereof I should bee very gladd, yf it lay in mee to doo him any good. As hee tells mee, hee hath ye place of an Ancient, or lieftenant already; and is in some hope when new Regiments shall bee raised, of further advancement. I assure my selfe that you may have opportunity to doo him yt favour in such a busines, wch I have not. Wch yf it shall please you to doo when time serves, I doubt not but you shall therein bee a means of promoting a serviceable young man, & of good abilities. As for mee, I shall account ye obligation wholy mine, & shall bee alwaies willing to requite your kindenes, in any thing that may fall wthin my power. And thus committing you to ye blessing of ye Almighty, I rest

Westminster   Your very loving friend.
April ye 8th 1628.   Io: Sarw.[33]

The author of this letter, John Davenant, Bishop of Salisbury, was well disposed toward his distant cousins from Oxford. When Robert, the poet's elder brother, had taken orders, the Bishop preferred him as his chaplain and later as prebend-elect of Salisbury.[34] He had no children of his own, his predecessor in the bishopric having died "in a mean condition," the father of

---

[33] State Papers in the Public Record Office, 16: 100, item 59.
[34] John Aubrey, op. cit., I, 204; Anthony à Wood, Fasti Oxonienses, II, 239.

fifteen children, and King James having commanded (not without reason) that the next bishop "should not take to him a
wife." [35] This concession to high church would have been no
hardship for the devout John Davenant, but he must have subsequently regretted the days when he was simply Margaret
Professor of Divinity at Cambridge. His leanings were Presbyterian and he represented England at Dort during the council
on the modernistic doctrines of Socinus, but when he continued
to show a fondness for the subject of predestination he was driven
to submissive knees before Archbishop Laud. He was a good
man. Had all the bishops been like him, they would never have
become the symbol of all things hated by Puritan England. It
is worth noticing that such a man, even though his acquaintance
with him must have been of the slightest, considered William
"a serviceable young man and of good abilities."

Whether or not William got the commission he was after, and
went on the second Rochelle expedition, is not certain. Apparently he did go on the expedition in some capacity. The
Earl of Newport participated in these campaigns and Davenant
was later to serve in the ordnance department under Newport.
A letter from Suckling to Davenant dated November 1629 indicates that the two had a mutual friend named Brett, and the
Bretts were a family of soldiers who performed notable service
in the attacks on the Isle of Rhe.[36] This is tenuous evidence, but
it is supported by testimony more explicit. Under what unhappy
auguries Buckingham's second expedition set out is well known.
After months of struggle to collect money and men, the Duke
was ready to sail from Portsmouth in August of 1628. On the
twenty-third of the month, he was stabbed by the most beloved
assassin of history, John Felton, and his army sailed on Septem-

[35] The predecessor was Robert Tounson, John Davenant's brother-in-law; cf.
Anthony à Wood, op. cit., I, 283. Particulars of Bishop Davenant appear in
M. Fuller, Life of John Davenant, D.D., the D. N. B., and elsewhere.

[36] Calendar S. P. D., 1627-28, 1628-29, passim; for Suckling's letter see
below.

ber 7 under the Earl of Lindsey. In October it returned inglori-
ously home, and England smarted under a humiliating peace.
Not long after the return of the army, Davenant's *Albovine*
was published and the commendatory verses written by Thomas
Ellice contain the lines:

> Wise Fame shall sing the praise of thy deserts,
> And voice thee glorious both in Arms and Arts.
> Whilst thou, releast from the Wars sad mishaps,
> Rests in soft dalliance on the Muses' laps. . . .

This proof [37] that Davenant sallied forth the second time as well
as the first is made more conclusive by the fact that his first four
plays were licensed for the stage and for the press, before and
after, but not during, the two expeditions to aid Rochelle.

One phrase in Ellice's tribute, "glorious both in Arms and
Arts," might have struck Davenant with somewhat rueful amusement. There had been nothing glorious about the Rochelle expeditions, and thus far the *Arts* had proved equally stinting of
triumphant garlands. His plays were failing upon the stage.
Albovine had not been acted at all, and although it is unknown
what fate greeted *The Siege,* it is certain that the Blackfriars
audience showed no enthusiasm for either *The Just Italian* or
The Cruel Brother. In his dedication to the first of these plays,
Davenant spoke of the age having "grown unworthy to receive
such truths," and in his dedication to the second he told how
"The uncivil ignorance of the People had deprived this humble
Work of life." His complaint in this second case is elaborated
by commendatory verses written by Thomas Carew which tell
how the sullen age loves only satire and has no taste for "strong
fancies, raptures of the brain, drest in poetic flames" or for anything that "exceeds Red-Bull and Cock-pit flight." Finally they
console the author:

[37] These lines suggested that there must have been an early military career
to Killis Cambell, *M. L. N.,* XVIII (1903).

> . . . men great and good
> Have by the rabble been misunderstood:
> So was thy Play, whose clear, yet lofty strain
> Wisemen, that govern Fate, shall entertain.

It is a fact that the high astounding terms of Davenant's plays were of a romantic fashion no longer acceptable and would have been better received twenty years before. The first two of them at least were, in a special sense, too Shakespearean.

Carew's contrast of the "rabble" and the "wisemen that govern fate" is significant in view of the manner in which the author brought out his plays in quarto form. In 1629–30 when these first quartos appeared, the feeling between the English people and their rulers was approaching mutual antipathy. London was nine-tenths Puritan, and nine-tenths opposed to Stuart absolutism. It was a time for choosing sides, and that Davenant had made his choice is clearly indicated by the men whom he selected as dedicatees: They might have been selected solely on the basis of their offensiveness to the English citizenry. *Albovine* was dedicated to Robert Carr, Earl of Somerset, *persona non grata* ever since the favoritism of King James had saved him from the consequences of the murder of Sir Thomas Overbury. *The Just Italian* was dedicated to Edward Sackville, Earl of Dorset, alive in the long memory of London Puritans for having killed Edward Bruce in a duel during an alleged liaison with Venetia Stanley.[38] *The Cruel Brother* was dedicated to Richard Weston, Lord High Treasurer and Buckingham's successor as the most detested man in England. Davenant had certainly elected to be a Royalist. The influences that had been acting upon him were of a kind to make him so, but a hurt vanity over the reception the populace had given his plays may also have had its weight.

The names of the great lords appearing in these early quartos should not deceive us into thinking that William had already

---

[38] *D. N. B.,* L, 90.

been recognized in courtly circles. He had made his entering wedge, but he was still on the outside looking in. It was to be several years yet before he was to emerge as the successful courtier poet. We get our truest picture of him at twenty-three or twenty-four if we see him simply as a young man strongly attracted by the glamour of fashionable circles, sincerely devoted to poetry, but alert to find advancement whether as a poet, a soldier, or a courtier. Affable and vivacious, he was finding popularity in a widening circle of friends. Most of these friends were young men of his own age, better connected than he, but as yet of no more importance in the world. Unfortunately for him, they were inclined to set up as *bon vivants* as well as wits, and he shared their pleasures. Drama and war did not occupy all of his time. His youth had this third and more festive side— a side which culminated in a disaster worse than the hisses of groundlings or the superior strength of military foes—three years of painful and devastating illness.

4

Davenant's companions were recruited from two groups, and neither of these groups—the smart set at the Inns of Court or the regimental officers in Buckingham's army—listed continence and sobriety among the distinguished accomplishments. Suckling is fairly typical of the Inns of Court gallants, and a letter sent to his comrade "Will" from Leyden, November 1629 breathes the spirit which must have pervaded many of their jollifications.[39] The letter describes the Netherlands in terms to prove that "the country is stark naught, and yet too good for the inhabitants," and is a swashbuckling, smutty document, full of bumptious wit. It hints at pleasures less innocent than "sitting up to lose money at threepenny gleek," and leaves a very decided impression that if its recipient was anything like its dispatcher, "Will" at this

---

[39] *Suckling's Works*, II, pp. 173–75. It is probable although not certain that this letter was sent to Davenant. Further details of his friendship with Suckling will appear below.

time was pretty much of a coxcomb. Yet in fairness it must be said that not all of Davenant's Inns of Court friends could have been like Suckling. Mingled among them, however, especially during the hectic year of 1628, were the regimental officers, and according to one informant at least, these were a corrupting influence. In his autobiography Edward Hyde has left the following account of the year during which he shared his lodgings with Davenant:

It was Michaelmas following before he [that is Hyde himself] returned to the Middle Temple, having by want of health lost a full year of study; and when he returned, it was without great application to the study of the law for some years, it being then a time when the town was full of soldiers, the king having then a war both with Spain and France, and the business of the Isle of Ree shortly followed; and he had gotten into the acquaintance of many of those officers, which took up too much of his time for one year: but as the war was quickly ended, so he had the good fortune quickly to make a full retreat from that company, and from any conversation with any of them, and without any hurt or prejudice from their conversation; insomuch as he used often to say, "that since it pleased God to preserve him whilst he did keep that company, (in which he wonderfully escaped from being involved in many inconveniences,) and to withdraw him so soon from it, he was not sorry that he had some experience in the conversation of such men, and of the license of those times" which was very exorbitant; yet when he did indulge himself that liberty, it was without any signal debauchery.[40]

Davenant did not escape the "many inconveniences" which Hyde alludes to with such masterful use of understatement, but it is doubtful if the fate which overtook him is more distasteful to contemplate than his friend's mealy-mouthed self-gratulation. We are apt to infer, since Hyde does not mention Davenant either here or later when he lists the poets and wits with whom he associated at this period, that he had Davenant in mind as

[40] *Life of Edward Earl of Clarendon written by Himself*, I, 8.

one of the military officers from whose conversation a divine providence so discriminately rescued him. But this does not follow; by the time Hyde wrote his autobiography, he had come to consider the poet disreputable—disreputable, however, for political reasons: We shall see how Davenant incurred his contempt by aligning himself with his political rivals, Colepepper and Jermyn. Incidentally Edward Hyde was the most plausible self-justifier of his age, and much that he says must be taken with the proper seasoning.

Putting it bluntly, the inconvenience which Davenant's entire circle no doubt risked and which he failed to escape was a complaint which was at that time sonorously known as the Grand Pox. Suckling alluded to it later, in the usual cliché, as a "foolish mischance, that he had got lately travelling in France," [41] while Aubrey, with the engaging particularity he always showed in such matters, traced it definitely to a "black, handsome wench that lay in Axe-yard, Westminster." [42] These open, one might say light-hearted, allusions to the affair remind one of the sharply defined conceptions of morality current in the day: One social stratum viewed as the merest peccadillo behavior that another social stratum was within a few decades to make punishable by death. Owing to the disparity in the accounts by Suckling and Aubrey, one is justified in making the at least chivalrous suggestion that his illness came upon Davenant just after he had been cashiered from Buckingham's ragtag, bobtail army, which literally carried contagion in its wings. However, he himself was resigned to letting stand its obvious and inevitable explanation; in a verse epistle to Endymion Porter he vowed never again to grow "valiant in a strange bed." [43]

The exact nature of the disease is known only by implication, but the injury to the sufferer's nose is a certainty. This was to prove a hard cross to bear. Such a nose was a distinguishing

[41] *Suckling's Works*, "Session of the Poets."
[42] John Aubrey, *op. cit.*, I, 205.
[43] *Folio*, 1673, p. 218, l. 6.

characteristic, and the poet's friends and enemies alike greeted it with a touching enthusiasm. There was never a period of worse taste, and no one in mentioning Davenant after 1630 failed to allude to his defect. Taunts were bad enough, but it must have been hard to get used to such sincerely intended praise as,

His Art was high, although his Nose was low.[44]

One may say without the least humorous intention that his nose henceforth became a vital part of his career. That is why it is mentioned here with what may seem distasteful insistence. Davenant achieved dignity and prestige in a generation predisposed, because of his peculiarity, to patronize him or to view him as a comic figure.

As annoying as the endless witticisms concerning his nose must have become, Davenant made it a point never to reply to them. It would be a mistake, however, to attribute his silence in the matter to any corroding sense of shame. Allusions to his illness are scattered freely, although in no sense brazenly, through the poems in *Madagascar* published in 1638. Anyone touched by a disease almost epidemic in that day, a disease often familiarly known to kings and magistrates, was considered a lazar neither by himself nor others; the attitude toward it was humorous rather than otherwise. Not until two centuries later did it occur to anyone to remark that Queen Henrietta Maria must have lacked any true delicacy to have selected for herself a servant such as Davenant. The lack of perspective thus quaintly revealed has not been confined to a few. I am convinced that the neglect accorded Davenant by critics of the nineteenth century is attributable to the fact that his injured nose offended the nice sensibilities of the age in a way undreamed of in his own times, and that the fulminations upon him by the exquisitely sensitive Edmund Gosse arose unconsciously from this same repulsion.[45] It is a curious

[44] *Spenser Society,* "Great Assizes Holden on Parnassus . . ." (1645), p. 20.
[45] Gosse deplores the laurel upon the "grotesque" head of Davenant; see below, p. 282.

commentary on this fact that Davenant was not a roué, and that
in an age too much given to literary indecencies, he was never in-
decent. He produced none of that bawdy verse which smudges
the works of Suckling, Denham, and the rest; and his serious
works do not suffer except in one or two early plays from the
sensual-mindedness which was the affliction of the era. Viewing
the works of Davenant and his Royalist contemporaries as a whole,
his are by all odds the cleanest of the lot.

The acuteness of the poet's three years of illness was due to
poisoning from the mercury used clumsily at this time in anoint-
ing all kinds of skin lesions. The Queen's own physician, Dr.
Thomas Cademan, a man whose widow Davenant was one day to
marry, attended upon him, and in a peculiarly intimate poem this
ministrant was rendered thanks for conquering "that no God but
Devil Mercurie":

> For thy Victorious cares, thy ready heart;
> Thy so small tyranny to so much Art;
>   For visits made to my disease
>   And me, (alas) not to my Fees:
>
> .   .   .   .
>
> May (thou safe Lord of Arts) each Spring
> Ripe plenty of Diseases bring
> Unto the rich; they still t'our Surgeons be
> Experiments, Patients alone to thee:
>   Health to the Poor; least pitty shou'd
>   (That gently stirs, and rules thy blood)
> Tempt thee from wealth, to such as pay like me
> A Verse; then think they give Eternety.[46]

It seems that Davenant's illness was complicated by poverty, so
that it was fortunate that he had made at least a few substantial
friends. The one who proved the truest in need was the kindly
Endymion Porter. During the long months while the sick man
tossed in fever that robbed him of sight and reason, or lay

---

[46] "To Doctor Cademan, Physitian to the Queen," *Folio*, 1673, pp. 234–35.

> In darkness thick as ill-met Clouds can make,
> In sleeps wherein the last Trump scarce could wake,[47]

it was the "large heart" of Porter that preserved him, and a number of poems remain to attest his heartfelt gratitude.[48]

The conclusion of this unhappy episode introduces one note of cheer. The activity of his ensuing years, the mental and physical fertility of his age, the health of his many children, argue at least an effective cure. By the latter part of 1633 he was abroad again, and was about to assume a new and more brilliant poetic rôle. As we take up his career at that point, we shall notice that he is a bit more worldly wise, a bit less volatile. Naturally so, for he had had, as I once heard a student preacher say of Job—a "sobering experience."

[47] "To Endimion Porter," *Ibid.*, p. 233.
[48] *Madagascar and other Poems*, 1638, *passim*.

III

THE QUEEN'S SERVICE

I

UPON recovering from his long illness, Davenant was forced
to inform certain acquaintances that he had not died.[1]
The fact soon became apparent: During the next six years
he made himself felt in London and Westminster with seven
plays, five masques, a volume of non-dramatic verse, and with his
rôle as prime mover in a varied host of activities. He had been
active only a year when he was received into the service of the
Queen, and it was the Queen—the admirable, unwise Henrietta
Maria—who then became the center of his universe. For him
she was Luminalia—Light—a light reflecting itself upon all his
diverse interests:

> Faire as unshaded Light, or as the Day
> In its first birth, when all the year was May;
> Sweet as the Altar's smoak, or as the new
> Unfolded Bud, sweld by the early dew;
> Smooth as the face of waters first appear'd,
> Ere Tides began to strive, or Winds were heard;
> Kind as the willing Saints, and calmer farre,
> Than in their sleeps forgiven Hermits are:
> You that are more than our discreter feare
> Dares praise, with such full Art, what make you here?
> Here, where the Summer is so little seen

[1] "To the Lady Bridget Kingsmell, sent with Mellons after a report of my Death," *Folio*, 1673, p. 219.

49

That leaves (her cheapest wealth) scarce reach at green
You come, as if the silver Planet were
Misled a while from her much injur'd Sphere,
And t' ease the travailes of her beames to night,
In this small Lanthorne would contract her light.[2]

The loveliness of these lines may be maintained in the face of all
that has been said about the egregious flattery produced by Davenant and his kind. Let us admit that such verses do offend
certain democratic convictions against self-abasement; yet these
convictions, however admirable, and necessary among us today,
do not apply when we consider a young man of the seventeenth
century, placed as Davenant was placed. He was a taverner's
son, and his patron was the Queen. More than that, she was a
charming queen—young, beautiful, gay, and to Davenant, always
kind. We are apt to see Henrietta Maria as the historians have
shown her to us, amidst the ruinous political intrigues of her
middle years, and not as the naïve and joyous girl with sparkling
eyes and bewitching accent, who was adored at Westminster as
his Majesty's sweetheart wife. The adulation for her expressed
in Davenant's poems and masques is beyond all question sincere.

Time has fixed on Davenant the character of a court toady—
in Restoration days, a sort of King Charles spaniel. The fact is
that his relations with the second Charles were always most distant, and that, although he was an opportunist who never missed
a chance for advancement if a polite poem would serve his turn,
he was anything but servile and parasitic. That he was no wor-
shipper of rank is implied in his remark to Aubrey that Suckling
"did not much care for a lord's converse, for they were in those
days damnably proud and arrogant, and the French would say
'My lord d'Angleterre, comme un mastif-dog.' "[3] For the Duke
of Buckingham whom he had known only as a gallant com-

[2] "To the Queen, entertain'd at night by the Countess of Anglesey," *Folio*,
1673, p. 218.
[3] John Aubrey, *op. cit.*, II, 241 ("Life of Suckling").

mander, he felt hero worship; [4] yet when William Chilling-worth marred an otherwise splendid record by informing upon his friend Doctor Gill, who had toasted Felton's health, Davenant branded his act "the detestable crime of treachery." [5] Satire upon the common multitude (especially that part of it which was Puritan) is common in his plays, but so also is satire upon the court, that place "where little intelligences of little things will serve for universal knowledge." [6] He believed, of course, in royal prerogative, and the attendant practice of court favoritism, but this belief was qualified by his ideal of what a royal favorite should be. In *The Cruel Brother,* a play by the way which launches an attack on court monopolists, Lucio, the favorite, is catechized by his friend, Foreste, on the way he has used his power. When Lucio affirms that he has never traduced justice, ignored the learned, or despised the poor, Foreste tells him that his decline from power would be the people's loss. This was an early play, but that the poet retained his ideal at the height of his career at court is attested by *The Fair Favorite,* in Act III of which there is an ingenuous display made of Eumena's im-partial justice in distributing the King's largess.

Davenant had to accustom himself to the clash of the ideal and the actual. His best friend, Endymion Porter, was a grievous sinner in the matter of court monopolies (specializing in salt and soap), and another valued friend, Henry Jermyn, was far from using his great power with the Queen in the manner of Lucio and Eumena. Davenant made compromises, in a manner to be described hereafter, and that these compromises were a debit to his conscience is suggested by a speech which he has put in the mouth of a *friend* of a court favorite:

[4] See "Elizium," and especially "To the Duchess of Buckingham," *Folio,* 1673, pp. 214, 319-20. An elegy to Buckingham, full of impassioned praise, was written by Davenant. It survives in Brit. Mus. Add. MSS. 33, 998, pp. 41-42.

[5] John Aubrey, *op. cit.,* II, 171 ("Life of Chillingworth"); for the incident in history, see S. R. Gardiner, *England under Buckingham and Charles I,* II, 343.

[6] *The Fair Favorite,* Act I.

What throngs of great impediments besiege
The virtuous mind! So thick in multitude
They jostle one another as they come.
Hath vice a charter got, that none must rise
But such who of the devil's faction are?
The way to honour is not evermore
The way to Hell;—a virtuous man may climb.

.   .   .   .

Here I dismiss my fears. If I can swell,
Unpoisoned by those helps which heaven forbids,
Fond love of ease shall ne'er my soul dehort:
Maugre all flattery, envy, or report.[7]

This much must be said: The pattern of a court flatterer and parasite is inconsistent with that of a man who pays his way; Davenant offered the full measure of his poetic talent and personal service both in peace and war, giving his royal masters in the end far more than they had ever given him.

2

It was Endymion Porter who sponsored Davenant at court. As early as 1630 the poet had written a New Year's ode to the King,[8] and had won the friendship of his gifted cupbearer, Thomas Carew. From the dedicatory epistles he had written to Lord Weston and the Earl of Dorset, as well as from subsequent poems to these powerful nobles,[9] it appears that they had given him some encouragement. Then had come the delay of his long illness, when only Porter had remained faithful. In 1634 he was receiving enclosures from Porter when the latter wrote to his wife,[10] and this indication that the poet had removed from Clerkenwell to a vicinity near the Porter house in the Strand next Durham House Gate is supported by one of his poetic

---

[7] *The Cruel Brother*, Act I.
[8] *Folio*, 1673, p. 220.
[9] *Ibid.*, pp. 230, 246.
[10] *Calendar S. P. D.*, 1634-35, p. 178.

epistles to Porter in which he mentions "our Fleet Street altars," [11] and by the site which he later selected for a projected playhouse. It is in connection with the production of *The Wits*, the comedy (excellent enough to have been called the best of its period) by which Davenant proved that he had returned to health, that we have our first intimation that he was known to the King through the active intercessions of Porter.

On January 9, 1634, Sir Henry Herbert, his Majesty's master of the revels, wrote:

This morning being the 9th of January, 1633 [i. e., 1634], the King was pleasd to call me unto his withdrawinge chamber to the windowe, wher he went over all that I had croste in Davenants playbooke, and allowing of *faith* and *slight* to bee asseverations only, and no oathes, markt them to stande, and some other few things, but in the greater part allowed of my reformations. This was done upon a complaint of Mr. Endymion Porters in December. The kinge is pleasd to take *faith, death, slight,* for asseverations, and no oaths, to which I doe humbly submit as my masters judgement; but, under favour, conceive them to be oaths, and enter them here, to declare my opinion and submission.

To this delectable bit, the censor added on the following day:

I returned unto Mr. Davenant his playe-booke of *The Witts*, corrected by the kinge. The Kinge would not take the booke at Mr. Porters hands; but commanded him to bring it unto mee, which he did, and likewise commanded Davenant to come to me for it, as I believe: otherwise he would not have byn so civill.[12]

Apparently the dour and dutiful master of the revels had found little obsequiousness in the young playwright, nor was he to find much in later years.

The Wits was licensed on the nineteenth of January,[13] and was acted at Blackfriars. Davenant had got wind of the fact that a

[11] *Folio,* 1673, p. 218.
[12] *Dramatic Records of Sir Henry Herbert,* p. 22.
[13] *Ibid.,* p. 35.

claque had been organized to condemn the play, and his prologue was an attempt at conciliation:

> Bless me, you kinder stars! how are we throng'd!
> Alas! whom hath our long-sick Poet wrong'd,
> That he should meet together, in one day,
> A session, and a faction at his play? . . .

If we can rely on Herbert, conciliation failed, and the play had
to be saved from the public stage by a performance at court.
He wrote, "The Witts was acted on tusday night the 28 January
1633 [1634], at court, before the Kinge and Queene. Well likt.
It had a various fate on the stage and at court . . ." [14] It was un-
doubtedly Porter again who procured this court performance,
and when the play was published, it was dedicated "To the
chiefly belov'd of all that are ingenious and noble, Endymion
Porter, of his Majesty's bedchamber," who "hath preserv'd life
in the author; then rescu'd his work from a cruel faction." [15]

Who composed this cruel faction does not appear. Davenant
had made enemies. He was a downright soul and had already
caricatured the satirist George Wither, and his *Abuses Stript
and Whipt*.[16] But it was probably neither Wither nor any other
Puritan who had formed the cabal against him. Hissing down a
play bears the stamp of a different set, and the inciters were no
doubt hangers-on at court, offended at his rising star. The poet
was to be persecuted by a band of cleverly satirical "cavaliers" for
the rest of his life, and it is little wonder that in his *Salmacida
Spolia,* one of the quacks in the antimasque of mountebanks
offers for sale "Treacle of the gall of serpents, and the liver of
doves to initiate a neophite courtier."

The fact that *The Wits* was "well likt" at court, and that a
tragi-comedy, *Love and Honour,* produced later in the same year,
reflects the influence of French romances such as formed Hen-

---

[14] *Dramatic Records of Sir Henry Herbert,* p. 54.
[15] See also a poem on the subject, *Folio,* 1673, p. 235.
[16] Castruccio in *The Cruel Brother;* see especially Acts I and II.

rietta Maria's favorite reading matter, partly explains why, early in 1635, Davenant received his first commission from the Queen. It happened that the court was in need of a writer of masques. The two irascible old gentlemen, Ben Jonson, who had long monopolized this species of authorship, and Inigo Jones, royal architect and scene-maker, had found that they could no longer work together. In 1631 they had had their final rupture over whose name should have precedence on the title page of *Chloridia,* and they were now amiably engaged in attacking each other, the one from the stage and the other from the pit, at the Blackfriars playhouse. Jonson had the right of the quarrel, but the court found its deviser of gorgeous scenes, machines, and costumes less dispensable than its poet, and someone was sought who could work congenially with Inigo Jones—or, as Jonson variously called him, Iniquo Jones, In-and-In Medlay, Dominus Do-all, and Vitruvius Hoop. Carew and Townshend had filled the gap for a time, and now Davenant was given his trial. His success in this trial was to assure him the position of chief entertainer of the court until the Civil Wars—an honor, even though on the title pages of his published masques his name was always to follow modestly after that of Inigo Jones.

The subject which the Queen assigned him for his first masque is a token of the curious spirit which pervaded her court. To entertain a circle in which the royal pair, however virtuous themselves, found it impossible to avert scandals among their own ladies- and gentlemen-in-waiting, Davenant was to compose a piece celebrating platonic love!

Henrietta Maria was in some respects a *précieuse;* [17] that is, she had been influenced throughout her youth by the Hôtel de Rambouillet, calculated to reform French manners and speech, and by that love-bible, *L'Astrée* of Honoré D'Urfé, accepted as canonical by all followers of the ideal of platonic love expounded in Castiglione, Marguerite of Navarre, and, supposedly, in Plato's

[17] J. B. Fletcher, "Précieuses at the Court of Charles I," *Journal of Comparative Literature,* I, 120–53.

Banquet. Transplanted to England, she and her lieutenant, the beautiful though far from irreproachable Countess of Carlisle,[18] dabbled at establishing the cult of the *précieuses* in the court of Charles; and while here its success in reforming morals was only that of a cosmetic, the impulse behind it and the character of the King and Queen did effect a trend toward refinement and away from the crudeness and bestiality which had tarred the court of the effete anti-feminist, King James. However, among the Caroline courtiers, the doctrine of platonic love *per se* fell upon stony ground. They were amused, and a trifle bewildered. On June 3, 1634, James Howell wrote to Philip Warwick at Paris:

The Court affords little News at present, but that there is a Love call'd *Platonick Love,* which much sways there of late; it is a Love abstracted from all corporeal gross Impressions and sensual Appetite, but consists in Contemplations and Ideas of the Mind, not in any Carnal Fruition. This Love sets the Wits of the Town on work; and they say there will be a Mask shortly of it, whereof Her Majesty, and her Maids of Honour, will be part.[19]

Howell was not the only one interested in the event, and later in the year both Elizabeth, Queen of Bohemia, and Thomas Wentworth, Lord Deputy of Ireland, received letters telling them that the Queen and nine lords and fifteen ladies were to appear in the masque at Shrovetide.[20]

Davenant was puzzled how to treat his subject. In his prologue to *The Platonic Lovers,* a play in which he later brought the subject of the cult to the popular stage, he speaks of the currency of the word "platonick" at court, and tells that

> . . . there he learnt it first, and had command
> T' interpret what he scarce doth understand.

---

[18] Davenant has a poem to this remarkable woman, cf. *Folio,* 1673, p. 244.
[19] James Howell, *Epistolæ Ho-Elianæ,* pp. 317–18.
[20] *Calendar S. P. D.,* 1634–35, p. 482; *Strafford Letters,* I, 360.

He could understand simple chastity, and he revered it, and he could understand the sublimed love of happy wedlock like that of Charles and Henrietta; but this other thing, a woman-devised regimen of unclimaxed dallying, left his intelligence cold. He has left a definition of love which helps to illustrate why he was scarcely the man to interpret D'Urfé:

Indefinite Love is Lust, and Lust when it is determin'd to one is Love; this definition too but intrudes itself on what I was about to say, which is, that Love is the most acceptable imposition of Nature, the cause and preservation of Life, and the very healthfulness of the mind, as well as of the body; but Lust (our raging Feaver) is more dangerous in Cities, then the Calenture in Ships.[21]

A sturdy conception this, but rather far removed from that of "Contemplations and Ideas of the Mind." The masque which he finally produced, *The Temple of Love,* presented at White-hall on February 10, 1635, with the Queen taking the part of Indamora, is a graceful and amusing piece alternating between poetic praise of love and virtue, and whimsical guying at platonic nonsense. At one point the page of the nine Persian youths seeking the Temple of Pure Love leaps on the stage shouting

Hey! hey! how light I am, all soul within,
As my dull flesh were melted through my skin.

The names of the nine young gentlemen cast as Persian youths is appended to the printed version of the masque. That of George Goring is among them, and it would be spiteful to men-tion at this point subsequent episodes in the life of him and others of these seekers for the Temple of Pure Love.

In spite of the masque's equivocal treatment of her ethical hobby, and in spite of the fact that Sir Thomas Roe moaned that it had been performed "with much trouble and wearisome-

[21] *Preface to Gondibert.*

ness," [22] the Queen approved it and graced the author with her livery. On the title page of *The Temple of Love* and of subsequent publications, Davenant designates himself her Majesty's servant.

Three years were to pass before Whitehall witnessed another masque, for Charles feared that the lights in these ever more elaborate productions would injure his precious paintings in the banqueting hall. But just one year later a similar entertainment was staged elsewhere. Again Davenant was the author, and again his work was graced by the approval of the Queen. In the winter of 1635–36 the Middle Temple set up a Lord of Misrule, one Mr. Vivian who as the Prince D'Amour maintained his *opera bouffe* state among the students; [23] and it was decided that an entertainment be given to celebrate the visit to England of the King's nephews, the youthful Elector Palatine and his brother, Prince Rupert. Davenant was called upon, and was given three days in which to write. There resulted *The Triumphs of the Prince D'Amour,* which consisted almost entirely of semi-comic spectacles such as would please youngsters, and ended with the performers setting before their highnesses a table of refreshments. Sir Henry Herbert has left this notice of the occasion:

On Wensday the 23 of Febru. 1635 [1636], the Prince d'Amours gave a masque to the Prince Elector and his brother, in the Middle Temple, wher the queene was pleasd to grace the entertaynment by putting of[f] majesty to putt on a citizens habitt; and to sett upon the scaffold on the right hande amongst her subjects. The queene was attended in the like habitts by the Marquess Hamilton, the Countess of Denbighe, the Countess of Holland, and the Lady Elizabeth Feildinge. Mrs. Basse, the law-woman, leade in this royal citizen and her company. The Earl of Holland, the Lord Goringe, Mr. Percy, and Mr. Jermyn, were the men that attended. The Prince Elector satt in the midst, his brother Robert on the right hand of him, and the Prince d'Amours on the left. The Masque

[22] *Calendar S. P. D.,* 1634–35, p. 510.
[23] *Strafford Letters,* I, 506–07.

was very well performed in the dances, scenes, cloathinge, and musique, and the queene was pleasd to tell mee at her going away, that she liked it very well.[24]

Not only is the Queen's presence interesting, as a token of her condescension, but by a coincidence so also is that of her gentlemen attendants. Within a few years a plot fostered by the Queen, and involving Holland, Jermyn, Percy, and Goring, was to bring Davenant within the shadow of the scaffold.

When *The Triumphs of the Prince D'Amour* was presented, only two years had passed since the poet's return to health; yet he had produced not only *The Wits, Love and Honour,* and the two masques, but also a second comedy, *News from Plymouth,* better in many ways than its predecessor. This comedy, written during the summer of 1635 and hence not for the Blackfriars but for the Globe,[25] is a reminder that Davenant was faced by the continuous need of earning a living. Thus far he was receiving nothing from the Crown except perhaps when he produced a masque or a New Year's ode for the Queen, and his plays meant bread and butter. A revealing bit of autobiography occurs in a burlesque poem, "The Long Vacation in London." This vacation, evidently the same that gave birth to the comedy, witnessed the poor poet out-sneaking duns and protesting

> . . . do noble Numbers chuse
> To walk on feet, that have no shoose?

until finally

> . . . forth he steals, to Globe does run,
> And smiles, and vowes Four Acts are done;
> *Finis* to bring he does protest,
> Tells ev'ry Play'r his part is best:
> And all to get, (as Poets use)
> Some Coyne in Pouch to solace Muse.[26]

---

[24] *Dramatic Records of Sir Henry Herbert,* p. 56; a corresponding account occurs in *Strafford Letters,* I, 525.
[25] See Herbert's *Records,* p. 36, and the epilogue as reprinted, *Folio,* p. 245.
[26] *Folio,* 1673, p. 290.

A character in *News from Plymouth* receives a beseeching letter from a creditor, one Gregory Thimble, offering the touching plea, there "has been but one bunch of turnips among twelve of us these four days," and the whole play is eloquent of its author's familiarity with Gregory Thimble's kind.

If industry could mend matters, Davenant did not intend to remain poor. He continued to write, averaging two plays each year the theatres were not closed by the plague. Most of these plays were modish productions, tragi-comedies of love, honor, and friendship among impossibly noble personages brought into hazard by passion or the chances of war. They are not uninteresting, lacking neither dramatic effectiveness nor verbal felicity, but they reflect a fad rather than life. The taste for such plays was bringing into the field of play-making such simon-pure courtiers as Carlell, Cartwright, Killigrew, Suckling, and Berkeley, and the invasion of such plays and such playwrights was troublesome to dramatists of the old school. In his prologue to *The Court Beggar,* 1638, Brome wrote:

> We've come to fear yours or the Poet's frown
> For of late days (he knows not) how y'are grown
> Deeply in love with a new strayne of wit
> Which he condemns, at least disliketh it.
>
> .   .   .   .
>
> He'll treat his usual way, no gaudy scene
> Shal give instructions what his plot doth mean,
> No handsome love-toy shall your time beguile
> Forcing your pitty to a sigh or smile. . . .

Davenant's position was peculiar. He had looked to the stage before he had looked to the court, and he shared much in common with such writers as Brome, Ford, Shirley, and Massinger. Shakespeare had been his first love, and Jonson's farcical vein is as dominant in his comedies as in those of Brome. Yet the age desired "love-toys" and his position among the courtly circle made him especially aware of the fact. He supplied the want, and to reward his adaptability his plays were usually called for several performances at court. This was lucrative, and what with the pension he later received and the bounty of his high-born patrons he was soon able to walk in London without fear of constables or the Clink.

3

All in all this is Davenant's sunniest period. Not only was he escaping poverty, but his dramatic activities were bringing his name to the fore in contemporary lists including those of Jonson, Shirley, and their greatest predecessors.[27] He was gaining favor at court. *The Platonic Lovers,* published in 1636, was dedicated to Henry Jermyn in such terms as to show that he had won the friendship of this most cherished (and most ill-chosen) favorite of Henrietta Maria. His acquaintance among poets was especially. wide. Thomas Carew continued to applaud his plays and poems, an attention which he reciprocated.[28] Sir John Suckling, who had been absent indulging himself in war and travel during our dramatist's illness, had returned by 1633, thereafter to cut an elegant figure about the town, and Davenant "was his intimate friend and loved him intirely." [29] If we may assume anything on the basis of mutual friendships, Davenant knew such acquaintances of Porter as Herrick, May, and Dekker; and on the testimony of commendatory verse written by him and with him, he knew also Sandys, Quarles, Vaughan, Massinger, Townshend, Carey, Montague, Bendlowes, Habington, and many others.[30] Later Waller, Cowley, Butler, and Dryden were of his circle, while an equal number, including Denham and Villiers, singled him out for their satiric shafts.

Intimacy with the poets would have meant much to one with

[27] See below, p. 270.

[28] See his poem to Carew, *Folio,* 1673, p. 252.

[29] Aubrey, *op. cit.,* II, 241, "Life of Suckling" (for which Davenant supplied many facts). See also Suckling's poem to Davenant, *Works,* I, 25.

[30] Wood, *Athenae Oxonienses,* II, 658, III, 516, 776; *Fasti Oxonienses,* II, 358.

Davenant's genuine devotion to literature. The group that had once foregathered at The Mermaid had passed on, but one portentous member of that group remained. Tradition reports [31] that once Ben Jonson, Suckling, Davenant, Porter, and Mr. Hales of Eaton had a long discussion about the poetry of the past and the present. During its course, Ben annoyed Sir John with the claim that Will Shakespeare had known too little of the Ancients, whereupon Mr. Hales confounded the staunch old classicist with the opinion that there was nothing in the Ancients which Mr. Shakespeare had not equaled or surpassed. This is only tradition, and it may be unjust to Jonson, the legend of whose imperfect sympathy with Shakespeare has such slender basis in fact. That Davenant admired Jonson as well as Shakespeare there is proof in his plays and elsewhere.[32]

It was no longer necessary for Davenant to swelter in town during the long vacation, nor to suffer the drabness of an entire London winter. Sometimes he traveled into the country with Porter;[33] and once he, Suckling, and Jack Young (a friend who was to survive him and write his epitaph) disported themselves at Bath. Aubrey tells of the trip, and of how "Sir John came like a young prince for all manner of equipage and convenience." They had a "cart-load" of books among them, and "twas as pleasant a journey as ever man had; in the heighth of a long peace and luxury, and in the venison season." One night they lay at Marlborough, where Suckling and Davenant played pranks on Young. Then they visited Sir Edward Baynton's "where they were nobly entertained severall dayes. From thence, they went to West Kington, to parson Davenant, Sir William's eldest brother, where they stayed a weeke—mirth, witt, and good cheer flowing. From thence to Bath, six or seven miles."[34]

William had evidently kept in touch with his family. His sister Jane was still at the Oxford tavern; Elizabeth had married

[31] Bradley & Adams, *Jonson Allusion Book*, p. 187.
[32] For a tribute to Jonson, see "To Doctor Duppa . . .," *Folio*, 1673, p. 253.
[33] See "A Journey into Worcestershire," *Folio*, 1673, p. 215.
[34] John Aubrey, *op. cit.*, II, 242.

Gabriel Bridges, rector of Letcombe, Berks, and was later to marry Richard Bristow, rector of Dedicote, in the same county; Alice had married Dr. Sherburne, minister of Pembridge, Hereford.[35] The Davenants were a marrying family: "Parson Davenant" himself married at forty during his incumbency at West Kington.[36] At the Restoration he was to receive a belated D.D., and was to make his bid for immortality by telling Aubrey that Suckling's "tract about Socinianisme was writt on the table in the parlour of the parsonage of West Kington." [37] This tract, *Religion by Reason,* was one of Suckling's few lapses into gravity, and its attitude toward religious free-thinking will occur to us later when we come to consider Davenant's own peculiar creed.

Neither religion nor reason occupied Suckling very often; more characteristic of him is the witty and bantering *Session of the Poets,* also written in 1637, and also of biographical interest in connection with Davenant, for it contains the first reference to him in regard to the laureateship. The poem describes an imagined meeting of upward of twenty of the poets of the day called together in order that Apollo may select from among them a poet laureate. Among the candidates are Sandys, May, Vaughan, Townshend, Berkeley, etc., as well as Ben Jonson, Davenant, and Suckling himself. It is interesting that this poem, written before Jonson's death in August, should show the literary dictator not as laureate but only as one of the candidates. It is a reminder that although Jonson had long been laureate in effect and in popular estimation, the title had never been officially accorded him and his patent for a royal pension had contained no mention of the office. It also hints that in the closing years of his life his obscuration at court had tended to edge him out of his nominal laureateship. In Suckling's poem Jonson and Davenant are the chief contenders for the laurel. When it comes Davenant's turn for consideration, a choice is almost made, and—

[35] *Ibid.,* I, 204; *Wood's City of Oxford,* III, 173.
[36] *Allegations for Marriage Licenses* . . . (Archbishop of Canterbury), p. 43.
[37] John Aubrey, *op. cit.,* II, 242.

Surely the company would have been content,
If they could have found any precedent;
But in all their records either in verse or prose,
There was not one laureate without a nose.

At length an alderman appears in the company, and to Davenant's chagrin, Apollo, who

. . . openly declared it was the best sign
Of good store of wit to have good store of Coin,

places the laurel on the alderman's head.

Not long after *The Session* was written, the rare Ben Jonson, whom Suckling had goaded by making him "mine host of his own New Inn," passed beyond the reach of flippant jests and official neglect; and Davenant, his defeat by the alderman notwithstanding, succeeded to the wreath. More than a year passed between Jonson's death and the issuing of the royal patent which gave Davenant his quasi-official standing. In the interim he had strengthened his right to consideration by publishing *Madagascar*.

In a sense this is a "state" poem. Prince Rupert, whom Davenant had entertained in his *Triumphs of the Prince D'Amour*, had remained in England, and his presence had suggested a project whereby he was to sail forth and conquer Madagascar. In a letter to his mother, the Queen of Bohemia, Sir Thomas Roe wrote that the plan was "absurd" and was "a course to lose the Prince in a desperate and fruitless action from which he wishes the queen to take him off." The Queen of Bohemia replied that the project sounded "like one of Don Quixote's conquests, where he promised his trusty squire to make him king of an island"; and she was no doubt relieved when Roe was able to write, "The dream of Madagascar, I think, is vanished. A blunt merchant, called to deliver his opinion, said it was a gallant design, but such as wherein he would be loth to venture his younger son." [38]

[38] *Calendar S. P. D.*, 1636–37, pp. 505, 559; *ibid.*, 1637, p. 82.

Davenant had viewed this gallant design not practically but poetically, and at its height he had composed the heroic verses in which his disembodied spirit hovers over the island and views the glories of Rupert during its conquest. *Madagascar,* together with many occasional verses to the Queen, to dignitaries about the court, and to his personal friends, as well as several interesting miscellanies, appeared in 1638, dedicated to those by whom the work had been "cherished," Endymion Porter and Henry Jermyn, and commended by three poets who have stood the test of time, Suckling, Habington, and Carew. This volume and the masques he was producing are sufficient testimony that Davenant was already functioning as court poet, and we are not surprised that on December 13, 1638, King Charles should have granted

. . . in consideración of seruice heretofore done and hereafter to be done unto us by Willm̃ Davenant gentĺ, one añuitie or yearlie penc̃on of one hundred pound^e of lawful money of England by the yeare . . . from the feast of the Anunceacon of the blessed Virgin mary last past . . .[39]

No mention of the term *poet laureate* occurs in the grant, and until Dryden no English poet could claim that title by letters patent; nevertheless the title was applied to Davenant by all his contemporaries. To all practical purposes he was from this time until his death England's laureate poet, an intermediate between Jonson and Dryden, and when all is said, a very worthy one.

The Princes of the Rhine had been involved in two episodes in Davenant's life at this period, and one of them, the elder one this time, also played a part in a third and rather curious episode. It will have been noticed how rarely Mary Davenant has come to the foreground in the career of this remarkably foot-loose married man. She appears for a moment in April 1638, only to disappear permanently thereafter. In the Public Record Office there exists an odd document:

[39] Patent Rolls, 14 Charles I, 2804, 33. This grant like a similar one to Jonson is printed by E. K. Broadus, *The Laureateship,* p. 225; Professor Broadus discusses fully the official status of Jonson and Davenant.

To the Kinges most Excellent Matie
The humble peticion of Mary: Dauenant

In all humility sheweth unto your Matie that whereas upon a
sodaine Causeless and intollerable prouocation given by one warren
being a Tapster or an ostler he received a small hurt by the said Will
Dauenant, your petitioners husbande wch by the said warrens owne
wilfull Neglect, and disorder, & by the letting of bloode, by wch he
lost 10 or 11 ounces of bloode, (was the cause of his own death as
by the annexed certificate may more clearly appeare. . . .^{40}

The document goes on to state that the negligence of the coroner
had caused a finding of criminal violence to be brought in
against the petitioner's husband, whereupon the King's nephew,
Prince Charles, Elector Palatine of the Rhine, had interceded in
his behalf. A pardon had been granted, but since this pardon
extended to the protection only of the offender's life, certain
"meane Lordes" were prosecuting him "to the outlawry, hoping
thereby to obtaine the estate of his landes to the ruine of his poore
wife and posterity, unless your Ma^{ty} wilbe gratiously pleasede to
make a gratious addition to your former fauors." The offender
was still absent at the time the petition was made, but on April
12, it pleased his Majesty to grant "the pet^{rs} husbande Will Davenant his gracious & free pardon for his life & landes and goodes."

The incident thus glimpsed has not previously been associated
with Davenant the poet because it has not been generally known
that he was married at this time. There is little doubt, however,
that he was the principal involved. It is unlikely that there
should have been two William Davenants, each with a wife named
Mary, and each with influence at court. There was a second
William Davenant of exactly the poet's age, but, fortunately for
the sake of distinction, his wife's name was Elizabeth.^{41} It
seems then that our poet followed the precedent of Ben Jonson,
the former laureate, by pinking his man. It is too bad that the

^{40} State Papers, 16: 323 (Entry Book of Petitions), p. 269.
^{41} *Allegations for Marriage Licenses* . . . (Archbishop of Canterbury), p. 29.

wilfully neglectful Warren should have been nothing more ex-
alted than a "tapster or ostler," but in the absence of fuller information about the affair we may hope that Davenant's was
not too inglorious a conquest.

The poet was certainly on the upgrade, even though there were
temporary setbacks. A year after he had received his pardon,
and three months after the grant of his pension, he received a
royal concession of a still more interesting nature. On March
26, 1639, a document was drawn up in which the King

upon the humble petition of our servant William Davenant . . .
granted . . . unto the said William Davenant . . . full power li-
cence and authority . . . to frame, new-build and set up . . . a
Theatre or Playhouse . . . containing in the whole forty yards
square at the most . . . upon a parcel of ground lying near unto
or behind the Three Kings Ordinary in Fleet Street. . . . And . . .
to gather together, entertain, govern, privilege and keep, such and
so many players and persons, to exercise action, musical presentments,
scenes, dancing, and the like, as he, the said William Davenant . . .
shall think fit. . . .[42]

In this enterprise as in so many things the poet had the backing
of Endymion Porter. On April 16, Porter wrote to Richard
Harvey to

. . . solicit my Lord Duke, who is now in London, to know what
he has done with my Lord Keeper concerning Mr. Davenant's
patent; if he has procured the passing of it, follow it close and attend the sealing. It has already passed the signet and privy seal,
and they are both paid for. Disburse money for it and keep the
patent until Davenant sends you the money, also by the next opportunity let me know how much it comes to.[43]

The playhouse in question was never built. Although the
poet's friends had the power to steer his patent past the seals,

[42] Thomas Rymer, *Fœdera*, XX, 377.
[43] *Calendar S. P. D.,* 1639, p. 49.

he lacked the financial resources to overcome the opposition which his scheme must certainly arouse among the citizens of Fleet Street and the managers of the other playhouses. These had their agent at court, and Davenant countered by seeking the aid of the Duke of Richmond. In a poem which cleverly compares Whitehall to a ship he tells how

> . . . this great Ship, the Court, takes dayly in
> Poor Traficquers who with small Stocks begin:
> They trade with Fortune, and her false Wares buy;
> One of this slight neglected Crowd am I.
> My little Venture I saw safely stow'd,
> Both Wind and Tyde serv'd outward from the Road,
> But making way, and bearing ev'ry Sayle,
> Proudly, as if I still could chuse my Gale,
> Strait I beheld (amaz'd as with a wrack)
> The sheets all rumpled and the Cordage slack. . . .[44]

Knowing that "some perverse and undiscover'd hand pulled an odd Rope," Davenant wished the Duke to use his influence with the King. But it was no use: His ship was hopelessly becalmed. On October 2, this same year, an indenture was drawn up between "the King's most excellent Majesty of the first part, and William Davenant of London, Gent., of the other part," wherein

William Davenant doth by these presents declare . . . His Majesty's intent . . . upon the granting of the license was and is that he, the said William Davenant . . . should not frame, build, or set up . . . the playhouse in any place inconvenient . . . and that the . . . parcel of ground . . . lying near or behind the Three Kings Ordinary in Fleet Street . . . is sithence found inconvenient and unfit for that purpose. . . .[45]

Although his venture had come to nothing, let it be noted that Davenant had already conceived the idea, not only to build a

[44] "To the Duke of Richmond in the Year 1639," *Folio,* 1673, pp. 293–94.
[45] J. P. Collier, *Annals,* II, 97. J. Q. Adams, *Elizabethan Playhouses,* pp. 424–31, reprints in part, and discusses, the grant and the indenture.

theatre of an unprecedented size, but also to bring to the public stage "musical presentments, *scenes,* dancing, and the like"—in other words the devices which had become familiar to him as a deviser of court masques. It was not by accident that during the Commonwealth and Restoration he was to evolve in England the first modern theatre.

The letter to Harvey concerning the theatre patent is the last of the concrete evidence of the fine friendship between Davenant and Porter. That it really was a fine friendship is certain. Beside all else he had done for the poet, Porter had even composed verses commending *Madagascar.* In this tribute he confesses

> . . . I guess at Poetry
> As when I hear them read strong-lines I cry:
> Th'are rare, but cannot tell you rightly why. . . .

and he tells how much these lines of his own are costing him:

> I twist my Face,
> As if I drew a Tooth, I blot, and write,
> Then look as pale as some that go to fight.
> With the whole Kennel of the Alphabet
> I hunt sometimes an hour, one Rime to get. . . .

But he consoles himself with the thought that Davenant has got in his labored efforts

> A foyle to set your Jewel off, which comes
> From Madagascar, scenting of rich gummes;
> Before the which, my lay conceits will smell
> Like an abortive Chick, destroy'd i' th' shell.

How the poet responded to Endymion's esteem is illustrated all through his non-dramatic poems. In fact he wrote more often in honor of Endymion and Olivia than in honor of Charles and Henrietta Maria. These poems are personal and fervid, after the manner of the day. To this friend he writes,

Thou art my wealth, and more than Light ere spy'd,
Than Eastern Hills bring forth, or Seas can hide. . . .[46]

In a sense Porter was his wealth other than figuratively, and the
poet was conscious that he could not respond in kind to his
friend's material favors. To Olivia Porter he addressed these
pleasantly rueful lines as "A Present upon a New-years day":

Goe! hunt the whiter Ermine! and present
His wealthy skin, as this dayes Tribute sent
To my Endimion's Love, though she be farr
More gently smooth, more soft than Ermines are!
Goe! climbe that Rock! and when thou there hast found
A Star, contracted in a Diamond,
Give it Endimion's Love, whose glorious Eyes
Darken the starry Jewels of the Skies!
Goe! dive into the southern Sea! and when
Th'ast found (to trouble the nice sight of Men)
A swelling Pearle, and such whose single worth
Boast all the wonders which the Seas bring forth,
Give it Endimion's Love! whose ev'ry Teare
Would more enrich the skilfull Jeweller.
How I command! how slowly they obey!
The Churlish Tartar will not hunt today;
Nor will that lazy, sallow-Indian strive
To climbe the Rock, nor that dull Negro dive.
Thus Poets like to Kings (by trust deceiv'd)
Give oftner what is heard of than receiv'd.[47]

Olivia's disposition was not so gently smooth as her beauty, but
let us hope she shared her husband's uncritical love of poets and
poetry.

Endymion Porter was a minor court favorite—one of those
who fattened in the public trough. Yet, strangely enough, the

---

[46] *Folio*, 1673, p. 224.

[47] *Folio*, 1673, p. 229. A copy of this poem exists among MSS of St. John's
College, Cambridge, 416, 13 written in a coeval hand although not in the
author's.

more we know of him the more we realize that he was a lovable soul—gentle, kindly, enlightened. He served his King not only in halcyon days, but afterwards through long adversity, faithfully and to his ruin. It is to William Davenant's credit that he cherished such a friend, and proved loyal to his survivors.[48]

4

Davenant and Porter were parted most of their later life by the chances of war. In 1639 war clouds were already black on the horizon. It will have been noticed that when Porter was engineering the sealing of the theatre patent, Davenant was away from London. Although the fact has never attracted attention, he was serving at this time in the King's army in the First Bishops War, that skirmish with the Scotch Covenanters in the Spring of 1639 which sounded the prelude to the Great Rebellion. This "war"—it consisted solely of feinting at the borders—was the result of Charles's obtuse efforts to saddle Anglican prelates and prayer books upon Scotland. Its three months of maneuvering gave the Cavaliers their first chance to parade military colors, Davenant's friend Suckling subsidizing for his Majesty a troop of one hundred horse, romantically clad in white doublets and scarlet coats, breeches, hats, and plumes.[49] It was not in Suckling's troop that Davenant served, however, but in the ordnance department under Mountjoy Blount, the Earl of Newport. We know of his service through a single episode.

In May about four hundred horses used in drawing the King's ordnance were pastured on the grounds of one James Fawcett at Goswick near York. Some time later Fawcett petitioned Arundel, the Lord General of the army, to protect him from a star-chamber suit which had resulted when "Wm. Davenant, the paymaster" complained that some of the horses had been hurt in being turned out of the corn.[50] Since Arundel was inclined

[48] See below, pp. 157, 167.
[49] *Suckling's Works,* I, xxxix.
[50] *Historical Manuscripts Comm.,* III, 35.

to favor Fawcett, the case might have been dropped, but the stout northern yeoman erred by indulging in large talk. He was then hauled to London and tried before the House of Lords. When it was deposed that he had called Newport and Davenant knaves, and had said that "he had done the King better service than either Mr. Davenant or my Lord of Newport, and they were base Fellows for prosecuting the suit against him," he was judged guilty, forced to kneel in submission at the bar, and to pay Newport (not Davenant) £500.[51] The Earl was a rapacious soul, and the judgment probably consoled him fully for any injury done to the King's horses and to his own (and Davenant's) reputation.

Davenant's activities, military and dramatic, are oddly crossed at this period. In May 1640 the King's expedition to the North was referred to offensively in an unlicensed play acted by the King and Queen's Boys at the Phoenix or Cockpit in Drury Lane. As a result their manager, William Beeston, was driven from his post. On June 27, it was recorded in the office-book of the Lord Chamberlain that "William Davenant, Gent., one of Her Majesty's servants" should henceforth govern the company, the members of which should "obey the said Mr. Davenant and follow his orders and directions, as they will answer the contrary. . . ."[52] This appointment as theatre manager, the most substantial favor the poet had yet received, was perhaps a compensation for the surrender of his right to build a new theatre.

However, he had little opportunity to develop at the Cockpit the schemes he had in his mind, for the demands of these troublesome times were growing daily more strident.

Just as Davenant received his new appointment, the Second Bishops War began. Again Charles made a feeble attempt to humble the Scots, and again Davenant served in his army. He was still in the ordnance department, for on July 17, 1640, Viscount Conway, badly in need of horses and cannon at Newcastle,

[51] *Lords Journals,* IV, 118, 131.
[52] Printed in J. Q. Adams, *Elizabethan Playhouses,* pp. 361–62.

wrote to Secretary Windebank that "There is only one man sent down, a deputy of Mr. Davenant; if another man should do so, he would put it into a play." [53] This war lasted until August when it was, ostensibly, concluded by the Treaty of Ripon, and it appears from Conway's letter that Davenant coöperated in its mismanagement with everyone from the King down. However, he had other things to think about besides horses and gross cannon. Henrietta Maria was very timorous during her husband's military sallies into the North, and one of Davenant's duties as her servant seems to have been to dispatch letters from the court at York. Suckling was also at York, and he wrote to a friend in London that he need expect no news of the treaty because "unless I had one of Master Davenant's Barbary pigeons (and he now employs them all, he says, himself for the queen's use), I durst not venture to send them. . . ." [54] Dispatching royal love letters on the wings of Barbary pigeons! an odd occupation this, for an officer of ordnance, or even for a poet laureate.

Davenant had remained through these six years a servant of the Queen. After a three-years intermission, between 1635–1638, masques had returned to the court—masques of a hectic splendor presaging that the end of these costly toys was near. Davenant had been retained as the author, and six months before his departure for the Second Bishops War, he had produced *Salmacida Spolia*, the last of the Caroline masques. Two years before, he had written *Britannia Triumphans* and *Luminalia*, dazzling productions for which a special building had been erected at Whitehall. One of these masques had featured the King, another the Queen, and the third the King and Queen together; in all of them the poet had been allowed to take astonishing liberties in disposing the actions of his royal puppets. In *Salmacida Spolia*, Henrietta Maria, enceinte at the time, was hoisted in an engine that she might make her entrance descending from a cloud. New times had brought new manners. Queen Elizabeth might have

[53] *Calendar S. P. D.*, 1640, p. 483.
[54] *Suckling's Works*, II, 217.

enjoyed such aerial adventures, but her ideas of majesty were not so flexible as to permit the indulgence.

Yet Henrietta Maria could never have taxed Davenant for irreverence. These masques contain songs of praise ardent enough to prove that his mistress was for him still the Goddess of Brightness, Beauty, Noblesse. He could expect bounties from her no longer, for the court had come suddenly to realize that it was bitterly poor. The Second Bishops War lasted only until the summer of 1640, but it was not until the following Spring that Davenant was paid for his service, and then he was given £40.[55] In the meantime he must have returned to manage the company at the Cockpit, but if so, it was his last peaceful occupation for many years. The Bishops Wars had been only symptomatic, and in 1641 real war was brewing—war in England between the ruler and the ruled. The Long Parliament was meeting, and was sending the King's right hand, Thomas Wentworth, Earl of Strafford, to the scaffold. William Davenant was the Queen's servant, and a year before armed hostilities actually began, her service—a new kind of service now—almost decreed that his humbler blood should follow Strafford's flowing upon the block.

[55] *Calendar S. P. D.*, 1640–41, pp. 545–46.

IV

THE KING'S CAUSE

I

I N following the career of one soldier through a war, we must
be careful not to write a history of the war.[1] This is not so
easy to avoid, for in wartime the movements of individuals
are governed by the movements of armies, and when the war is a
class conflict, a struggle over principles, it is also a gauge of the
character of each participant.   As a Royalist, Davenant was pitted
against a righteous cause, but we must not be amazed if he, lacking the perspective which several centuries have given us, seemed
largely unaware of that fact.   The English people, or a substantial
portion of them, rebelled against their King in 1642 because he
imposed Anglican discipline upon their Puritan convictions, and
arbitrary taxation upon their love of freedom and the legality of
Parliamentary government; they executed him seven years later
because they suspected, with good cause, that he was treacherous.
Yet the King and many of his adherents were sincere, and were
just as devoted to an abstract principle—royal prerogative—as
their opponents were to liberty of conscience and inviolability of
pocketbook.   The fact that right was not on their side makes
their mental processes only more interesting.

Davenant's works contain a number of clues to his political
attitude during the years preceding the crisis.   The Puritans were
the enemies of his craft, and like all playwrights, or actors, he did

[1] Only the facts referring specifically to Davenant are documented in this
chapter; for the rest see the works of Clarendon, Gardiner, and other authorities.

not care for them. He wrote scarcely a play which did not gird
at them in some part; yet his satire was never ill-natured, and he
never presented a caricature so subversive as Jonson's Zeal-of-the-
Land Busy. To him the Puritan seemed simply amusing. When
Captain Cable is impelled by circumstances to turn "precision" in
Act V of *News from Plymouth,* he vows to listen to the "silenc'd
party" till he is deafened; to forswear drinking because "the dew's
enough to satisfy a temperate man, so he travel by night and with
his mouth open"; and to cut down his mainmast "for no other
reason but because it looks like a may-pole." When Davenant
consented to be serious on this subject, he echoed Shakespeare's
"Dost thou think, because thou art virtuous, there shall be no
more cakes and ale?" and impugned the idea of a "tyrannous"
heaven frowning upon the harmless pleasures of man

> . . . as if the fawn and kid were made
> To frisk and caper out their time, and it
> Were sin in us to dance. . . .[2]

His attitude in other issues was not so clear-cut and logical.
We arrive at his opinions chiefly through what may be called
his political masques. In 1638 King Charles had set himself up
as sovereign of the seas, actually in order to countenance the
levying of ship-money, and *Britannia Triumphans,* presented in
January of that year, celebrated that pretentious claim. The King
(garnished in a costume costing £150) [3] was posed behind a
proscenium arch symbolizing "right government" and amidst a
scene depicting variously London, The Palace of Fame, and a
harbor welcoming a stately fleet of ships. He is "Britonocles, the
glory of the western world [who] hath by his wisdom, valour
and piety, not only vindicated his own but far distant seas."
Counterposed to those who praise him is the character Imposture,
a cynical apostle of fraudulence and detraction, who requests

[2] Action's speech in *Britannia Triumphans.*
[3] *Calendar S. P. D.,* 1637–39, p. 19.

Merlin, the magician, to raise the spirits of the "mean and low."
These invoked spirits, cavorting amidst a "horrid hell," furnish
the antimasque. Actually they represent the many-headed multitude, or that part of it most in contrast with the ruling classes;
among them are not only pedlars, ballad singers, and mountebanks, but such historic rebels as Cade, Kett, and Jack Straw.
Now as it happened, those figured as "mean and low" were also
British subjects: The sins of this masque were remembered
sixty years later by a supporter of Jeremy Collier, who in 1698
devoted to it a lengthy section in his *The Stage Condemn'd.*[4]

It is debatable whether Davenant was such a sinner against
democracy as this masque would indicate, or that he really saw
Charles only as wise, valiant, and pious, and his enemies only as a
ridiculous mob. No doubt he did what many have done since—
confused Charles's virtues as a man with his qualities as a ruler.
We shall see in a moment that he was not blind to the justice of
the People's demands, or to the abuses in the court. Among the
"mean and low" of the antimasque described above, he included
"Four old-fashioned Parasitical Courtiers" evidently in an attempt to strike a balance. This group appears elsewhere in his
court masques, the qualifying adjective "old-fashioned" indicat-
ing not that he considered Charles's courtiers any better, but that
he had to be circumspect in criticizing the class for which he
wrote. Davenant had a philosophical turn of mind, and the
knowledge and sagacity which packs such a work as his *Preface
to Gondibert* makes us wonder at the cloudiness and contradiction
in his political opinions. As we examine them we are apt to
think him either hypocritical or muddle headed. But the truth
is that he was simply a thinking man constrained to allegiance
to an irrational cause. He had a conscience, so he rationalized,
but he rationalized badly because he was not a learned man. He
did not become hard and cynical like most of those in his position;
instead, he forced the King's cause to become his intellectual

[4] Paul Reyher, *Les Masques Anglais,* p. 309.

blind spot, and took refuge in a kind of political sentimentalism.

What is meant by political sentimentalism is fully illustrated by *Salmacida Spolia,* a masque presented in January 1640, and even more allusive to national affairs than *Britannia Triumphans.* There is an opening scene of tempest and confusion, which is calmed at last by Concord and Good Genius of Great Britain. The people are invited to "honest pleasure," represented by an antimasque of no less than twenty entries. The scene then changes to represent a craggy mountain range through which lies "the difficult way which heroes are to pass ere they come to the throne of honour." That throne of honor is gained, however, and by none other than King Charles, represented as Philogenes or Lover of his People! His beloved people "of the better sort" sing choruses in his praise, and how the other sort shall be won over is indicated in the explanation of the title of the masque. Charles, like the sweet waters of the Fountain of Salamacis in Caria, can turn barbarians from their barbarism. Not war, but this good King, descending as a "Secret Wisdom," will compose all strife in the dominions.

The wisdom of Charles was so secret that one might scarcely have suspected its existence. Everything that could be done to fan the spark of rebellion, he did. Davenant realized what was coming in 1638 when he wrote his play, *The Distresses,* in Act III of which a character with Puritan tendencies is described as "a very great misleader of weavers" who "may in time breed a rebellion." Like many Royalists he deplored the approaching conflict. In one aspect *Salmacida Spolia* is pacifist propaganda. An even better proof of his desire for peace, and a proof likewise that he respected the case of the other party, is his poetic epistle "To the Queen" written during the gloomy days after his return from the Second Bishops War. In this poem he prays Henrietta to urge her husband to set less store by "that mystick word, Prerogative," and to

> . . . perswade him (in the Peoples Cause)
> Not to esteeme his Judges more than Laws.

There is courage in the lines,

> Accurst are those Court-Sophisters who say
> When Princes yield, Subjects no more obey,[5]

and in his earnest plea for her intercession lest what she may "gain
with Tears, cost others Blood."

2

Henrietta Maria had no talent for the rôle of Angel of Peace.
For her, Puritanism was the symbol of England's apostasy from
the Catholic Church, to which she was becoming daily more devoted. To relieve her husband's straits she preferred, not to soften
his policies, but to crush his domestic enemies with aid to be
got by intriguing with foreign powers and with the Pope. These
aids failed to materialize, and in the spring of 1641 while the
Long Parliament was trying Strafford, she mothered an abortive
coup which involved Davenant and did much to precipitate the
Civil Wars.

Ever since the Treaty of Ripon had halted the Second Bishops
War, two armies had been encamped in the north of England
—the King's army, and the army of Scotch Covenanters. It was
the armed threat from Scotland which lent force to London's
opposition to the King, and while Parliament was obliged to pay
the soldiers in both camps, it tended to stint the English to pay
the Scots. This policy offended a number of English officers,
some of whom were themselves members of the House of Commons; and Henry Percy, brother of Northumberland the Lord
General, began to discuss with several of his fellows the possibility of signing a declaration wherein they should pledge their
troops to the King in the event that Parliament should go too far
in opposing him. But while they were proceeding, cautiously
-and within their rights, another scheme for using the northern

[5] *Folio*, 1673, pp. 298–99.

army had occurred to the Queen and her group of favorites. During March and April, Henry Jermyn, Sir John Suckling, and William Davenant became her agents in a plot to replace Northumberland with Newcastle as Lord General, to place George Goring in the post of Lieutenant General, and to have the army march on London, free Strafford, and dissolve the Parliament.

It is impossible to detail all the ramifications of these concurrent movements. Both groups, the Parliamentary officers and the Queen's courtiers, broached their propositions to the King, and while he saw the infeasibility of the march on London, he was, after his manner, unable either to accept or reject either plan. Instead, he prevailed on Percy to allow the courtiers to meet the officers, hoping that they might effect some brilliant compromise. Henceforth Goring and Jermyn attended the secret councils in Percy's lodging. The officers were reluctant to admit Jermyn; and the two poets, Suckling and Davenant, they would "not medle with at all." As one of them, Captain Pollard, said in his deposition on the plot during the subsequent investigation by Parliament, "Wee disliked them [that is the proposals to march on London and free Strafford] because Sir John Suckling and they were in it. . . . Wee did not very well like the men, for Suckling, Jermaine, and Davenant were in it. . . ."[6] Davenant had acted thus far only as liaison officer and companion of Jermyn and Suckling. But he was "in it." How far he was in it he soon learned to his sorrow.

The officers and courtiers were unable to agree on a scheme to aid the King, splitting primarily on the question of who should command the northern force. When George Goring, trusted favorite of the Queen, found that Percy's group had no stomach for him as Lieutenant General of their army, he forgot his oath of secrecy long enough to breathe a few words about their proposed declaration into the ear of the Earl of Newport, who was at this time aligned with the popular party. The information soon reached Pym, the Parliamentary leader, and no one knew

[6] *Historical Manuscripts Commission*, XXIX, I, 17.

better than Pym how to nurse such a bit of knowledge until it could be used in the right place.

During Strafford's trial, London was in constant tremors over rumors of royal treachery, French aggression, and popish plots. It would not have surprised many of the populace if half the city had been blown up by underground mines, or if a new Armada had appeared in the Thames with the Pope as its admiral. It added nothing to the public peace of mind when the irrepressible Suckling displayed his original notions of conspiracy by convening sixty armed men for a conference in a Bread Street tavern, or when one Captain Billingsley, who had been active with Suckling in raising troops "for the Portugese service," appeared with a hundred soldiers to replace the Tower guard. The Queen's group, despite its repulse by the Parliamentary officers and finally by the King himself, had gone ahead with the army plot unaware of Goring's treachery. Then, during the first week of May, Pym rose in the House and told all he knew. The Commons, in fact all of London, was thrown into an uproar—an uproar which subsided only after it had witnessed the Protestation, Strafford's execution, and the bill against the dissolution of Parliament.

The Queen's conspirators did the worst thing possible under the circumstances. Upon Pym's revelation in the Commons, Percy, Jermyn, Suckling, Davenant, and Captain Billingsley fled the city. Contemporary correspondence reveals how this flight put the sensational climax to the affair. One Puritan sympathizer wrote,

Here has been the greatest treason discovered this week that was in England since the powder plot. . . . The conspirators were Mr. Jermyn, Mr. Percy, Sir John Suckling, Davenant the Poet, and such youths (unsworn counsellors), and, as my lord of Essex called them in the House, the new Juntillio. They are all fled. . . . My lord of Carnarvon and Mr. Crofts did happen to go a private journey at the same time, and so are come to the honour of being reported traitors.[7]

[7] *Historical Manuscripts Commission,* LXIII, I, i, 134.

A Royalist was writing at the same time, "Mr. Percy, Henry Jermyn, Sir John Suckling, Wm. Davenant the poet, and the Earl of Carnarvon are gone for France or Holland. It makes strange discourses . . . and they are esteemed much more culpable than I hope they are." [8]   Many similar letters survive, among them one written by the Venetian ambassador noising the scandal, persistent ever afterwards, that Jermyn was not only the Queen's adviser but her lover as well.[9]

On May 6, Northumberland issued a writ for the stopping of all the ports,[10] and on May 8, a proclamation was published to effect the return of the fugitives to the Parliament.[11]   Then came an almost laughable twist to the affair. Jermyn, Suckling, and the rest escaped to the Continent, while Davenant—the humblest pawn in this queer game—was captured at Feversham in Kent as he was scurrying toward Dover. He was hauled back to London to hear the Lions roar.

Parliament had in its power Wilmot, Ashburnham, Pollard, and others of Percy's group, but these had been less at fault than the courtier conspirators of whom Davenant was now the sole representative. Possibly the poet was ill equipped to elude pursuit. There exists a jingling account of the army plot written just after his capture, which concludes:

> Soon as in Kent they saw the Bard,
> (As to say truth, it is not hard,
> For Will has in his face, the flawes
> Of wounds receiv'd in Countreys Cause)
> They flew on him, like Lions passant,
> And tore his Nose, as much as was on't:
> They call'd him Superstitious Groom,
> And Popish dog, and Curre of Rome;
> But this I'm sure, was the first time,

[8] *Calendar S. P. D.*, 1640–41, p. 571.
[9] *Ibid.*, p. 574; *Historical Manuscripts Commission*, LXIII, I, i, 136; *ibid.*, III, 295; *Calendar S. P. Venetian*, 1640–42, pp. 149, 153.
[10] *Historical Manuscripts Commission*, IV, 413.
[11] *Rymer's Fœdera*, XX, 461.

That Wills Religion was a crime.
What ere he is in's outward part,
He is sure a Poet in his heart,
But 'tis enough, he is thy friend,
And so am I, and there's an end.[12]

However it may have struck his acquaintances, the poet's predicament was not comic. On May 15, he was summoned a prisoner to the House,[13] and on May 17, after lengthy examinations, he was committed to the custody of the Sergeant of Arms who had orders that his prisoner was not to communicate with his friends.[14] This week saw the execution upon Tower Hill of Thomas Wentworth, Earl of Strafford, the most powerful man in England next to the King himself. Parliament had the bit in its teeth, and one poor plotter could have had little hope that it would show more consideration for him than for a King's minister. That Davenant would be convicted of treason and executed was the general opinion. On June 29, Sir John Pennington received the news that "Wilmot, Ashburnham, and Pollard were committed to several prisons. 'Tis thought Jermyn, Suckling, and Davenant will be judged guilty of death." [15] Another bit of doggerel appeared in print, and contained, besides the inevitable reference to the poet's nose, the lines:

> But Davenant shakes and Buttons makes
> As strongly with his breech-a
> As hee ere long did with his tongue
> Make many a bombast speech-a.
>
> And yet we hope hee'le scape the rope,
> That now him so doth fright-a:
> The Parliament being content
> That he this fact should write-a.[16]

---

[12] *Musarum Deliciae*, I, 26.
[13] *Commons Journals*, II, 147; Nalson, *Impartial Collection*, II, 245.
[14] *Commons Journals*, II, 148; Nalson, II, 246; Rushworth, *Collections*, IV, 245.
[15] *Calendar S. P. D.*, 1641–43, p. 29.
[16] Anon., "Letter sent by Sir John Suckling from France . . .," London, 1641.

There is much more of this none too luminous drollery which the reader may be spared. It is worth noting that both these and the rimes previously quoted express a rough good will toward the culprit, and this spirit was not altogether lacking among the Commons themselves.

There is little use in being a man of the pen if one cannot turn his talents to account in a pinch, and Davenant now prepared a petition to be distributed as a folio sheet among members of the House. This shall be quoted in full: It is not readily available elsewhere, and it supplies a glimpse at the character of our man.

To The Honorable

KNIGHTS, CITIZENS

And Burgesses Of The House

of Commons, assembled

in Parliament

The humble Remonstrance of William Davenant, Anno: 1641.

I humbly beseech you to conceive, that I have absented to appeare before this honourable Assembly, rather from a befitting bashfulnesse, as being an ill object, then of outward sence of guilt, as being a delinquent. I did beleeve if I were layed aside awhile, my Cause would be forgotten, because I knew nothing stronger but suspicions and meere opinions can be brought against me; unlesse I may particularly suffer for the old infirmity of that Nation which hath bin ever bred with liberty of speaking: and the very Mechanicks of *Spaine* are glad they are *Spaniards,* because they have liberty; and thinke, when over-speaking becomes dangerous, that then they chiefely lose the liberty of Subjects.

Confession is the neerest way to forgivenesse, therefore I will make haste to accuse my selfe, and say it is possible I may be guilty of some mis-becoming words, yet not words made in dangerous principles and maximes, but loose Arguments, disputed at Table perhaps, with too much fancy and heat. And as in speaking, so in writing, I meane in Letters, I have perhaps committed errours, but never irreverently or maliciously against Parliamentary government.

I have beene admitted into the company of these noble Gentelmen

that are absent, but never was taken into their councels: and sure
for two of them, Master *Iarmin* and Sir *Iohn Suckling,* with whom
I was more particularly acquainted, they were strangely altered, and
in a very short time, if it were possible they could design any thing
against your happy and glorious proceedings, who both in their writing, and speech have so often extold the naturall necessity of Parlia-
ments here, with extreame scorne upon the incapacity of any that
should perswade the King he could be fortunate without them.

And it is not long since I wrote to the Queenes Majesty in praise
of her inclination to become this way the Peoples advocate, the which
they presented to her; for the Arguments sake it is extant in good
hands, and now mentioned, in hope it may be accepted as a Record
of my integrity to the Common-wealth.

It becomes not me to meddle with businesses so farre above my
reach, but that I perceive I am unfortunately mistaken to be ill-
affected.

I doe not certainly know, I protest before God and you, that I
have spoken or written any thing that may endanger me, but as I
urged before, it is generally whispered, and upon the publication of
your Warrant men did avoid me, even my old friends, like one
stricken with an infectious kinde of death, so terrible already is every
marke of your displeasure growne; therefore I humbly beseech your
pardon if a single courage flye from your anger, and begge you
would not interpret as disobedience my not appearing, since it did
rather proceed from a reverend awe your displeasure bred in me;
which two wayes I conceive I might incurre.

First, by knowing of the departure of an ingenious Gentleman
named in the Proclamation, who lay in my house. And secondly,
by something which might either have escaped my tongue or
pen.

Lastly, I most humbly implore, that as you daily leave to future
times some examples of your Iustice, so this day you will leave me
to posterity as a marke of your compassion, and let not my flight
or other indiscretions be my ruine, though contrary to *David's*
opinion, I have fled from Divine power, which is yours by derivation, and chose to fall into the hands of men, which are your Officers
that apprehended me.[17]

[17] British Museum, 816. m. 1. (56).

We may smile at the "befitting bashfulnesse" which had caused the poet to flee, or his willingness to be spared simply that Parliament might leave to posterity the proof that it had tempered justice with mercy, or at his use of biblical cant dear to the hearts of many of his intended readers; yet we should not miss the fact that his petition contained something besides unconscious humor. Davenant was fighting for his life, but he remained loyal to Suckling and Jermyn, and did not deny his cause. Contrast his behavior with that of the highborn Goring, who was at this moment telling all he knew and shifting responsibility upon his closest friends.[18] The attempt to make the Queen the "Peoples advocate" alleged by the petitioner alludes to his poem already mentioned, and to an open letter of similar purport which had been sent by Suckling to Jermyn.[19]

The petition had its effect, and Parliament showed the moderation which so often surprises us in the actions of both sides during this struggle. On July 8, "Upon Reading of Petition of Mr. Wm. Davenant, it was Resolved upon the question That Mr. Wm. Davenant be bailed upon such Bail as this House shall allow of." [20] On the next day the bail was fixed at £4,000, half to be offered by Davenant and half by Dudley Smith and William Champneys, Sewers to the King.[21] The sum seems large, but not so in comparison with the £10,000 fixed as the bail of Sir John Berkeley, one of the army officers involved. Although Davenant was now at liberty, the proceedings in the Commons continued. A bill was prepared, and on August 12 the House voted Percy, Suckling, and Jermyn guilty of high treason—"and then falling out about Mr. Davenant there was great debate, but broke off till further consideration of the evidence against him.[22]

---

[18] *Calendar S. P. D.*, 1641–43, p. 29; *Verney's Notes of the Long Parliament* (*Camden Soc.*), p. 88. In evidence of the friendship between Goring, Jermyn, Davenant, (and Porter), see the elegy written by the poet when Goring was supposedly lost at the siege of Breda, *Folio*, 1673, p. 247.

[19] *Suckling's Works*, Vol. II.

[20] *Commons Journals*, II, 203.

[21] *Ibid.*, II, 205; Nalson, II, 377.

[22] *Verney's Notes*, p. 117.

The rest is anticlimax. Parliament was very busy during the next few months, and it seems simply to have forgotten about the poet. There is no evidence of two more attempted flights described in existing notices of his life and based on a misapprehension by Anthony à Wood.[23] Subsequently Berkeley, also on bail, was allowed to leave London in the royal household, and Davenant probably grasped a similar opportunity, perhaps accompanying the Queen when she sailed for the Continent in February. The honorable knights and burgesses in the Commons assembled knew the value of £4,000 and may have preferred it to another celebration on Tower Hill. Certainly Davenant would not have complained of his inglorious omission from the bill of high treason.

During the months preceding the Queen's departure and while the action against him was being allowed to lapse, he seems simply to have lain low and avoided public attention. When his friend Suckling, after a season of illness and misery on the Continent, ended his own life, Davenant did not commemorate the event. One elegist noticed the fact:

What is become of Davenant, who alone
And onely he, is able to bemone
So great a losse? . . .
Speake, learned Davenant, speake what was the reason?
To praise thy friend, I hope, will not prove treason!

After suggesting that their friendship has been so great that the death of one has meant the death of the other, or that the other though alive "dares not speak for fear," Suckling's admirer concludes:

That hee was constant ever unto the end,
Aske Davenant who was once, and still, his friend,

[23] Aubrey had given Canterbury as the place of capture, and Wood, having heard of Feversham, assumed that there were two arrests, and added a third flight to get the poet out of England.

His hundred Horses hoofes doe yet still ring
His liberall loyalty to his King.[24]

Like pyrotechnic displays in general, Sir John's life had been brilliant but brief. If his hundred horses were to help the King, their riders were now to exchange their white and crimson silks for more durable garments. A long road stretched before them.

3

Practically nothing has ever been said of Davenant's career during the Civil Wars. It has been known that he was knighted, and in his *History of England* Oldmixon remarked "if he deserved nor more for his chivalry than he did for his poetry, it was a dubbing thrown away." [25] Such gruffness is often mistaken for the honest truth. The fact is, however, that Davenant deserved a great deal for his chivalry. He fought in the King's cause longer and more continuously than any other Cavalier poet, though we include in that category the poet by privilege, Newcastle himself. It will be no more than justice if we remember, as we trace his movements at this time, the polite evasions during the same period by that other Royalist poet, Edmund Waller.

In August 1642 King Charles followed a mad attempt to seize the Parliamentary leaders by raising his standard at Nottingham. Henrietta Maria was trying to swell her husband's lean war chest by pawning the crown jewels in Amsterdam. The Earl of Newcastle was raising a Royalist army in the North. The northern army, chiefly because it commanded a port into which the Queen was sending supplies, became known as the popish army, and Davenant's first service in the war was as shuttle between his mistress in Holland and Newcastle in Yorkshire.[26] When the

[24] *Suckling's Works*, II, 282.
[25] II, 235.
[26] *Letters of Queen Henrietta Maria*, p. 121. That Davenant before departing for Yorkshire had, together with Percy, Jermyn, and Montague, been acting as Henrietta's agent in pawning jewels is made known in *Three Letters of Dangerous Consequence*, July 1, 1642; this is one of the news sheets referred to in the foreword as discovered by Hotson.

work of organization had been done, he traded his occupation for one at the battle front.

The poet was already an experienced officer of ordnance, and it was in that capacity and in Newcastle's army that his actual fighting began. Henry Jermyn, and George Goring (who had returned penitent to the Royalist fold) had, like Davenant, been with the Queen in Holland. Jermyn was retained as her personal aide, and Goring was dispatched to Newcastle to become General of the Horse. On October 11, the Queen wrote Newcastle to reserve the place of Master of Ordnance because she had in mind one "very fit for it, and with whom you will be satisfied." [27] Apparently she alluded to Davenant, for by November 1 [28] he had made his final departure from Holland to become Newcastle's Lieutenant General of Ordnance, and ninth ranking staff officer in the northern army.[29] A contemporary in commenting on this appointment said:

The Earle of Newcastle . . . was a Gentleman of grandeur, generosity, loyalty, and steddy and forward courage, but his edge had too much of the razor in it; for he had a tincture of a Romantick spirit, and had the misfortune to have somewhat of the Poet in him; so as he chose Sir William Davenant, an eminent good Poet, and loyall Gentleman, to be Lieutenant-generall of his Ordinance. This inclination of his own and such kind of witty society (to be modest in the expression of it) diverted many counsels, and lost many opportunities. . . .[30]

All of which is amusing—but we must repeat the formula that it does not square with the facts. Davenant served under Newcastle only for nine months. These months, not because of the poet's presence but certainly in spite of it, were Newcastle's only successful period. When the two parted company, the northern

[27] *Letters of Queen Henrietta Maria*, p. 131.
[28] *Historical Manuscripts Commission*, XV, 89.
[29] Margaret Cavendish, Duchess of Newcastle, *Life of the Duke of Newcastle*, p. 165.
[30] Sir Philip Warwick, *Memoirs of the Reigne of Charles I*, p. 235.

army had defeated the Fairfaxes and subdued nearly the entire North.

There is no reason to linger over these early campaigns, for nothing remains to inform us of Davenant's specific engagements. This lack of evidence in itself is an assurance that he performed adequately, for the military records of the day are most eloquent on the subject of failures. John Aubrey has left us only one anecdote as his contribution to the record of the poet's life during the seven years of the war, but as it happens this anecdote relates to the time when he was with the northern army.[31] It appears that two aldermen of York were taken prisoners and turned over to Davenant as investment possibilities. He entertained them with the lavish civility dictated as correct by the most approved authorities on wartime chivalry. But as time wore on and no ransoms were forthcoming, he decided he could not stand the upkeep, so he suggested to them "privately and friendly" that they would oblige him by escaping. They took the hint, but when they had got halfway back to York, they decided that they should have thanked him for his hospitality. They returned, and Davenant narrowly escaped having his soldiers deliver to him the same two prisoners for another prolonged visit. This story may be apocryphal, but not necessarily so. War was then not quite the strenuous exercise it has been made by modern efficiency.

During these months while the poet was with Newcastle, Henrietta Maria had sailed from the Continent with money and munitions, and had joined the northern staff at York. Then with a miniature army severed from the northern forces, she had marched southward, joining her husband at his headquarters in Oxford on July 14, 1643. Just one month later Davenant followed her south with dispatches from Newcastle, and although it was originally intended that he return, he actually remained to fight with the King's army.[32]

[31] John Aubrey, op. cit., I, 206.
[32] Letters of Queen Henrietta Maria, p. 225.

It was just at the juncture when the Royalist forces under Charles, Newcastle, and Hopton and Prince Maurice were expected to make a three-part drive upon London. Instead, each commander elected to besiege isolated Parliamentary strongholds in his own territory. A few days before Davenant's arrival at Oxford, Charles, against the advice of the Queen and of many others, had undertaken the siege of Gloucester, and the poet now followed his King to that front. He was certainly not seeking the quiet sectors. The Earl of Essex at the head of 18,000 Londoners was on his march west. Early in September he arrived at Gloucester, drove the Royalist forces from their position, and entered the city. Later in the month the King attempted to cut off his return march to London, and there ensued the great First Battle of Newbury. Had good management among the King's forces equaled their gallantry, the attempt would have been successful, but officers blundered, ammunition ran low, and Essex broke through. Among the heavy Royalist losses was the death of the poetic and melancholy Falkland who, sick of bloodshed and strife, had stepped into a breach where he was sure he would be killed. The other poet, William Davenant, had one thing to console him for having participated in these sad reverses. At Gloucester the King had conferred upon him the honor of knighthood.[33] When Parliament again found him in its clutches several years later, it had difficulty getting used to his new station and finally compromised by designating him "William Davenant otherwise called Sir William Davenant."

The King's army followed the campaign about Gloucester by going into winter quarters at Oxford. Davenant must have spent only a fraction of the winter with the Court, for he continued his work as agent of the Queen in securing money and munitions at Rotterdam; one news writer reported that among the many

[33] The earliest authority I have found for the place where the honor was conferred is *Walkeley's catalogue of the Dukes . . . of England, Baronets, Knights, &c*, 1653, p. 163; cited by Andrew Kippis, *Biographia Britannica*, IV, 634.

agents who had visited the city the "chief was Davenant the Poet (now Knighted)."[34]   At Oxford the King and Queen set up their state, and a Royalist Parliament assembled. This winter of 1643–44 was one of lame negotiations, futile peace proposals, and nasty bickering. Davenant expressed his disgust with the situation in a poem wherein he distributed the Queen's various excellences among those who needed them:

> Your Patience now our Drums are silent grown,
> We give to Souldiers, who in Fury are,
> To find the profit of their Trade is gone,
> And Lawyers still grow rich by Civil Warr. . . .[35]

It is true that the crusading enthusiasm on both sides was already warping under the stress of private and mercenary interests. Davenant's pessimism was only momentary, and most of his poem expresses his unflagging devotion to his mistress. Ever the Queen's servant, he had begun to compose tributes to her the moment she had landed in England. His knighting in September may have occurred at her suggestion, for she was then successfully seeking honors for Newcastle and Jermyn. Yet on the whole, royal favor meant little in these days. Although the King's cause was more prosperous than it was ever to be again, Royalist morale was low, and as the winter progressed the Queen declined in spirits and in health. Probably Davenant's pleasantest moments during his intermittent stay at Oxford were spent at his old home, the Corn Market tavern still kept by his sister Jane.

In the spring the King again decided to take the field. Had Davenant been seeking a non-combatant's berth, he might have secured a place in the Queen's retinue when in April she left Oxford for Exeter, thence to retire to the Continent. He remained instead with the King's army and, in June, took part in the campaign of Cropredy Bridge.

[34] *The True Informer*, Jan. 13, 1643[4]; see also *The Parliament Scout*, Nov. 24, 1643. (H.)
[35] *Folio*, 1673, p. 296.

For several weeks Charles maneuvered through the Oxford district, badgered at first by both Essex and Sir William Waller and finally by Waller alone. On June 13 he held a council of war at Bewdley, and Davenant, evidently on reconnoitering duty —for he was stationed on the line of march at Haleford—improved his time by writing a letter of military advice, addressed to no less a person than Prince Rupert. At this time the Prince was faced with the alternative of relieving Newcastle, whom an invasion of Scots from the north had forced to retreat into York, or coming to the aid of the King. Davenant argued very sensibly that the loss of the North would be disastrous and that the King's army was in no immediate danger. There is no need to quote this letter: [36] From the point of view of military strategy it is quite sound, and compares extremely well with one sent to Rupert by the King on the following day. The King's letter tells Rupert either to go to Newcastle, or to come south, or to do both. Incidentally the situation in the North culminated in the victory of Cromwell, Manchester, and Fairfax at Marston Moor, an event which forecast the doom of the Royal cause and so discouraged Newcastle that he left for the Continent and proceeded to write plays and train horses.

Although Davenant had the honor of being reported killed at Marston Moor, by Parliamentary news writers,[37] he seems not to have left the King's army. The Battle of Cropredy Bridge itself consisted only of a few sallies by the Cherwell between Waller's sluggish levies and Charles's cavalry. If Davenant was craving a chance to grace his newly acquired knighthood, this would have seemed a poor climax to weeks of forced marches about the Cotswold. It took place on June 29, just a few days before Marston Moor, and was followed by the King's decision to lead his army to Cornwall in pursuit of Essex. The march westward began, and by the beginning of August the King had

---

[36] Reproduced in facsimile by W. W. Greg, *English Literary Autographs*, Part I, number xxvi. The King's letter on the same subject is an historical curiosity, printed by R. S. Gardiner, *Great Civil War*, I, 435.

[37] *The Parliament Scout*, July 18–25, 1644. (H.)

reached Liskeard and was in a position of advantage to treat with the enemy at Lostwithiel. That Davenant had shared in this pursuit we know from a new development which came at this juncture of his military career. For the present the King had the upper hand in the West, for Essex was cornered and out-numbered; and Davenant, scenting a new means by which he might be useful, decided to forsake land service for the sea.

On August 16, he was at Boconnock, a post near Lostwithiel just seized by the Royalists, and had got in touch with George, Lord Digby. Digby, a rising official lately created principal Secretary of State, gave him a letter describing him as his "very good friend" and addressed to Edward Seymour, commander of the port of Dartmouth.[38] Three days later, the poet had returned along the King's line of march to Exeter and had received another letter to Seymour from Sir Hugh Pollard. From this second letter we get our first inkling of his design. Pollard wrote: "I join with Sir William Davenant in desiring you let him know whether you have any ship or bark in your harbour that will transport him into France; . . . secrecy and speedy answer is desired, and I am sure when you consider what business he car-ries with him, you will need no quickening."[39] One month before Davenant had set about getting these letters, the Queen and Lord Jermyn had sailed for France, and only one week be-fore, Lord Goring, fresh from Marston Moor, had joined the King at Liskeard and had replaced Wilmot as General of the Horse in the western army. It is obvious that Davenant, either of his own or Goring's volition, was now to secure a packet boat to run through the Parliamentary blockade munitions sent to the western army by the Queen.

The boat was obtained, and the poet-soldier now became the poet-marine. For the remainder of 1644 and throughout 1645 he engaged in this hazardous and presumably useful service. In all he delivered over £13,000 worth of arms and ammunition,[40]

[38] *Historical Manuscripts Commission*, XLIII, 73.
[39] *Ibid.*, pp. 78–79.
[40] *Ibid.*, LXX, 302; *Calendar S. P. D.*, 1645–47, pp. 23–24.

about £1,000 worth of which seem to have been purchased with his own money.[41] That one man at least considered him a dangerous enemy is attested by a letter sent from Paris in December, 1645, by a rabid Parliamentarian: "Sir William Davenant, the poet—*now the great pirott*—and he that was the agent in projecting and bring[ing] up the northerne army three years since [sh]ould be putt into the exceptions for life. No man hath don you more hurt, and hath been a greater enemy to the parliament."[42]

During 1645 Henrietta Maria was seeking armed aid from the Duke of Lorraine and, on condition that the Dutch would give similar aid, a marriage contract between her son and the Princess of Orange. Sir William had not yet been accepted into the councils of the Royalist leaders, but that he knew of the Queen's projects is indicated in a letter he carried across the channel in May. It was addressed by Jermyn to Digby, and reads in part:

This bearer, Sir William Davenant, is infinitely faithful to the King's cause; he hath been lately in Holland, so that he met there with the knowledge of our treaty so that it was neither possible nor needful to conceal it from him. The treaty of the marriage and the proposition [for Dutch alliance] he knows, but the design of the Duke of Lorraine he does not; of the other two he will speak to you, but charge him with secrecy, for the Queen does still desire the business of the marriage may not be divulged, and the other is destroyed if it yet take wind. Pray if Davenant have need of your favor in anything else use him very kindly for my sake, and let him know [who] conjured you to do so.[43]

These are friendly sentiments, even though they show more confidence in the poet's faith than in his discretion. All this secrecy, incidentally, was wasted. A few weeks later, the terrific defeat

[41] *Calendar S. P. D.,* 1661–62, p. 359.
[42] *Historical Manuscripts Commission,* XXIX, I, pp. 323–24.
[43] *Calendar S. P. D.,* 1644–45, p. 430.

of the Royalists at Naseby dampened what little ardor the Queen's prospective allies may have had.

The entire year was one of disasters. For any good they did the western army, Davenant's munitions might have remained across the channel. The Commander, Lord Goring, as the far more estimable Newcastle had done before him, conceived a jealousy of Prince Rupert, and spent most of his time sulking at Exeter. Sinking himself at last into absolute debauchery, he allowed the West to be wrung practically without resistance from the Royalist grip. In December, ill from his excesses, he asked the King for permission to leave England, and without awaiting a reply, he sailed for the Continent. Davenant concluded his service at sea by conducting this precious warrior to Havre,[44] and thence to Rouen and Paris.[45]

At the time, the poet did not realize that his experiences in running the Parliamentary blockade were over. At Paris he was met by an express from the Queen, who was hoping that she could retrieve the losses in the West with five thousand troops which France (as she thought) had consented to let her raise. These troops were to be conducted to Dartmouth by Davenant, and to be commanded by Goring, when he was "passed his cure." [46] But if the others at St. Germains had not yet lost faith in Goring, Sir William had. In a long letter sent to Colepepper and Hyde on January 17, 1646, he discusses the project. He is highly optimistic, having just received word that the Dutch fleet will help to transport the troops, but he adds:

The last thing now will bee to consider in what manner and by what persons the western businesse is to bee managed. That it may bee so designed at least that Sober men may expect such events from it as good men ought to wish . . . is onely to bee hoped for from that which humane nature is least capable of, Self Deniall.s . . . I look upon this bodie, which will bee a mixt one of Strangers and English,

[44] *Calendar of Clarendon Papers,* I, 290–91.
[45] *Historical Manuscripts Commission,* VI, 453.
[46] *Ibid.,* XXIX, I, 335.

not easily to bee governed but by one accustomed to both. . . . I
cannot reverence the Princes [i. e. Charles's, whom he has suggested
as the leader] age and experience so much, though I doe his other
parts, that I would have this work fall into his hands but with the
greatest assistances. . . . Sr P. Ball, Sr G. Pary & Mr Muddiford are by
the reputation wee have of them excellent persons. . . .[47]

No mention is made of George Goring in this letter, or in one he
sent on the same subject to Sir Hugh Pollard.[48]   The letter to
Pollard was sent in February, at which time Davenant was still
confident he would soon be bringing over the French troops.
Needless to say these troops never materialized.   Reverses in England continued, and early in the spring King Charles laid down
his arms and surrendered his person to the Scots.

Davenant remained in Paris, and occupied part of his time in
writing hopeful letters to Chancellor Hyde,[49] and in adding his
arguments to those of Henrietta Maria and Jermyn in favor of
removing Prince Charles from Jersey to Paris.   In February there
fell into the hands of Parliament a Scotchman, "a famous
Engineer, and servant to Sir William Davenant, who hath promised to make the Port of Dartmouth impregnable."   At the time
Dartmouth had already surrendered.[50]   The poet's optimism
never flagged, and was, like the continuance of his service, almost
unique among the literati (and others) who served the King.
Absence of morale and of "Self Deniells" lost the war.   Newcastle
served just the length of time that it should have taken, by perfect management, to win the victory.   Rupert retained his high
spirits, but only because he loved the fighting game, and he
alienated whole counties from the King by his wholesale plunder-
ing.   Falkland died at Newbury, not a sacrifice to his cause, but
a mere suicide.   Many others showed a marked preference of
exile to the English war zone.   It is true that Davenant's zeal may

[47] Tanner MSS (Bodleian), LX, 371.
[48] Ibid., LX, 489.
[49] Calendar of Clarendon Papers, I, 315, 320, 323.
[50] The True Informer, Feb. 6, 1646. (H.)

have risen from the same naïveté and quixotism that had made him, years before, offer to blow up Dunkirk. But the Royalists would have been better off if more of them had shared his simplicity.

4

Although it was not to conduct troops, Davenant did make one more journey to England in the Royal cause. The Queen and her advisers, that is, the group centering about Jermyn as opposed to the group centering about Hyde, believed that the King's safety now lay in abandoning Episcopacy and in uniting with the Scottish and English Presbyterians against the English Independents and antimonarchists. Efforts were made to bring about this step, and Bellievre, the French ambassador at Newcastle, constantly preached expediency to the captive King. But Charles, who had wavered in so many things, clung to the rock of Anglicanism. As winter drew on, the Queen resolved to send her husband a special envoy from Paris. The problem arose of whom to send. Since the task was to be one in dialectics, a literary man seemed to be indicated. Hobbes was considered (a rare thought!), but finally Sir William Davenant was selected.

He arrived at Newcastle in October, and was admitted, together with Will Murray, into the presence of the King. Hyde has left the following account of the interview:

The queen, who was never advised by those who either understood or valued his [Charles's] true interest sent sir William Davenant, an honest man and a witty, but in all respects inferior to such a trust, with a letter of credit to the king, who knew the person well enough under another character [i. e. as a poet] than was like to give him much credit in the argument in which he was intrusted. . . .

Sir William had, by the countenance of the French ambassador, easy admission to the King; who heard him patiently all he had to say, and answered him in that manner that made it evident he was not pleased with the advice. When he found his majesty unsatisfied and that he was not like to consent to what was so earnestly desired by them by whose advice he was sent, and who undervalued all those scruples of conscience which his majesty himself was so strongly possessed with, he took upon him the confidence to offer some reasons to the king to induce him to yield to what was proposed. . . . [Hyde here ascribes to the King speeches condemning Colepepper and Jermyn of irreligion, and praising the superior worth of Hyde himself.] Davenant then offering some reasons of his own, in which he mentioned the church slightingly, as if it were not of importance enough to weigh down the benefit that would attend the concession, his majesty was transported with so much passion and indignation that he gave him more reproachful terms, and a sharper reprehension, than he did ever towards any other man; and forbade him to presume to come again into his presence. Whereupon the poor man, who had in truth very good affections, was exceedingly dejected and afflicted; and returned into France, to give an account of his ill success to those who sent him.[51]

Luckily we are able to determine how much of the above account is the writer's embellishment. Hyde's source of information was a copy of a letter sent by the King to Colepepper, Jermyn, and Ashburnham. It does contain a reprimand, but one couched in most conciliatory terms:

This letter will need a preamble, for otherwais, what I shall wryte may be easily mistaken. Wherefore know and be assured, that I am so well satisfied of the loyallty, fidelity, and affection of you three to my crowne, cause, and person, as what I shall heer after is without any detriment to this my profession; in which if you were not firme, I should not think you worthy of this ensewing freedome. . . . I found Davenant's instructions to be such both for matter and circumstance, that my just greife for them had been unsupportable, but that the extraordinary and severall kynde expressions of my wyfe (meeting casually at that tyme) abated the sharpness of my sorrow. . . . I am condemned of willfulness. . . . And who causes me to be condemned but those who either takes courage and morall honesty for conscience, or those who were never rightly grounded in Religion according to the Church of England. . . . Wherfor instruct your-

[51] Edward Hyde, Earl of Clarendon, *History,* IV, 223–25.

selfes better, recant, and undeceave those whom ye have misinformed. . . . Only one particular I must mention, wherwith Davenant hath threatned me; which is 351 [the Queen] retyring from all businesses into a monostary. This if it fall out, (which God forbid) is so distructife to all my affaires—I say no more of it; my hart is too bigg. . . .[52]

Charles had been strongly moved, but Davenant had neither been blasted with his displeasure nor forbidden the presence. As a matter of fact he remained at Newcastle a week and continued to urge his reasons. We get a true knowledge of the episode, not from the partisan Hyde, but from the above letter, and a similar one sent to the Queen. In this, Charles, after protesting his "perfect reall and unchangable love," says, "I asseure thee that the absolute establishing of Presbiteriall governement would make me but a titulary King. And that this is so, both the Wills, Davenant and Murray confesses; but then they say, that a present absolut concession is the only way to reduce the governement, as I would have it. . . ."[53] There is no sign of that passion which according to Hyde had withered Davenant—mentioned here familiarly as one of the "Wills." The King made the poet his return messenger, and anxiously awaited the Queen's response.[54]

The envoy returned to Paris in November. According to one, no doubt imaginative, report, he had been forced to smuggle himself out of the country in a chest.[55] He had left behind him letters of high courage written by Henrietta Maria to hearten Charles: *"Mes esperances sont grands; pourveu que vous soies constant et resolu, nous serons Maistres encore; et nous nous reverrons avec plus de joye que jamais. A Dieu, mon cher Coeur!"*[56] But now she could only write: "Davenant hath given me a large account of the business where you are, upon

[52] *State Papers collected by Edward, Earl of Clarendon,* II, 270.
[53] *Ibid.,* II, 270.
[54] *Camden Society Publications,* "Hamilton Papers," pp. 127–28.
[55] *The Kingdomes Weekly Intelligencer,* Feb. 23–Mar. 2, 1647. (H.)
[56] *State Papers collected by Edward, Earl of Clarendon,* II, 271.

which I must conclude with more feare than hope. . . ." [57]
The Queen's love for Charles was genuine, and her fears for his
welfare were amply justified.

Davenant had failed in the most important service that his
mistress had ever entrusted to him. It is true that he had shown
himself a sheer opportunist, and to gain his end had used the
lever of Charles's love for his wife. He had "threatened" the
King. But the case was extreme. Edward Hyde would never
have done such a thing, and this man who had once shared with
the poet his lodgings in the Inner Temple could, now that he had
risen to such heights of dignity, treat him with tolerant contempt. Nevertheless, in this instance the Poet had been wiser
than the Chancellor. A few months after his mission, the Scots
surrendered Charles to the English commissioners—not, as the
Royalists claimed, for English gold, but because he had rejected
the Presbytery. In the period which followed, the King made
concessions equaling those which the poet had urged at Newcastle. It was now too late. There were months of turmoil, and
at the end of them Cromwell was in the saddle. On January 30,
1649, Charles stood in the Banqueting House at Whitehall, looking for the last time upon the Vandykes and Titians which he had
guarded so solicitously from the gay lights of Davenant's masques.
When he left the room, it was to step from the window to his
scaffold. The cause was lost to which Davenant, in the words of
Lord Jermyn, had been "infinitely faithful."

[57] *Letters of Queen Henrietta Maria*, p. 329.

V

THE VENTURER

I

FOR over four years Davenant lived in France, his mission to the King being only an interlude in an exile which lasted from late winter of 1645 to early spring of 1650. In the midst of this period there were five months of fighting in England —the second Civil War—and while the poet was not there to bear arms, he shared in the activities of the little court at St. Germains which instigated this desperate Royalist attempt. He was now the agent and confidant of his former friend and fellow conspirator, Lord Jermyn, chief officer of Henrietta Maria and the Prince of Wales, sharing with him his apartments at St. Germains and in the Louvre, and going with him on his journeys about the Continent. Between the time when he had arrived in Paris hoping to conduct five thousand French troops to Portsmouth and the time when he had been sent to Charles at Newcastle, he had already accompanied Jermyn on an important mission. In June 1646 the Queen had sent her favorite, together with Wentworth, Digby, and Wilmot, to the Island of Jersey to fetch Prince Charles to Paris. The Prince's council, headed by Edward Hyde, was opposed to his removal from English soil. For several days Hyde and Jermyn squared at each other; when the Prince finally elected to join his mother, the Chancellor refused to accompany him, and he never forgave that group, including Davenant,[1] which had usurped his authority over the heir apparent.

[1] *Calendar of Clarendon State Papers*, I, 323.

Opinions of Lord Jermyn vary, but only in negative degree. Hyde indicted him of covetousness and the vanity of thinking he could please all and displease none, while Bishops Burnet and Warburton shared the none too Christian suspicion that he was kept by the Queen and was the father of one of her children. Any scandal about Jermyn, in so far as it relates to Henrietta Maria, is unfounded. He was loyal to the King and as zealous in his cause as his love of self and the creature comforts would permit. His own opinion that he had a flair for diplomacy was quite mistaken, but it was flattered by the unlimited opportunities cast his way by the favor of his mistress. He was a courtier miscast as a statesman, and he brought to the arena of international politics talents only qualifying him to dominate the intrigues of Whitehall. Yet when we pierce beyond his incompetence and defects of character, we find in Davenant's patron more to attract than to repel. It is difficult to analyze why we of today feel more at home with Jermyn's type, the new seventeenth-century type, than with the more admirable Elizabethans. Between us and the courtly Philip Sidney or the stalwart Walter Raleigh stands a medieval barrier—the barrier of their determinate thought. We are embarrassed. But among Jermyn's kind, a certain intellectual and emotional equipoise, an urbanity, call it what you will, convinces us that they would have been more open to the complexities, perhaps the equivocations, of modern thought. Perhaps it is simply that they shared our own taint of scepticism. It is to Jermyn's credit that his mastery of *savoir vivre* dictated a choice for literary companionships. He extended his protection at this time not only to Davenant but to another poet very much like him, Abraham Cowley, whom he selected as his secretary. He was in a position to be hospitable, for according to Hyde "he loved plenty so well, that he would not be without it, whatever others suffered who had been more acquainted with it. All who had any relation to the prince were to implore his aid; and the prince himself could obtain nothing but by him." [2]

[2] Edward, Earl of Clarendon, *History*, V, 343.

It was lucky for Davenant that Jermyn received him. The
exiles were impoverished as a class, and mere food and lodging
were at a premium. Moreover the poet had not only himself to
think of. At some time during the Civil War his wife had died,
and his two children, William and Mary, were now sent to join
him in exile. In August 1646 he wrote to Sir Richard Brown, the
Royalist minister at Paris:

Sir,

I understand that I have 2 children newly arrived at Paris, which
a servant of my wives hath stolne from an obscure country education in which they have continued during this Parliament now in
London: And I shall desire you will be pleased to contribute a little
of your care toward the provision of such necesserie things as shall
refine their bodies, and for their mindes, I will provide a magiciene
of mine owne. M^m Porter tells me Mistresse Sayers will upon your
intreaty take this paynes: and I will intreat you to give her mony to
furnish them cheap and handsomely which upon sight of your hand
shall be returnd you by
                Your most humble and affectionate servant
                        Will Davenant [3]
St Germains
Aug 14

Since William Jr. was an adult by this time and Mary was probably not much younger, Davenant (unless he had younger children of whom we know nothing) must have intended his "magiciene" simply to give them a certain polish in deportment. In one
respect their Commonwealth education stuck, for although a
friend of Madame Porter was selected to tutor them, both retained their Protestant faith. At this period Davenant himself is
reputed to have turned Catholic.

There would be nothing very surprising about such a step, considering the length of time he had come under the influence of
the Queen. To be of her circle had long been enough to invite

[3] Montague MSS (Bodleian), d. 1, f. 40.

suspicion, and we have seen that as early as 1641 he was referred to as "Popish dog and curre of Rome." Henrietta Maria was constantly converting those about her, and since five or six years prior to 1641 it had been fashionable to be thus converted. At first, men prominent in court life had found it politically inexpedient to desert the Anglican faith of the King, but their wives had suffered no such restraint. Endymion Porter remained a Protestant, but Madame Olivia became not only a Catholic but a violent proselytizer.[4] A number of male courtiers simply objected to the high cost of recusancy, and attended mass in the Queen's chapel but evaded fines by attending Anglican services as well. Many of Davenant's chief associates had been Catholics, among them the friendly physician, Thomas Cademan. During the exile many of the barriers against declaring for new faiths had been removed: During 1647 there was some indecision at St. Germains whether the Prince of Wales was to be a Roman Catholic, an English Episcopalian, a Scotch Presbyterian, or a French Huguenot. Such men as Thomas Hobbes and Jermyn himself remained Protestants, not through any deep religious conviction but because they found certain terrestrial comforts in the Church of England.

Aubrey says nothing of Davenant's conversion, and Anthony à Wood, whose testimony[5] has been sufficient to win the poet a place in all Catholic cyclopedias and anthologies, may have been misled by the fact that his third wife was French and apparently Catholic. He himself was given a Church of England burial.[6] There is little point in debating the question (except that it might help to remove from him the stigma of timeserving), because Davenant's religious beliefs can be determined without reference to any particular creed. The basis for these beliefs was a kind of regretful agnosticism. For him, life after death was

---

[4] D. Townshend, *op. cit.*, p. 150.
[5] *Athenae Oxonienses*, III, 805.
[6] John Aubrey, *op. cit.*, I, 208; *Calendar of Treasury Books*, 1669–72, p. 772.

The place of absence, where we meet, by all
The guess of learned thought, we know not whom;
Only a prompt delight we have in faith
Gives us the easy comfort of a hope
That our necessity must rather praise
Than fear as false. . . .[7]

Coupled with this was an insight into the practical application
of Christianity—an insight not shared by certain archbishops of
his day, and since:

Christian Religion hath the innocence of a village neighbourhood,
and did antiently in its politicks rather promote the interest of Mankind than of states; and rather all states than one, for particular en-
deavors onely in behalf of our own homes are signs of a narrow
moral education, not of the vast kindness of Christian Religion,
which likewise ordain'd as well an universal communion of bosomes,
as a communion of wealth. Such is Christian Religion in the pre-
cepts, and was once so in the practice.[8]

Davenant had seen at first hand the politico-religious travesty of
Buckingham's overtures to Rochelle. He had marched with
Charles on the crusade to force Anglicanism on Scotland—a crusade during which his superior officer, Newport, had driven a
private trade in selling the Royal munitions. Denominational
conflicts had left him few illusions, and he had concluded that
religion and creed have little in common. The most interesting
sentence in Aubrey's rough jottings about Davenant is the irrele-
vant addendum—"His private opinion was that Religion at last,
—e. g. a hundred years hence,—would come to settlement, and
that in a kind of ingeniose Quakerisme." [9]

All through his exile Sir William espoused Jermyn's interests
with the loyal zeal so characteristic of him. In the winter of

[7] Love and Honour, Act III.
[8] Preface to Gondibert, Folio, 1673, p. 4.
[9] John Aubrey, op. cit., I, 208. One commentator on the side of Parliament
branded Davenant's type of heresy as Gnosticism; cf. The Cavalier's Bible,
1644. (H.)

1647–48 the two went to Calais, where the Prince of Wales hoped to take command of the revolted Parliamentary fleet. While there, Davenant rendered Jermyn the delicate service of sheltering him from the attentions of one Griffin, a duellist and bully, who later followed them to Paris and proclaimed his intention to "cause Davenant to be pistolled and Lord Jermin to be gelt." [10] Griffin's aggressions were the result of his anxiety to be received by the exiled English court; and the rivalry to gain influence with Prince Charles caused feuds among Royalists supposedly more responsible than chance swaggerers. The chief bone of contention was the personnel of the Prince's council. No one could approve of anyone but himself as a member, and on one occasion Davenant came out with the blunt statement that Charles's advisers were so only "by virtue of my Lord Jarmins pleasure, who might, if he pleased, as well have appointed him for one and, if he found itt inconvenient to continue them all or any of them, he might and would att his pleasure remove and change them. . . ." [11]

It was no sinecure to be mixed up in the "wayes and small policies of St. Germains," and a letter written by Lord Hatton in the summer of 1648 hints at the range of the poet's duties. [12] Lord Digby, having taken offense at Jermyn's monopoly of the heir apparent, challenged him to a duel. The two were to fight it out with swords at Nanterre, and since Jermyn had selected Davenant as his second, the poet was to encounter the challenger's brother, Sir Kenelm Digby. Both the Digbys were notoriously capable swordsmen. According to Hatton, who was well disposed to neither of the principals, the fight never came off because of a mutual distaste for cold steel. After he had sent his challenge, Lord Digby failed to make sure that the duel would take place, as he might have done, by keeping out of sight; and Jermyn ordered Davenant to set a guard upon him. The upshot was

[10] Christopher Lord Hatton to Secretary Nicholas, *Camden Society Publications*, "Nicholas Papers," I, 94.

[11] *Ibid.*, I, 96.

[12] *Ibid.*, I, 90 ff.

that the quarrelers were brought before the Queen, and Lord
Digby, instead of giving the "home charge" which everyone expected, rendered Lord Jermyn the necessary satisfaction. Whereupon Sir Kenelm Digby left Paris, disgusted at the lost opportunity to kill Davenant. The poet's relations with Jermyn were
not calculated to win him popularity, and among others who
took umbrage at him at this time was Sir Balthazar Gerbier, once
the assistant master of ceremonies at Whitehall. Gerbier, who
seemed to suffer from delusions of persecution, complained that

> . . . the malice of men was so great, as that they endeavoured to
> make the world beleeve that the disaster which then befell me, be-
> tween Roan and Deepe was but a fixion; and who should be the
> authour of this abominable falsehood, but William Crafts and Dav-
> enant the poet, who reported it frequently at the Louvre, and up and
> down Paris.[13]

Of course all of the poet's time was not taken up with these
dissensions. There were amenities. In 1646 a strolling company
of English actors entertained the Prince.[14] The French stage
was in full flower, and Cardinal Mazarin was bringing Italian
opera to Paris. There was no lack of good company for a
literary man. Thomas Hobbes was at hand to tutor the Prince
in mathematics, and Buckingham was there to tutor him in mys-
teries less cold. Davenant became very intimate with Hobbes,
and also struck up an acquaintance with Edmund Waller—a
friend well chosen, for he was the only exile besides Jermyn who
could afford to keep a table. Other wits and writers were there
at intervals—Cavendish, Killigrew, Denham, Crofts, Murray, etc.
Occasionally his old friend, Endymion Porter, visited Paris as a
messenger to the Queen.

Davenant's most constant companion must have been his part-
ner in Jermyn's service, Abraham Cowley. These two had much

<hr>

13 *Manifestation by Sir Balthazar Gerbier,* 1651, quoted by Maidment and
Logan, *Davenant's Dramatic Works,* II, 262.
14 L. Hotson, *Commonwealth and Restoration Stage,* p. 21.

in common; Cowley himself has told us that his head was first
filled with the chimes of verse from the pages of the *Faerie
Queene*,[15] and although he is usually listed among the precursors of Classicism, he belonged like Davenant partly to the
former age. He was the author of the unfinished epic, *Davideis*,
and his influence may help to explain why his companion now
embarked on an epic venture of his own.

During 1649, Davenant wrote the first two books of *Gondibert*,
bringing to the task all the dammed-up zeal of a poetic urge
frustrated for nearly ten years. This poem was to be his bid for
lasting fame and he put away from him "as papers unworthy of
light, all those hasty digestions of thought which were published
in youth," for "those must needs prophecy with ill success who
make use of their Visions in Wine." [16] His aim was to shatter
the gyves of epic tradition and lead the way to a new poetic
ideal—a heart-warming aspiration, however inadequately realized. Hobbes read his verses from day to day, and on January
2, 1650, the poet addressed a long prefatory epistle to the philosopher, not only introducing the poem but setting forth his
literary creed and his philosophy of life as well. No one can
read this essay without yielding to the personality behind it.
What little prose of Davenant comes before—a thin sheaf of military and official correspondence—has the wary solemnity of a
man talking over his head. But in the *Preface to Gondibert*,
the author was in his own true world. Not only is it full of
wisdom and originality, but it is written with a richness of flavor
that convinces one that any critic who ignores Davenant is ig-
norant of his own craft. Abstracts will be given hereafter, but
even the few sentences already quoted give a notion of its color
and tone:

Christian Religion hath the innocence of a village neighbourhood.

*Those must needs prophecy with ill success who make use of their
Visions in Wine.*

15 "Essay on Himself."
16 *Preface to Gondibert*, Folio, 1673, pp. 9–10.

Nor does the merit lie solely in the phrasing and the sententious-ness. For the first time we are able to glimpse Davenant's ma-turer personality: He is a very human person who speaks to us familiarly, with honest sincerity, humor, and a mellow fullness of tone.

Hobbes wrote a very complimentary answer to the preface, and although the poet preferred not to publish any of his epic (which, in spite of him, was turning out to be a rimed romance) until he had completed the remaining three books, he published imme-diately his own and Hobbes's epistles.[17] When the itinerant Cavaliers learned that one of their number was writing neither drinking songs nor ribald satires but a heroic poem designed to give a "familiar and easie view" of human life, and to teach the politic and moral virtues, they emitted a whoop of derision which echoed for several years. They had decided they would not like this work before they had seen it, and the more jovial element among them began to sharpen their barbs for the author.

In 1650 Davenant was forty-four years old, homeless and pre-cariously placed. To his credit it can be said, he did not wish to spend the rest of his life as the underling of Henry Jermyn. He was a Quixote, born to action and experiment, and three great ventures compose the pattern of his middle years. The first of these ventures was *Gondibert,* and in his preface to the epic there is mention of the second. His poem, he told Hobbes, would be completed in America. King Charles was dead, England was in the grip of Cromwell, and the poet faced toward the New World.

2

In September 1649, while Charles II (at present "King of Scots") was enduring another sojourn at Jersey, Davenant re-ceived an appointment to be Treasurer of Virginia in the absence of Sir John Berkeley, who had been named to replace William

---

[17] Paris, 1650; see Bibliography.

Clayburne because the latter "was affected to the Parliam^t." [18]
It is possible that Davenant was in Jersey at the time, for he
seems to have been associated with Sir George Carteret, Governor
of the island and himself interested in the colonization of "New
Jersey." Five months later Charles signed a new commission ap-
pointing the poet to an office important enough to be startling.
The document is dated February 16, 1650, and authorizes Davenant
to sail to Maryland and oust the proprietary, Lord Baltimore.
He is to be the new Governor, because the old one "doth visibly
adhere to the rebels of England, and admit all kind of schismatics
and sectaries and other ill-affected persons into the said planta-
tion of Maryland." [19] There is a certain consistency shown in
this appointment, for Sir William Berkeley's selection as Governor of Virginia seems to prove that the Royalists were partial
to playwrights as the masters of American colonies. In fact
Berkeley's commission includes the name of Sir William Davenant as a member of the council which was to fortify Virginia
against Parliamentary invasion.[20] Aubrey's account of the poet's
project is at variance with all of these contradictory official documents. According to him, Sir William

. . . layd an ingeniose designe to carry a considerable number of
artificers (chiefly weavers) from hence to Virginia, and by Mary
the queen-mothers meanes, he got favour from the King of France
to goe into the prisons and pick and choose. So when the poor
damned wretches understood what the design was, the[y] cryed *uno
ore*—'*Tout tisseran!*' i.e. We are all weavers! Will [took] 36, as
I remember, if not more, and shipped them . . .

Although there is something suspicious about this anecdote—lying perhaps in the fact that Aubrey came so near remembering
thirty-six as the exact number of weavers—information has re-

[18] *Historical Manuscripts Commission*, LXX, 284, 302.
[19] W. H. Browne, *George Calvert and Cecilius Calvert, Barons Baltimore*,
pp. 141–42.
[20] *Calendar S. P. Colonial*, 1574–1660, p. 340.

cently come to light to give substantiation to certain of its details. In the *Journal* of Jean Chevalier, wherein Davenant's venture is identified with Carteret's attempt to establish a colony on Smith Island in Chesapeake Bay, the Jersey chronicler mentions certain craftsmen (fourteen or fifteen in number) whom Davenant had taken to ply their trades in the New World.[21]

Whether it was to become Treasurer or Commissioner of Virginia, Governor of Maryland, or to plant the textile industry in the trans-Atlantic wilds, Davenant went about his preparations during the early months of 1650. He must have had considerable financial backing, for by spring he had obtained and provisioned a ship, and enlisted his company. He took with him Jean Bernard, a Frenchman, as his personal servant,[22] Thomas Crosse, his future stepson, as his secretary,[23] and no doubt his two children, William and Mary. Early in May he weighed anchor and put out to sea.

At Paris his friends anxiously awaited news that he had cleared the channel. On May 10, Abraham Cowley wrote to Henry Bennet, future Earl of Arlington, "We have not heard one word from Sir W. Davenant since he left us; be pleas'd to give me some account of him and his Voyage." [24] Just two weeks later the news arrived, and it was tragic. Cowley again wrote to Bennet:

I should write to Sir G. Carteret but have not now time, be pleased to let him know the Misfortune that is befallen Sir Will Davenant (in which I believe he has a share) it is he is taken, and now Prisoner with all his Men in the Isle of Wight. We are strangely pursu'd in all things, and all places, by our evil Fortune, even our retreats to the other World (except by death) are cutt off.[25]

[21] W. R. Richardson, "Davenant as American Colonizer," *ELH*, I (1934), pp. 61–62.

[22] *Calendar S. P. D.*, 1651, p. 251.

[23] For documentation see below, note 76. The point of departure was the Island of Jersey, whither Davenant went from Paris during the second week of January, 1650, in the company of Sir John Berkeley; cf. *A Briefe Relation*, Jan. 8–15, 1650. (H.)

[24] *Miscellanea Aulica*, p. 133.

[25] *Ibid.*, p. 137.

It was true. Parliamentary ships had swooped down upon the venturer's bark before it had fairly started. Davenant had been cast into prison at Cowes Castle, and by May 17 the Council of State had instructed Col. Sydenham to keep him there until further orders, "he having been an active enemy to the Commonwealth." [26] It was sad news for the Royalists, and even Edward Hyde professed himself "exceedingly afflicted for the misfortune of Will Davenant." [27]

The poet's misfortune was greater than the mere loss of his venture. It was his fate to fall into the hands of the enemy at unseasonable moments. The last time, Parliament had been executing Strafford, and this time, it was not only convalescing from the execution of the King himself but was preparing for further exercises of the same kind. The beheading of Charles had been followed by a stupid Royalist reprisal. In April 1649 Dr. Dorislaus, the Parliamentary envoy to the States General, had been murdered by English or Scottish exiles. The Commonwealth was just recovering from its rage when Davenant was captured, and he had been in Cowes Castle less than a month when Antony Ascham, a second Parliamentary envoy, was murdered by exiles in Madrid. London was beside itself, and the officials prepared to exact reprisals of its own. The new government had made provision for such Royalists as wished to compound and live peacefully in England, but Davenant was one of the "Malignants" whom the act of pardon did not save.

Parliament passed a resolution to "pitch upon" six of the Royalists distributed in various English prisons and to bring them before the new high court of justice. By June 28 four had been selected, and on July 3 six more names, including that of the poet, were brought up for consideration in the Commons.[28] A

---

[26] *Calendar S. P. D.,* 1650, p. 167.

[27] *Calendar of Clarendon State Papers,* II, 67–68. Chevalier's *Journal* (cf. note 21) adds to our knowledge of the details, that the capture took place May 4 in the Channel, off Falmouth, and that Davenant's company was stripped of all possessions down to the very clothes worn by their leader. Considerable silver money belonging to Davenant and Carteret was taken.

[28] *Commons Journals,* VI, 434; *Calendar S. P. D.,* 1650, p. 228.

fifth victim was selected, and then the House voted upon Davenant. There were 27 yeas to 27 noes on the motion to include him in the bill, and he was saved by the speaker's vote.[29] This gave rise to the inevitable jest on Davenant's facial peculiarity; a news sheet issued the next day reported that "some Gentlemen, out of pitty, were pleased to let him have the Noes of the House, because he had none of his own." [30]   But on the next day another ballot was taken, and he was selected as the sixth man.[31] On July 9, an act was ordered to be printed, to the effect that the high court should

. . . hear and determine all Treasons, Murthers, felonies, Crimes and offenses done or committed by *Sir John Stowell* Knight of the Bath; *David Jenkins,* Esq; *Walter Slingsby,* Esq.; *Brown Bushel, William Davenant,* otherwise called *Sir William Davenant,* and Colonel *Gerrard* . . . and to proceed to their . . . Tryal, Condemnation and Execution. . . .[32]

The specific charges against them thus far were simply that they had borne arms against Parliament, and belonged to the same faction as did those whose abominable Villainies had caused the "detestable, barbarous, and horrid Murthers" of Doctor Dorislaus and Antony Ascham. Parliament was making a "publique Manifestation of their just Resentment."

During the entire summer of 1650 Davenant remained a prisoner at Cowes Castle. He spent his days working on *Gondibert,* and by fall had completed half of the third book. His impending trial then required that he be moved to the Tower, and on October 22 he wrote a postscript to the reader and laid down his pen. This postscript is touching as a testimony of an abiding love for poetry, and of a quiet courage:

[29] *Commons Journals,* VI, 436; *Calendar S. P. D.,* 1650, p. 229.
[30] *Mercurius Politicus,* June 27–July 4, 1650. (H.)
[31] *Commons Journals,* VI, 437.
[32] *An Act for the Tryal of Sir John Stowel* . . . etc., British Museum, 506. d. 9. (102).

. . . 'tis high time to strike sail, and cast anchor (though I have run but half my course) when at the Helme I am threatened with Death; who, though he can visit us but once, seems troublesome, and even in the innocent may beget such a gravity as diverts the Musick of Verse. And I beseech thee (if thou art so civill as to be pleas'd with what is written) not to take ill, that I run not on till my last gasp. For though I intended in this Poem to strip nature naked, and clothe her again in the perfect shape of vertue; yet even in so worthy a Designe I shall ask leave to desist, when I am interrupted by so great an experiment as Dying, and 'tis an experiment to the most experienc'd, for no Man (though his Mortifications may be much greater than mine) can say, *He has already Dy'd.*

The trial was under way by December,[33] but a report was not rendered to Parliament until five months later, in May 1651.[34] In the meantime the poet remained a prisoner in the Tower and awaited his fate.

A needless mystery has been made of Davenant's escape from death. Aubrey explains on one occasion that he was saved by the two godly aldermen of York whom he had befriended during the Civil War, and on another occasion that he was saved by one of the jests of Col. Henry Marten, who protested that only lambs without blemish should be offered as sacrifices, not tainted old rascals like Davenant. (Incidentally Aubrey gives this same jest as the means by which Marten himself was saved when tried as a regicide at the Restoration.) [35] The more widespread legend is that Milton saved Davenant and thereby won the friend through whose mediations he escaped the wrath of the restored Royalists.[36] This is a pleasant story, and one wishes that it were true. There is, however, not a scrap of evidence; moreover it is improbable that Davenant would have had the influence to save

---

[33] *Commons Journals,* VI, 511.
[34] *Ibid.,* VI, 569.
[35] John Aubrey, *op. cit.,* I, 208.
[36] Anthony à Wood, *Athenae Oxonienses,* III, 805; and all subsequent authorities.

Milton, or that Milton—let the truth be told—would have had the inclination to save Davenant. What actually happened is clear —and sadly commonplace. Parliament calmed down and became legal again. Davenant simply shared the escape of the five other Royalists named in the bill. None of them was executed, the Commonwealth preferring not to assume the responsibility for a vicarious atonement.[37]

The poet had now been in durance for over a year, and he began to agitate for his release. On July 8 he wrote to Henry Marten: "I would it were worthy of you to know how often I have profess'd that I had rather owe my liberty to you than to any man, and that the obligation you lay upon me shall for ever be acknowledg'd. . . ."[38] Although he had been the King's most open enemy from the very beginning, Marten's honesty and courage, and his signal lack of sanctimony, had won him the respect of the Royalists. But although he was occasionally able to do something for those who were his political enemies but his kindred spirits, Marten could do nothing for Davenant. For some reason Parliament clung on to this particular prisoner. In November, Col. Bingham got the permission of Blake to exchange Davenant for one Captain Clark, held prisoner by the Royalist garrison of Castle Cornet in Guernsey. Clark was set free, but the officials at London, not having been consulted in the arrangement, saw to it that the poet remained in jail.[39]

These were dreary months. Davenant wrote nothing except a little commendatory verse, an activity in which he shared once with James Shirley, and a second time with Jeremy Collier the elder.[40] He was forgotten by all except those to whom he might be of some small use. Lord Baltimore remembered him to the extent of producing his commission to be Governor of Maryland,

[37] S. R. Gardiner (*Commonwealth and Protectorate*, I, 343) says they were held instead as hostages against further outrages on the Continent.

[38] *Historical Manuscripts Commission*, XXXI, p. 389.

[39] *Calendar S. P. D.*, 1654, p. 107.

[40] See John Ogilby's *Fables of Æsop* (1651), and Edward Benlowe's *Theophila* (1652).

thus assuring his own reputation as loyal to the Common-wealth.[41] To darken his life further, William, his "beautifull and ingeniose son," died and was buried in the family church of St. Martin's, Oxford.[42] Finally, on October 7, 1652, the Council of State, apparently at the solicitation of Bulstrode Whitelocke who had known the poet in their Inns of Court days, granted him the liberty of the Tower.[43] Whitelocke received a letter of thanks, the obsequiousness and tortured phrasing of which seems to reveal a man at the end of his tether:

My Lord,

I am in suspense whether I should present my Thankfulness to your Lordship for my Liberty of the Tower; because when I consider how much of your Time belongs to the Publick, I conceive that to make a Request to you, and to thank you afterwards for the Success of it, is to give you no more than a Succession of Trouble, unless you are resolved to be continually patient and courteous to afflicted Men, and agree in your Judgement with the late wise Cardinal, who was wont to say, If he had not spent as much time in Civilities as in Business he had undone his Master.

But whilst I endeavour to excuse this Present of Thankfulness, I should rather ask your Pardon for going about to make a Present to you of Myself, for it may argue me to be incorrigible, that after so many Afflictions, I have yet so much Ambition as to desire to be at liberty, that I may have more opportunity to obey your Lordship's commands, and show the World how much I am, My Lord,

Your Lordship's most obliged, most humble and obedient Servant,

Will Davenant.[44]

Tower, Oct
9th, 1652.

His Lordship must have done something, for within a few weeks, after two full years in the Tower, not to mention the half year

[41] The Lord Baltamore's case concerning the Province of Maryland . . . 1653.
[42] Wood's City of Oxford, III, 173.
[43] Calendar S. P. D., 1651–52, p. 432.
[44] B. Whitelocke, Memorials of the English Affairs . . . (1732), p. 546.

on the Isle of Wight, the poet was set free.[45]   First, however, he
was forced to furnish bail, and to promise that he would not stir
outside of London.[46]

Davenant's actions are always surprising. He had scarcely left
the shadows of the Tower when he married a second wife—a
widow and the mother of four children. The incongruity of this
step appears less when we discover that his bail had evidently
been the £800 belonging to his bride. He had known her for
some years, for she was Dame Anne Cademan, the widow of the
physician who had tended him in his illness over twenty years
before and who had served with him in the Bishops Wars.[47]
Dame Anne was partial to cavaliers in distress, for she had be-
stowed herself, her fortune, and three children by one Crosse, a
previous husband, on Dr. Cademan after he had suffered ship-
wreck and destitution at the beginning of the Civil Wars. The
children whom Davenant inherited from her two former spouses
were all boys, the eldest twenty-two and the youngest nine, and
he was engaged by bond to supply them lodging, washing, linen,
woolen, meat, drink, and "physick," and by February 1655 to
give each £100 of their mother's portion or to find them suitable
employment. It had not been a brilliant match, but a case of
any port in a storm—"Sir William being at the time of their inter-
marriage in a very low condition." [48]

Dame Anne owned a house on Tothill Street, Westminster, left
her by Dr. Cademan, and here the poet took up his residence.
But he was still at an impasse. Apparently there was nothing
left of the £800, and the condition of his release forbade him to
leave London to seek the means to recoup his fortunes. Several
writs for debt were served on him, and when scarcely a year was
out, he was back again in prison.[49]

[45] *Calendar S. P. D.,* 1654, p. 106.
[46] See below—note 49.
[47] See above, Chapter II, and *Calendar S. P. D.,* 1640–41, pp. 545–46.
[48] See below—note 76.
[49] For this information, and that in the following paragraph, see *Calendar S. P. D.,* 1654, pp. 106–107.

By this time—and it was none too soon—the Parliamentary army officers who had arranged the exchange of prisoners at Cornet Castle began to feel that their honor was involved. Blake himself certified that he had passed his word for the poet's release in 1651. Col. Bingham wrote to Bradshaw that Davenant had already been unjustly detained for two years, and that he should be allowed "some further time to follow his occasions; as his sufferings, contrary to the articles of war, have been great." But officialdom moved with a deliberation befitting the example of the prophets. Bingham's letter was dated February 1654. In the following month the poet was allowed to state his requests— for liberty, for six months of protection from actions for debt, and for "a general pardon that he may live as a faithful subject." Three months later the Council of State found time to consider the report on his petition and to order his release from prison.[50] And *two months later* this order was carried into effect! [51]

It was August 4, 1654, when the release came. On March 5, 1655, the burial register of St Andrew's, Holborn, received a succinct entry: "Anne, wife of Sr William Davenant, K^{nt}, out of Castell Yard." [52] The poet was again a widower, penniless, threatened by suits of outlawry, and responsible for the welfare of four stepsons, to each of whom he owed £100. It was time for another venture.

3

There was, of course, no possibility of organizing a new voyage to America, even if the four years of consequences of the first attempt had left any taste for such a project, so Davenant selected London itself as the field of his operations. He had but one trade other than that of the courtier and soldier—writing plays; and the Parliament had passed an ordinance against stage plays in 1642, extended it in 1647, and in 1648 commanded the poor actor

[50] *Calendar S. P. D.*, 1654, p. 224.
[51] *Ibid.*, p. 439.
[52] *Gentleman's Magazine*, 1850, p. 367.

"never to act or play any plays or interludes any more" on penalty
of being publicly flogged "as an incorrigible rogue."[53]   It was
not a pleasing prospect; yet Davenant, already suspect as a malignant Royalist, took up the gage, and working between the out-
stretched claws of Parliament and the Council of State, brought
back a quasi-legitimate theatre to England.

The venture began with overtures to John Thurloe, Secretary
under the Protector.   On June 15, 1655, the poet wrote:

Sir,

I humbly desire to make a proposition to you, which will inferr
my going into France; and consequently give occasion to dedicate
my service to you during my short abode there.   This doth continue
that request, which I made to you not long since, by this way of
address, to receive an appointment, when you have leisure to heare,
Sir

Your most humble and most faythful servant. . . .[54]

This cryptic message resulted on August 10 in a pass to France,[55]
and the poet's object becomes clear at once.   Money was necessary to relieve his immediate needs, and he was acquainted with
a French widow with a dowry.   That he had a list of such eligi-
bles at his disposal, and kept in touch with each prospect, suggests
itself, for with almost magical celerity he espoused his third wife,
"Henrietta-Maria du Tremblay of an ancient family in St. Ger-
main Beaupré."[56]   He brought his wife to London, and prepared to set his scheme in motion.

There had, of course, been illicit performances of plays from
the beginning, but Davenant was planning to operate on a
grander scale.   During the winter of 1655–56 he joined with one
William Cutler in organizing a company; a theatre was to be
built near the Charter House and plays were to be presented with
Davenant as the poet in chief.   Four sanguine citizens were per-

[53] S. R. Gardiner, *Great Civil War*, IV, 69.
[54] *State Papers of John Thurloe*, III, 554.
[55] *Calendar S. P. D.*, 1655, p. 595.
[56] *Registers of Westminster Abbey*, p. 168.

suaded to invest a total of £925 in this project, with the under-standing that if the government should interfere, the assets of the company would be divided. The government did interfere, and according to Cutler and Davenant there were no assets to divide. Later both of them were sued by the citizen adventurers for fraud, and Davenant was accused of going on with his theatrical activi-ties "in another place which did not concern them." [57]

This other place was Rutland House, a nobleman's mansion at the upper end of Aldersgate Street, once occupied by friends of the poet [58] but recently confiscated and sold up by the Common-wealth. There is no definite reason to suppose that when he transferred his operations to this spot Davenant had done the investors in his company a greater wrong than to have sunk their money in a desperate enterprise. The Commonwealth would certainly have made short and thorough havoc of any attempt to build a new theatre, and according to a contemporary satire the poet had been considerably badgered in several attempts to use the theatres already in existence.[59] Rutland House, however, was not to be a theatre but a private home. Davenant moved his family from Tothill Street and prepared to invite the public to be his guests, and to enjoy (at a fee) musical entertainments and moral representations with scenes.

The whole thing was carefully calculated. The terminology of the playhouse was studiously avoided. It is interesting to ob-serve that the word *opera* penetrated into the English language because Sir William Davenant had to find some substitute for the offensive words *theatre* and *play*. Bills were modestly distrib-uted, and on May 23, 1656, came the formal opening. The piece presented was called simply *The First Dayes Entertainment at Rutland-House, by Declamations and Musick: after the manner*

[57] Leslie Hotson, *op. cit.*, pp. 139–40.

[58] "Elegie on Francis Earl of Rutland," *Folio*, 1673, p. 242.

[59] "How Daphne pays his Debts"; see below. Aubrey (*op. cit.*) mentions Sergeant Maynard as one of the "engagers" for Davenant's theatre. John Maynard was interested in theatricals and was the author of an unpublished masque; cf. Nichols, *Progresses of James I*, IV, 941.

of the Ancients. Among the auditors was a government spy, and we may let his official report describe the piece:

The Bills for Sʳ Will: Dauenants Opera are thus Intitled. / The Entertainment by Musick and Declarations after the manner of the Ancients/.

Vpon friday the 23 of May 1656 These foresaid Declarations began att the Charterhouse and 5ˢ⁺ a head for the entrance. The expectation was of 400 persons, but there appeared not aboue 150 auditors. The roome was narrow, at the end of which was a stage and on ether side two places railed in, Purpled and Guilt, The Curtayne also that drew before them was of cloth of gold and Purple.

After the Prologue (wᶜʰ told them this was but the Narrow passage to the Elizium theire Opera) Vp cam Diogenes and Aristophanes, the first against the Opera, the other for it. Then came up a Citizen of Paris speaking broken English—and a Citizen of London and reproached one another wᵗʰ the Defects of each Citty in theire Buildings, Manners, Customes, Diet &c: And in fine the Londoner had the better of itt, who concluded that hee had seene two crocheteurs in Paris both wᵗʰ heavy burdens on theire backs stand complementing for yᵉ way wᵗʰ, ceste a vous Monsʳ: Monsʳ: uous uous Mocquies de Moy &c: which lasted till they both fell down under their burden.

The Musick was aboue in a loouer hole railed about and couered wᵗʰ Sarcenetts to conceale them, before each speech was consort Musick. At the end were songs relating to the Victor (the Protector) The last song ended wᵗʰ deriding Paris and the french, and concluded.

> And though a shipp her scutchen bee
> yet Paris hath noe shipp at sea.

The first song was made by Hen: Lawes, yᵉ other by Dʳ Coleman who were the Composers. The Singers were Capᵗ Cooke, Ned Coleman and his wife, a nother wooman and other inconsiderable voyces. It lasted an howre and a haulfe and is to continue for 10 dayes by wᶜʰ time other Declamations wilbee ready.[60]

---

[60] Among the state papers; printed by Leslie Hotson, *op. cit.,* p. 150.

Five shillings seems rather high for the amusement offered (although the speeches are not dull, contrary to whatever critics have taken each other's word for that fact), but the price of admission was really an assessment. Most of the Royalists were now back in London, starving for entertainment, and Davenant gave them to understand, now and subsequently, that they must coöperate with him in getting it. *The First Day's Entertainment* was only an entering wedge for something better to come.

The "opera" must have seemed innocuous even to the government, for the producer was not molested. Similar entertainments probably followed, although we have nothing to go upon except the survival of certain ambiguous titles: *Satyricall Declamations by Sir William Davenant Knight*,[61] and *An Essay for the New Theatre representing the Preparacon of the Athenians for the Reception of Phocion after hee had gained a victory*.[62] Now the poet was not interested in entertainments but, regardless of what it was advisable to call them, in plays. He was interested in music —but only as an auxiliary to drama. Opera itself was a Renaissance product suggested by the discovery that the speeches in Greek tragedy had been accompanied by music. The use of musical background to heighten the tone of dramatic passages had frequently been employed by Davenant and his predecessors, notably Shakespeare, and cadenced recitation with instrumental accompaniment—"music within"—may have been little different in general effect from the Italian *recitativo secco*. True *recitativo* had appeared early in England, a full musical score having been written for one of Ben Jonson's masques,[63] and masques were the true precursors of English opera. Even if he had been inclined to do so, Davenant had not the means to import the ballet and the miraculous mechanical and panoramic effects which floated the thin mythological contents of Italian opera of the

---

[61] *Ibid.*, p. 151; from a book catalogue of 1660.
[62] *Stationers Register*, December 7, 1657.
[63] By Alfonso Ferrabasco; cf. *Grove's Dictionary of Music and Musicians*, III, 696.

period. He had, however, fallen truly in love with *stilo recita-tivo:* Poems other than those he had written for the theatre were designed at this time to make use of this device;[64] and even *Gondibert* (he had the optimism to hope) was some day to be sung, for did not "Homer's spirit, long after his bodies rest, wander in musick about Greece"?[65] Within three months of his opening at Rutland House, he had composed *The Siege of Rhodes,* "a heroique story in Stillo Recitativo," declamatory in character and divided into "Entries" instead of "Acts"; despite its complement of music, it was less an opera than a play.

To complicate the risks the author was taking, official nerves were on edge because of impending Royalist invasion and rebellion, and political ferment in London. It was necessary to get some kind of permission, so he wrote to Bulstrode Whitelocke, Lord Commissioner of the Treasury and one of the few beaurocrats (besides Oliver himself) who had a sense of proportion:

My Lord,

When I consider the nicety of the Times, I fear it may draw a Curtain between Your Lordship and our Opera; therefore I have presumed to send your Lordship, hot from the Press, what we mean to represent; making your Lordship my supreme Judge, though I despair to have the Honour of inviting you to be a Spectator. I do not conceive the perusal of it worthy any part of your Lordship's leisure, unless your antient relation to the Muses make you not unwilling to give a little entertainment to Poetry; though in so mean a dress as this coming from, my Lord,

Your Lordship's most obedient Servant . . .[66]

This letter was dated September 3, 1656, and shortly after it was dispatched, the play was presented.

The Siege of Rhodes has been called the most epoch-making play in the English language. Dryden saw in it the "first light" of the Restoration heroic plays, and others date from it the be-

---

[64] See below, p. 139–40.
[65] *Preface to Gondibert, Folio,* 1673, p. 8.
[66] B. Whitelocke, *Memorials of the English Affairs* . . ., p. 650.

ginning of opera in England. It was presented with the accoutrements of proscenium arch, curtain, and movable scenes, and in its
limited cast was the first *English* woman to *act* upon the *public*
stage. This was Mrs. Coleman, the wife of one of the former
court musicians whom Davenant cautiously selected as his actors.
The music was composed by Henry Lawes, the friend and collaborator of Milton, together with other leading composers, and the
scenes were designed by John Webb, the protégé of Inigo Jones.
Henry Purcell the elder, father of the greatest composer of the
succeeding age, may have been associated in the enterprise.[67]
The combination of new elements in the production, even although some of them were not the innovations they have been
supposed, justify the acceptance of this play as the prologue to a
new dramatic era.

The next step in the producer's guerilla campaign was to get
into a regular playhouse. Rutland House afforded only a long
narrow hall for his purpose, and cramped his performances and
limited the number of his auditors. He set himself therefore to
the task of preparing a remarkable document, calculated to convince the government that the benign influence of his representations should have a wider usefulness. His arguments were
economic, moral, and political. The gentry were coming to town
only during the Term, and then only as lodgers. Thirteen noble
houses were to let! Retailers and mechanics were in danger of
becoming poor, because "money should at home be continually
spending; for parsimonie may advance particular families, but
stops the revenue and destroys the peace of a State. . . ." Moreover

. . . in seasons of hazard . . . States should never seeme dejected,
nor the People be permitted to be sad . . . [Foreigners have observed that Englishmen need amusement] . . . being otherwise
naturally inclin'd to that melancholy that breeds sedition: which
made our Ancestors entertaine them with publique Meetings for

[67] *Grove's Dictionary of Music and Musicians,* IV, 285.

prizes in archery, horse-races, matches at foot-ball, wakes, may-poles and sports of Christmas, theatres and other publique spectacles . . . [Amusements will] . . . recreate those who will too much apprehend the absence of the adverse party . . . [and will withdraw the younger generation] . . . from licentiousnesse, gaming, and discontent. . . .

The writer concluded in a manner which might have made Praise-God Barbon greet him as a brother and Oliver Cromwell accept him as an ally:

If morall representations may be allow'd (being without obscenenesse, profanenesse, and scandall) the first arguments may consist of the Spaniards barbarous conquests in the West Indies and of their severall cruelties there exercis'd upon the subjects of this nation: of which some use may be made. . . .[68]

The Commonwealth had in hand the expensive task of fighting Spain, and Davenant was not above offering his talents as a propagandist.

Whether he had now struck the right note with the authorities, or was simply resorting to effrontery, he had moved by July 1658,[69] and was presenting, "daily at the Cockpit in Drury-Lane, At Three after noone punctually," *The Cruelty of the Spaniards in Peru. Exprest by Instrumentall and Vocall Musick, and by Art of Perspective in Scenes, &c.* The first edition was printed while the piece was running, and contains the note that "notwithstanding the great expense necessary to scenes, and other ornaments in this entertainment, there is good provision made of places for a shilling." It is impossible to place this work in any known category. It is a succession of speeches, songs, and dances presented against a background of painted scenes representing panoramically the life of the Incas, the atrocities of Spanish in-

---

[68] Among the Thurloe papers in the Rawlinson MSS; discovered and printed by C. H. Firth, *English Historical Review*, XVIII, 320.

[69] Leslie Hotson, *op. cit.*, p. 156.

vaders, and the glories of an anachronistic English army.[70] Intercalated is a tight-rope dance by two mimic apes, and surprising behavior on the part of an attendant upon an Inca priest. From time to time, and for no apparent reason, this resourceful servitor indulges himself in acrobatics, performing successively the "Spring," the "self-Spring," the "double Somerset," the "Porpoise," and the "Sea-Horse." Davenant is not at his dramatic best in this work, and the reader of it feels that it could well be spared; yet he must regret that life has denied him the privilege of witnessing such delights as the "Sea-Horse" and the "Porpoise."

While scarcely an opera, for all its subordination of dramatic action to song, dance, and divertissement, *The Cruelty of the Spaniards in Peru* is even less a play. It has a theme but no plot or dialogue, and the courts would have been puzzled what to accuse the author of presenting had they brought him to trial. Later in the year, having been tolerated in his public playhouse, he grew bolder and presented *The History of Sir Francis Drake*. This resembles *The Siege of Rhodes* in type although it is even more episodic and non-dramatic than that piece, dealing as it does merely with a few adventures of Drake *Senior*, Drake *Junior*, and Captain Rouse, as they penetrate the interior of "Peru" and make friends of native Symerons and Peruvians, and victims of colonizing Spaniards. The climbing of a tree from which may be viewed both the Atlantic and Pacific, the display of courtesy to a Spanish woman, and the capture of a mule train laden with Spanish gold, furnish the not too harrowing excitement of the piece. As in the other productions, there were the accessories of a symbolical proscenium arch, and scenes. The scenes in the case of each of the Commonwealth experiments seem to have been simply back-drops painted in perspective to represent the locale of the action. They were illustrative rather than realistic,

[70] L. Hotson, *op. cit.*, p. 157, finds the source for this in J. Phillips' translation of Las Casas, *The Tears of the Indians*, London, 1656. (Dedicated to Oliver Cromwell.)

and tended to compensate for deficiencies in the size of the cast. Fleets and armies were represented in the scene, and in the case of *The History of Sir Francis Drake* the mule train and the Spanish woman (treated diversely by the English) were presented to the audience by the same means. Since the scenes were changed on an average only of once for each of the five or six entries or acts, awkward inappropriateness was occasionally the result. Nevertheless all this was progress.[71]

The History of Sir Francis Drake contains dialogues in song, an operatic feature which had not yet occurred in Davenant's Commonwealth entertainments. There was still an absence of duets, and group numbers other than the chorus, and of many of the features of Italian opera of the period. Davenant no doubt felt that the *recitativo,* the airs, the choruses, the dancing, and the scenes would justify the classification of these things as opera, and, viewed historically, his contribution to the development of this *genre* in England was indeed as great as any before the early eighteenth century; [72] however, to the undiscriminating eyes of Parliament, especially now that the impresario was ensconced in a public playhouse, *The History of Sir Francis Drake* would have seemed parlously like one of those proscribed atrocities—*stage-plays.*

Davenant's entertainments were not nearly so dramatic as his nimble balancing feat in the midst of the godly party, and this display had its interested spectators. On October 15, 1658, the Reverend Thomas Smith wrote to Daniel Fleming:

. . . Its supposed the great Funerall [Cromwell died September 3rd] will be about All Saints; Henry 7[ths] vault is cleansing: after w[ch], its

[71] See "The designs for the First Movable Scenery on the English Public Stage," *Burlington Magazine,* XXV (1914), and all works on seventeenth-century theatre history.

[72] For discussions of Davenant's contribution to opera see besides the works of A. Nicoll, W. J. Lawrence, L. Hotson, etc., C. Meyers, "Opera in England from 1656–1728," *Western Reserve Bulletin,* IX (1906), 129–56; and D. M. Walmsley, "The Influence of Foreign Opera on English Operatic Plays of the Restoration," *Anglia Zeitschrift,* LII (1928).

said, a Parliam^t will be called, to sitt about February next. One thing, hee [i. e., a third correspondent] saith, hee wonders at (but so do not I) viz: that Sr Wm Davenant (Poet-laureate) hath obtained a permission for Stage-plaies, and the Fortune-playhouse is now trimming up against the Terme. . . .[73]

It may be that Davenant's successes had encouraged a second group to begin rejuvenating the Fortune; at least he was establishing a precedent. He himself remained entrenched at the Cockpit, and during 1659 he produced the second part of *The Siege of Rhodes*.[74] There is no ambiguity about the character of this: It is a full-length, fully equipped *play*, attractive enough to become, together with the first part, the favorite theatrical piece of Samuel Pepys and most of his contemporaries during the early Restoration.

As late as May 5, 1659, Davenant was still running his theatre. On that date John Evelyn noted in his diary:

I went to visit my brother in London and next day to see a new opera after the Italian way in recitative musiq and sceanes much inferior to the Italian composure and magnificence, but it was prodigious that in time of such public consternation such a vanity could be permitted. I being engaged could not decently resist the going to see it though my heart smote me for it.

As we shall see, others besides Evelyn deplored Davenant's immunity in the service of Satan—still another group jeered at him; yet many others frankly enjoyed what he had to offer. "You," said Thomas Pecke in 1659

> . . . in this Waspish Age;
> Are more than Atlas to the fainting Stage.
> Your *Bonus Genius,* you this way display
> And to delight us, is your Opera.[75]

---

[73] *The Flemings in Oxford,* J. R. Magrath, Ed., I, 116.

[74] Unlike the preceding pieces, *The Siege of Rhodes, Part II* was not printed until after the Restoration, and we cannot be certain when it was presented first. However, Aubrey (*op. cit.,* I, 208) lists it with the Commonwealth plays, and without it there would have been little to keep the theatre going.

[75] *Parnassi Puerperium,* 1659, p. 180.

For three years our venturer had bearded the lion, had worked toward the modernization of the theatre, and had provided an oasis of levity (however chaste) in the austere desert of London.

4

What the poet accomplished during the Protectorate is the more remarkable in view of his public and private distresses. We have followed thus far only the successes of his theatrical venture, and have omitted the sable background. Domestic troubles, official persecution, and the attacks of unfriendly wits complicated his life throughout this period to such an extent that, compared with it, even after his second release from prison, his exile had been a bed of silken ease.

In the first place Davenant was bitterly poor. His daughter Mary had been sent to his relatives in Oxford, probably soon after his capture by the Parliamentary fleet, but he had still his four stepsons to care for, Thomas, Paul, and John Crosse, and Philip Cademan. In 1655 he had not the £100 apiece due them from their mother's estate, so he resorted to the more troublesome alternative of providing them with a home and employment. Nearly twenty years after his death the eldest of his stepsons, Thomas Crosse, having been ousted from his office as treasurer to the widow Davenant's theatrical company, came finally to the conclusion that he had been grossly neglected in youth, and tried to recover on the old £800 bond. His and the widow's conflicting allegations in the case furnish interesting biographical material.[76]

"Sir William," said Crosse, "ought to have provided better for them . . . considering the fortune he had with . . . sayd mother." He himself from 1655 on had to act as his stepfather's clerk, and to serve in "constant hard writing and goeing of his Errands." His brother Paul "often wanted bothe meate, and

[76] These chancery documents, the Davenant v. Crosse Bill and Answer (C6 250/28), were discovered and printed by Leslie Hotson; cf. *op. cit.*, pp. 356–76.

drink and cloths," and all of them were "often put to shift untill after his Majesties happy restauration." On one occasion the poet had put £100 worth of furniture in the Tothill Street house in his stepson's name in order to evade his creditors.

All this is no doubt true, but the case which Crosse himself makes out shows that he and his brothers had only shared Davenant's own adversities. Thomas was given permanent employment in the theatre before and long after the Restoration. Paul lived for two years with his stepfather, and subsequently became a clerk and a soldier in Flanders. John was secured a position as page in the service of General Jephson. Philip Cademan was trained to act small parts in the theatre, and when he was permanently disabled by a wound in a stage duel he was given a pension of thirty shillings a week (a generous sum in those days), which was paid regularly for many years. All of them, including Thomas, had got on amicably with their stepfather until the day of his death.

These stepsons were not the poet's only hostages to fortune. His third wife blessed their marriage with distressing regularity. Their son Charles was born within a year of their marriage,[77] William in 1657;[78] then came Alexander, and Ralph, and Thomas, and Nicholas, and finally Richard.[79] Apparently there were no girls—further proof that boys preponderate in times of calamity. Estimating conservatively, Sir William had four infants in his house while he was still dueling with the Commonwealth; Rutland House was large, and domestic economy may have been differently managed in those days; still, four infants are no trifle in any historical era. Henrietta Maria, or "Lady Mary" as she was usually called, must have been considerably younger than her husband; she was an active and capable woman as we shall see, and she made the poet an excellent wife, quite aside from her fruitfulness and any dowry she may have brought.

[77] *Alumni Oxonienses,* I, 375.
[78] *Ibid.*
[79] For the careers of these sons, see below.

When we turn from the exigencies of Davenant's household to his life in town, the prospect is little more pleasing. He renewed old acquaintances in London, going to see on one occasion Gideon de Laume, once apothecary to the Queen and now a man over eighty years old; he found him in the chimney corner and "slighted not only by his daughter-in-law, but by the cookemayd, which much affected him—misery of old age." [80]   Davenant himself was no longer young; he was turning fifty at the time of his third marriage, and in the seventeenth century the average life span was considerably under forty years. He seemed to prefer quieter companionships now; his associates in the theatrical enterprise were anything but Bohemian, and he went about occasionally with Daniel Fleming,[81] and cultivated the friendship of Charles Cotton, and of his fellow pioneer in the rimed play, the Earl of Orrery.[82]   This was not through necessity, for nearly everyone with whom he had shared in the war and exile had returned; the Royalists had compounded and the wits were back in town.

For Davenant the wits were no blessing. In Paris they had laughed at his *Preface to Gondibert,* and accused him not only of piety but ostentation. When he wrote the postscript to the unfinished poem on the Isle of Wight, he explained to the future reader that "whilst others tax me with vanity, as if the *Preface* argu'd my good opinion of the Work, I appeal to thy Conscience, whether it be more than a necessary assurance, as thou hast made to thy self in like Undertakings." [83]   He had listed in his essay the epic poets from Homer to Spenser, not to disparage them but to point out wherein he intended to depart from their practice; it was a dangerous thing to do, and of course he had been misunderstood: Archbishop Ussher is said to have shouted "Out upon him with his vaunting preface, he speaks against my old

[80] John Aubrey, *op. cit.,* I, 216.
[81] Leslie Hotson, *op. cit.,* p. 55.
[82] See the long poem to Orrery, *Folio,* 1673, pp. 275–86; it had been entered in the Stationers Register on December 7, 1657.
[83] *Folio,* 1673, p. 198.

friend, Edmund Spenser." [84] Thomas Killigrew, writing a quasi-autobiographical play during the exile, included the passage: "we met Embassadour Will [Murray], and Resident Tom [Killigrew], with M. Sheriff's Secretary [Will Crofts], John the Poet with the nose [Denham]; all Gondibert's [Davenant's] dire foes." [85] When certain members of this group arrived in London, they united with kindred spirits in a campaign to blast the poem.

Gondibert appeared in its unfinished state in two different formats in 1651. In 1653 a small volume was issued with the title Certain Verses written by severall of the Author's Friends, to be re-printed with the second edition of Gondibert. The cleverest thing about this squib is the take-off on the practice of publishing commendatory verses, but its twenty-four pages contain everything from skilful parody to mere obscenity and abuse. A fair sample of its humor is,

> I am old Davenant, with my Fustian quill
> Tho' skill I have not
> I must be writing still
> On Gondibert. . . .

and so on into the unprintable. Even one of those contributions claimed for Sir John Denham concludes with the subtlety,

> We thought it fit to let thee know it,
> Thou art a damn'd insipid Poet.[86]

Later, certain town wits, less gifted than their predecessors, revived the attack with a second volume, The Incomparable Poem Gondibert vindicated from the Witt Combats of Four Esquires, Clinias, Dametas, Sancho, and Jack Pudding. This was more insidious than the first, because the report circulated that

---

[84] John Aubrey, op. cit., II, 233.

[85] Thomaso or the Wanderer, Part II, Act V, Scene 7; cf. the present author's Thomas Killigrew, Cavalier Dramatist, p. 100.

[86] The verses conjectured to be Denham's are included in his Works by T. H. Banks, pp. 317–24.

Davenant had written his own defense. Although it was a "defense" which besmirched him and his epic more than ever, the report persisted for years. After mentioning the first volume, Anthony à Wood added, "whereupon sir Will D'avenant came out with a little thing . . . which tho' it seems to be written by D'avenant's friend, yet he himself was the Author." [87]   Wood had probably read neither volume; yet Gerard Langbaine read both, and was completely taken in: He prints a stanza from the first publication and then follows it with the clumsy ribaldry of Davenant's supposed reply! [88]   Not until the time of Isaac Disraeli was the true nature of the *vindication* exposed in print.

Behind these elaborately planned pleasantries—they were anonymous of course—were George Villiers, Duke of Buckingham, Sir John Denham, and as it is variously conjectured Edmund Gayton, John Donne the younger, Will Crofts, Sir Allan Broderick, Sir John Mennis, and others.[89]   Lesser wits took up the game and in 1656 four of these, modestly self-styled "a Club of sparkling Wits," issued *Sportive Wit: The Muses Merriment,* which contains the satire "How Daphne Pays his Debts." [90]   Daphne, of course, is the laureled Davenant, and the author of the verses jibes *Gondibert,* the poverty of the poet, and his attempts to perform plays at various theatres before opening at Rutland House. In 1658 a satire was directed against the activities at the Cockpit, "A Ballad upon the Late new Opera, The Cruelty of the Spaniards in Peru." The writer had excellent material to work on in this case, and his verses take the form of an extended burlesque of the entertainment. The first and last verses will be an ample specimen of his gentle merriment:

[87] *Athenae Oxonienses,* III, 808. G. Thorn-Drury, *A Little Ark,* 1921, p. 30, names Edmund Gayton as the author.

[88] Gerard Langbaine, *op. cit.,* p. 113.

[89] See John Aubrey, *op. cit.,* I, 207; Gerard Langbaine, *op. cit.,* p. 112; Isaac Disraeli, *Quarrels and Calamities of Authors,* II, 241. A clue to the authorship of *Certain Verses* . . . is proffered by *The Incomparable Poem* . . ., p. 29, in the phrase "drolling gasmen Wal-Den-Do-Donne-Dego."

[90] Printed in part by H. Rollins, *Studies in Philology,* 1921, p. 322; and by L. Hotson, *op. cit.,* pp. 142–44.

Now Heaven preserve our realm
And him that sits at the helme
I will tell you of a new story
Of Sir William and his apes
With full many merry japes,
Much after the rate of John Dorie.

.   .   .   .

And so now my story is done,
And I'll end as I begun,
With a word, and I care not who know it;
Heaven keep us great and small,
And bless us some and all,
From every such pitiful poet! [91]

Davenant was a poet and a philosopher fallen, as Disraeli puts it, among an age of wits. There was a certain guilelessness about him which challenged such men as Denham and Villiers, and the sportsmanship of their circle included no rule against shooting at sitting pheasants. He attempted no *Apologia* and wrote no satires in reprisal. A few of his friends rose to his defense. James Howell wrote a poem "On some who, blending their brains together, plotted how to bespatter one of the Muses' choicest sons, Sir William Davenant." [92] Waller and Cowley (the most esteemed poets of their day, incidentally), and "Old Hobbs" had come in for a share of abuse for commending the poem; Hobbes wrote:

My judgement in poetry hath, you know, been once already cen-sured, by very good wits for commending *Gondibert,* but yet they have not, I think, disabled my testimony. For, what authority is there in wit? A jester may have it, a man in drink may have it, and be fluent over night, and wise and dry in the morning. . . . [93]

Among general readers the poem received respectful attention, and sober judges began to offer favorable opinions of it. Yet

[91] *Notes and Queries,* Fourth Series, IX, 49.
[92] Isaac Disraeli, *op. cit.,* II, 241.
[93] *Ibid.,* II, 247.

Davenant never completed it. Leisure and the first heat of enthusiasm were lacking, so we cannot say that the venture had
withered in the blasts of cruel laughter; still, this laughter was
poor reward for a labor undertaken in exaltation and with hope
of undying fame. Davenant had known laughter before, and
there is little wonder that he wrote: "Humor is the drunkenness
of a Nation which no sleep can cure." [94]

Throughout this period the poet's chief concern had been how
to keep out of prison—as a debtor, as a Royalist suspect, and
as the manager of an illicit theatre. There seems to have been
some kind of tacit and irregular understanding between Secretary Thurloe, Councilman of State Whitelocke, and Lord Protector Cromwell that Davenant was not to be molested. Thurloe
and Whitelocke were neither of them extremists, and Cromwell,
although he saw visions and made prophecies, had, with the
complexity of genius, a weakness for fun and fiddles. Shortly
after his death, however, opposition became pronounced. On December 14, 1658, a letter from London contained the observation,
"It is thought the Opera will speedily go down; the godly party
are so much discontented with it." [95] The next month Richard
Cromwell and the Council of State decided to examine Davenant
on his authority for acting at the Cockpit, and on February 5,
1659, the House of Lords ordered a committee to take action on
plays ". . . and things of the like nature, called Opera, acted,
to the scandal of Religion and Government." [96]

The producer persisted in running the gauntlet, and by April
he and his opera had become an issue in Parliament, rivaling
the problem of whether it might avert the impending counter-
revolution if three thousand Royalists were expelled from London.[97] Yet on May 5 the Cockpit was still open, for it was then
that it intruded its joys upon the reluctant Evelyn. But Davenant
was not only the manager of this theatre; his name was on the

[94] *Folio*, 1673, p. 5.
[95] Leslie Hotson, *op. cit.*, p. 159.
[96] *Ibid.*, p. 160.
[97] *Camden Society*, "Nicholas Papers," IV, 85.

list of the three thousand dangerous Royalists: It was decided that the safest place for him was the Tower.

Booth's rebellion coinciding with this fourth (and final) Parliamentary imprisonment, it has been assumed that Davenant was involved in it, although there is no evidence of the fact. It may be that his theatrical activities had at last forced a showdown, or that he merely suffered for his political taint. In either case he was held only for a short period; on August 16 Whitelocke made a memorandum that "Sir William Davenant was released out of Prison,"[98] and the next day the Council of State took security of him on the act against delinquents and granted him a belated "liberty to reside in England."[99]

The political balance was now turning, and England pined for her King. No one could have pined more deeply than Davenant. From Cromwell himself and a few of his lieutenants he had received decent treatment, but from the Parliamentary zealots—those who did

> . . . wrest and rack
> The good old Prophets, till they falsly draw,
> From ill translated Hebrew English Law,[100]

he had received a hounding, exercised through their wardenship of the Tower, compared to which the arrows and tomahawks of the American Indians would have seemed like gentle ministrations. The years of Parliamentary rule, whatever they had meant for England and the world, for him had meant war, exile, prison, quasi-vagrancy in London, and a series of arduous ventures nearly always futile. He had been in his prime when the Long Parliament met; he was an old man when the Rump Parliament dissolved. It is little wonder that when General Monck arrived in London to clear the way for the Restoration, Davenant composed a panegyric:

[98] B. Whitelocke, *Memorials of the English Affairs* . . ., p. 682.
[99] *Calendar S. P. D.,* 1659–60, p. 118.
[100] "To his Excellency the Lord General Monck," *Folio,* 1673, p. 255.

Auspicious Leader! None shall equal thee
Who mak'st our Nation and our Language free.

.   .   .   .

How soon, how boldly, and how safely too
Have you dispatch't what not an age could do . . .[101]

On March 17, 1660, a month before the assembly met which was to recall the Royal House, the poet received a pass for France.[102] He was off to Calais to join the son of Charles Stuart.

[101] "To his Excellency the Lord General Monck," Folio 1673, p. 255.
[102] *Calendar S. P. D.,* 1659–60, p. 571.

VI

PLAYERS RESTORED

I

THE Restoration brought Davenant morning prospects, and he soon became one of the most brilliant theatre managers that London has ever known. The mere return of the Royalists, however, did not mean that his path opened gently before him; a peculiarity in his situation required that he hew each step of his way. Charles II, although the civil eruptions of the last eighteen years had ordained that he return to a limited and circumscribed English monarchy, was able to establish a social régime of the purest royalism; in minor matters, at least, everyone's hope for advancement rested upon the favor of this clever and inebriate young slacker. Unhappily for Davenant, his own youth and buoyancy were spent, and the King's intimates were not such service-worn sexagenarians as he, but Rochester and Buckingham and the cynical wits of that very circle which had laughed at him in Paris and jeered at him in London. Moreover, this group thought it had definite grounds for viewing him askance.

What success he had known during the Protectorate was not calculated to recommend him to King Charles, the man who exhumed and quartered the corpse of Oliver Cromwell. It may be remembered that the Commonwealth agent sent to report on *The First Day's Entertainment at Rutland House* had observed that the piece concluded with songs in praise of the Protector. These songs were suppressed in the printed version of the entertainment; and a deviation of the same kind, "Epithalamium upon the Marriage of the Lady Mary, Daughter to his Highness, wth the Lord Viscount ffalconbridge to bee sung in Recitative Musick," although written for the nuptials of Oliver's daughter in November 1657, and subsequently entered in the Stationers' Register,[1] was either withdrawn from the press or bought up in the first edition, for not a copy of it was allowed to survive. But alas for the transgressor, there is always the largè memory of little men. Davenant's nemesis appeared in the person of his old antagonist, Sir Henry Herbert, the master of the revels. When the two began to contend over the government of the Restoration stage, Herbert was careful to remind the court that "the said Dauenant published a poem in vindication and justification of Oliuers actions and government, and an Epithalamium in praise of Oliuers daughter M^s Rich,—as credibly informed." With some embroidering he described how the poet

. . . exercised the office of Master of the Revells to Oliuer the Tyrant, and wrote the First and Second parte of Peru, acted at the Cockpitt in Oliuers tyme, and soly in his fauour; wherein hee sett of[f] the justice of Oliuers actinges by comparison with the Spaniards, and endeavoured thereby to make Oliuers crueltyes appear mercyes, in respect of the Spanish crueltyes, but the mercyes of the wicked are cruell.[2]

Nearly everyone has a taste for martyrdom in other people, and a theoretical contempt for authority, so that a person who may himself be demonstrative in his glee at the slender witticisms of his own petty employer will be hurt to the quick when some puny figure of history has failed to pull the whiskers of the lions of the land. Seen in their true light, Davenant's expediencies in Cromwell's time had been no impeachment of his loyalty. This is true even assuming that his poems were sincere, for many Royalists were able to reconcile an admiration for the

[1] S. R., December 7, 1657.
[2] Dramatic Records of Sir Henry Herbert, pp. 122–23.

man who could spread England's might over the nations of the world with a hatred for the faction through which he had risen. Every Cavalier who compounded implied his satisfaction with the Protector's rule, and some of them were quite vocal in their respect for it. A curious little volume issued in 1659 by three men who, one year later, appeared never to have been anything but devoted Royalists, contains the verse by Edmund Waller, "From Civill Broyles he [Cromwell] did us disingage" [3]—a denial of the Stuart cause such as Davenant never approached. The restoration of *Astraea* was haled by a triumphant chorus to which nearly every poet contributed his verses, and it is worth noting that Davenant's poem,[4] unlike many, does not insult the memory of Cromwell, and substitutes for that retrospective animus toward all Roundheads shown by the others a recommendation for general forgiveness and forgetfulness. Davenant's behavior stands up well in many comparisons. Cromwell was the man to bow all before him, and Charles himself is reputed to have once sent across the channel his seal and signature upon a blank sheet of paper, on which his adversary was invited to write any conditions whatsoever that would save the first Charles's life—an admirable action quite, but one the memory of which might have pleaded leniency for one powerless writer who in order to protect the enterprise which meant his bread and butter had written a few verses in praise of the greatest Englishman alive.

But the toll of the poet's trespasses is not yet complete. A man may have private opinions of a King which he does not express in his laureate poems, and such was the case with Davenant. When he crossed to the Continent in the early months of 1660 to join Charles, he had been preceded by a letter from Col. Whitley to Charles's secretary.

[3] Three / Poems / Upon the Death of his late / Highnesse / Oliver / Lord Protector / of / England, Scotland, and / Ireland. / written by { Mr. Edm. Waller Mr. Jo. Dryden Mr. Sprat of Oxford } / . . . /1659.

[4] *Folio*, 1673, pp. 256–261.

I cannot forbeare to tell you of an imprudent discourse that ye last weeke came from one that pretends to witt, but might very well have more discretion or loyalty, viz. Sir Wm Davenant. Hee being in company with two Parliament men and a confident of Monke, discoursing of the King and composing of differences, told a story how the King would not let Mr Cooley [i. e., Davenant's friend, Abraham Cowley] kisse his hand, though sollicited by and presented by Lo Jermin, which argued irreconcileablenesse in his nature, as is inferd by ye company and for the Kings disaduantage at this time whatever hee intended by it.[5]

Almost anyone might be guilty of such remarks—Clarendon often was, although he prudently kept them in manuscript—but it was the poet's luck that his should reach the King's ear, where they would have more weight than his years of sacrifice and suffering in the Stuart cause. Considering his age and character, his past relations with Cromwell, and this final obliquity, it is little wonder that Davenant never became a prime favorite with the Merry Monarch. Samuel Pepys was in the troop which surrounded Charles when the *Naseby* bore him triumphantly to England in May, and although he mentions the presence of the man who was to become Davenant's rival theatre manager, Thomas Killigrew, "a merry droll, but a gentleman of great esteem with the King," he does not mention Davenant. However, the poet had probably been received and permitted a place in the royal train—it was the more substantial favors he was denied.

After the reëstablishment of the court, Davenant, who was still the recognized poet laureate, and the holder of a patent from Charles I, should have received £100 a year and all his arrears on that pension. He was never given a shilling.[6] Killigrew, on the other hand, had his fist perpetually in the Treasury bags.[7] Killigrew was also protected, as a King's servant, from actions

[5] *Camden Society*, "Nicholas Papers," IV, 195.
[6] E. K. Broadus, *op. cit.*, p. 58.
[7] A. Harbage, *op. cit.*, pp. 111–12.

for debt—a great convenience for a theatre manager—but Davenant, while he should have enjoyed a corresponding immunity, could be reached by creditors through the Lord Chamberlain's office. While privileged, on occasion at least, to designate himself *Gentleman of the privy chamber*,[8] he received none of the emoluments connected with the position. In the theatrical world he was forced to play a distinct second fiddle to the enterprising but less experienced Killigrew.

It would have been impossible for the court to lay Davenant aside altogether. He had suffered too conspicuously at the hands of Parliament, and had retained too many influential friends. Even Edward Hyde felt at least tolerantly toward him, and was further conciliated by being chosen as dedicatee for his most popular play, *The Siege of Rhodes*. We can imagine his describing his needs to the Queen Mother and the now powerful Lord Jermyn, his old patrons, and it may have been through the intercession of these that he won the protection of his Highness the Duke of York,[9] and was given at least some consideration by Charles. Charles's favors were not magnanimous. In the first months of the Restoration Thomas Killigrew had expectations of replacing Herbert as master of the revels in England,[10] and Davenant, again playing second fiddle, was appointed to the same office in Ireland.[11] The rightful holder of the Irish office was John Ogilby, the same who had translated Æsop and had won thereby commendatory verses from Davenant, and from the Merchant Taylors' Company, whose livery he had once worn, the uncompromising sum of thirteen pounds, six shillings, and eight pence—"to encourage him."[12] Both Ogilby and Herbert succeeded in repelling the interlopers, but while Killigrew obtained the reversion of the office in his case, Davenant did not, and it was all he could do to prevent Ogilby from retaliating on him

[8] *Calendar S. P. D.*, 1661–62, p. 455.
[9] See the terms of the dedication to his Highness, *Folio*, 1673.
[10] A. Harbage, *op. cit.*, pp. 115–16.
[11] John Aubrey, *op. cit.*, II, 103; L. Hotson, *op. cit.*, 209–10.
[12] *Memorials of the Merchant Taylors Company*, p. 187.

by decoying his actors to Dublin.[13] He did receive from the Crown during the first five years of the Restoration grants total-ing £750,[14] but these were in just payment for plays ordered to be acted at court, and it is problematical if they were ever cashed. Killigrew's company had the honor of presenting the first play before the restored court when Jonson's *The Silent Woman* was revived in November 1660; and although Davenant was permitted to write the Prologue to the King, the distinction was rather dubious in view of the fact that Killigrew himself, although a dramatist and a wit, was chronically incapable of writing a single metrical line. Davenant, however, could do this sort of thing admirably, knowing how not only to laud Charles, but to exalt his own craft:

> This truth we can to our advantage say,
> They that would have no *King* would have no *Play:*
> The Laurel and the Crown together went,
> Had the same Foes, and the same Banishment . . .[15]

His eclipse as a courtier brought Davenant one advantage: He could live an unmolested private life—a genuine blessing in these baroque days. Satires upon him diminished in number and virulence. There are some allusions to him among the *State Poems,* a bit of mild raillery upon his epic in *Hudibras,*[16] and his nose was not forgotten by Buckingham when he ridiculed the heroic dramatists of the day in *The Rehearsal.*[17] However, the bookstalls were not again loaded with volumes devoted ex-clusively to the task of making him appear absurd. The phe-nomenal popularity of *The Siege of Rhodes* made the first few years of the new era the time of his greatest literary vogue, and the new devices at his theatre were the talk of the town; yet he

[13] *Calendar S. P. D.,* 1661–62, p. 455.

[14] A. Nicoll, *History of Restoration Drama,* p. 280.

[15] Printed entire by L. Hotson, *op. cit.,* p. 288.

[16] See the arguments to the cantos, and ll. 395–400 in Part I, Canto II.

[17] See Act II, Scene 5. Davenant's plays are alluded to frequently in the burlesque, and the composite figure, Bayes, adumbrates their author.

himself was a comparatively retired figure. Pepys knew Killigrew personally, for Killigrew mixed in the life of the court, but Davenant he rarely saw and he viewed him with some awe, listening attentively to everything he could gather about the poet from his gossip, shoemaker Wotton. The diarist's admiration for the theatre manager is amusing. Once when he made a duty visit to Dr. Clerke, he was disgusted not only because the dinner was "an ill and little mean one" but because criticism had been leveled at a great man:

. . . among other vanities, Captain Cooke had the arrogance to say that he was fain to direct Sir W. Davenant in the breaking of his verses into such and such lengths, according as would be fit for musick, and how he used to swear at Davenant, and command him that way, when W. Davenant would be angry, and find fault with this or that note—but a vain coxcomb I perceive he is, though he sings and composes so well. But what I wondered at, Dr. Clerke did say that Sir W. Davenant is no good judge of a dramatick poem, finding fault with his choice of Henry the 5th, and others, for the stage, when I do think, and he confesses, "The Siege of Rhodes" as good as ever was writ.[18]

Such gossip was harmless; happily for Davenant he never became the tidbit at dinner tables in the manner of his satirist, Sir John Denham; a young wife was not the most comfortable of possessions during the Restoration, and Denham was given cause to wish he had emulated in his home life the more old-fashioned ménage of the author of the despised *Gondibert*. The catalogue of Davenant's misfortunes was not destined to include the shattered integrity of his own hearth; he and Lady Mary lived peacefully together, and continued to swell the number of the King's subjects. The poet's home and his theatre were now his chief interests. They stood side by side in Lincoln's Inn Fields, and here he welcomed, both as authors and friends, such old comrades as Abraham Cowley and the son of Endymion Porter.

[18] February 13, 1667.

Here he realized ambitions conceived nearly a quarter century before.

2

So long as his favorite, Killigrew, was given preference, King Charles, however much he might disapprove of Davenant as a courtier, was not averse to using his talents as an entertainer. In March 1660, the same month when he had received his pass to France, the poet had made the first step in preparation for the new theatrical era which he knew the Restoration would bring. The French had found that the rectangular buildings housing tennis courts could be adapted as playhouses, and taking his cue from them, Davenant had leased the new building known as Lisle's Tennis Court running lengthwise behind the gardens of the gentlemen's houses along Portugal Row,[19] a site desirably convenient to Westminster. He now had a building to fall back upon, and he likewise had his old patent to manage a company granted him by Charles I in 1640. He was thus equipped in June when the reëstablishment of the court brought a jockeying for rights in theatrical enterprise.

The turn in government had brought actors, old and young, immediately into public stir, and three companies were already presenting plays, at the Cockpit, at Salisbury Court, and at the Red Bull. In July, Killigrew obtained a patent corresponding to Davenant's, and these two old-timers now coöperated in establishing a theatrical monopoly. By August 21, a warrant was issued authorizing each to conduct a playhouse over which he was to have absolute rule including rights of censorship, and, most important, authorizing both to maintain their houses as the only ones permitted to exist in London and Westminster. It appears that thus far Davenant was the strategist, and Killigrew was the active agent in obtaining official coöperation. By October, the two had exercised their rights of monopoly to the ex-

19 L. Hotson, op. cit., pp. 124-27.

tent of organizing a single company from the leading actors of the troupes already in existence, and this company, "His Majesty's Comedians," began to perform under their joint management at the Cockpit. Within a few weeks, Killigrew took the oldest and most experienced actors as a separate troupe to the Red Bull and thence to Gibbons's Tennis Court. Here, in what was equivalent to the old Elizabethan "private" playhouse, he was content to settle down and entertain the gentry and such citizens as were willing to indulge.[20]

Davenant's plans were more elaborate, and it took him longer to get under way. With such actors as Killigrew had left him, young men for the most part, he established himself in temporary quarters at Salisbury Court, and went about preparing his building in Lincoln's Inn Fields. His company was organized on the old actor-sharer basis, with this distinction, that once he was established at the new theatre, he was to hold ten out of a total of fifteen shares. The arrangement was fair enough, for Davenant was engaged as "sole Master and Superior" of the company to pay all the expenses of maintenance—house rent, costumes, stage accessories, actresses' wages, etc. A curious clause in his agreement with his actors indicates to what degree his rival patentee had been given precedence over him: Killigrew was to have a free box seating six persons at Davenant's theatre, although no corresponding convenience was offered him at Killigrew's theatre. Additional individual patents were issued to both monopolists during the following two years, the final one obtained by Davenant in January 1663 stipulating that his company should be known as the Duke of York's Players. Killigrew's company had the more august title—His Majesty's Players.

The building operations at Lisle's Tennis Court were consider-

[20] The chief source of our knowledge of the playhouses is the state papers in the Public Record Office, Herbert's records, the Lord Chamberlain's accounts investigated by A. Nicoll, and the chancery documents discovered by L. Hotson. For the most recent and detailed account, see the latter, *op. cit.*, Chapters V & VI.

able. They included alterations and enlargements such as would permit the manager to live in an annex adjoining the building [21] and, most significant, would provide a large scene room as the accessory to a new type of stage. This was Davenant's great contribution toward the development of the modern theatre. During the Commonwealth he had used the proscenium arch, curtain, and scenes, such as he and Inigo Jones had worked with in Caroline court masques, and now he made these adjuncts, with further elaborations, a permanent feature of the public theatre. All his contemporaries recognized the importance of the step, and modern scholars see in it the birth of our modern picture-frame stage.[22]

June 28, 1661, was the grand opening day. There must have been some previous interruption of the acting at Salisbury Court, for the first play presented at the new theatre had been rehearsed at Apothecaries Hall.[23]   Pepys was a little more tardy than usual in sampling a novelty, but as soon as he was sure that he would be entertained with the supplementary spectacle of royalty, he paid the entrance fee at Lisle's Tennis Court:

. . . went to Sir William Davenant's Opera, this being the fourth day that it hath begun, and the first that I have seen it.   Today was acted the second part of "The Siege of Rhodes." We staid a very great while for the King and Queen of Bohemia, and by the breaking of a board over our heads, we had a great deal of dust fall into the ladies' and men's hair, which made good sport. The King being come, the scene opened; which indeed is very fine and magnificent. . . .

Two days later he went to Killigrew's theatre, ". . . but strange to see this house, that used to be so thronged, now empty since

---

[21] L. Hotson, op. cit., p. 125.

[22] John Downes, Roscius Anglicanus, p. 20; James Wright, Historia Histrionica, p. 412; G. Langbaine, op. cit., p. 115; E. Phillips, Theatrum Poetarum Anglicanorum, p. 20; W. J. Lawrence, Elizabethan Playhouse, I, 100, 159, II, 121–47.

[23] John Downes, Roscius Anglicanus, p. 20.

the Opera begun; and so will continue for a while I believe."
The King's manager was feeling the knife of competition, and
it was not long before he had built a new theatre of his own
where his productions would not be shaded by Davenant's
magnificence.

Davenant lived at Lisle's Tennis Court until his death, and
except when public gatherings were prohibited because of the
plague, he continued to stage a long line of theatrical successes.
One pestilence he must have found worse than quarantine was
the series of lawsuits in which his activities involved him. In 1661
he was sued by the four citizens who had invested their money in
his Commonwealth project at the Charterhouse.[24] In 1662
he was sued by one William Crow, and in 1663 by one William
Creed, apparently for the recovery of debts.[25] In 1664 he was in
complicated difficulty with the owner and the subleaser of the
property adjoining his theatre. In making alterations he had
been permitted to encroach on this property, and now the owner
wanted the encroachment torn down, while the subleaser, because of the yearly rental of £4 which Davenant paid him,
wanted it to stay up. The poet was willing to satisfy either of
them, but could not perform the miracle of both remaining upon
the property and retiring from it. The courts must have been
similarly nonplussed, for they hedged by ordering a court of
armed neutrality among the contestants. In addition to all this,
from the winter of 1660 until the spring of 1662, Davenant, either
singly or together with Thomas Killigrew, was sued by Sir
Henry Herbert no less than four times.

It was not so easy to enjoy a monopoly and the right to censor
plays in the face of the traditional powers of the master of the
revels, and Herbert persisted in treating the two patentees just
as though they had been the old managers of Blackfriars and the
Cockpit, giving them at regular intervals peremptory commands
to cease acting. He insisted primarily upon his dignity as monarch

[24] See above p. 120.
[25] A. Nicoll, *op. cit.*, p. 275.

of the playhouses, but was also extremely solicitous about the licensing fees of £1 for old plays and £2 for new ones, and he proved so belligerent that Killigrew at last capitulated. Davenant held out for a while longer, but finally, having won some cases and lost others, and having found each simply the prelude to another, he petitioned the King in desperation to certify

. . . the just authoritie of the Master of the Revells, that so his Fees, (if any be due to him) may be made certaine, to prevent extorsion; and time prescrib'd how long he shall keep plaies in his hands, in pretence of correcting them; and whether he can demand Fees for reviv'd Plaies; and lastly, how long Plaies may be layd asyde, ere he shall judge them to be reviv'd.[26]

By some means all these uncertainties were finally resolved.[27]

In addition to Herbert, one George Jolly appeared on the scene as a cross to the patentees. In an expansive moment Charles, forgetting the exclusive rights he had granted the two managers, awarded this veteran trouper a patent to conduct a "nursery" or third playhouse where young actors could learn their craft at the public's expense. Killigrew and Davenant so manipulated the cards that Jolly awoke one day to find his rights in their hands. However, he proved as pugnacious as Herbert, and received from the monopolists a partial satisfaction; he was permitted to conduct his playhouse as their agent, and was allowed to retain two-thirds of the receipts, an arrangement which continued as long as Davenant lived.[28] To us for whom the Restoration appears to have been one vast holiday it seems curious that the patentees should have been so concerned to keep down the number of theatres. But the fact is that the city audience no longer existed, and the drama having become almost purely a gentleman's diversion, there were scarcely enough auditors to support the two houses.

[26] L. Hotson, op. cit., pp. 125–26.
[27] For details of the controversy, see Dramatic Records of Sir Henry Herbert, passim, and L. Hotson, op. cit., Chap. V.
[28] L. Hotson, op. cit., pp. 177 seq.

3

Lawsuits and quarrels are such a constant quantity in the theatrical world that it is a relief to step inside Davenant's playhouse and to taste its more individual features. First of all, the actors. Davenant trained and directed these himself, and it soon became apparent to the London critics that he had lost nothing by getting the younger men. The leading rôles were played by Thomas Betterton, Henry Harris, Cave Underhill, James Nokes, and Samuel Sandford. Of these, Betterton is universally remembered as one of the great actors of all time; he was Davenant's peculiar find, and was assigned such parts as that of Solyman the Magnificent in *The Siege of Rhodes,* Lear, Henry VIII, and, since he was versatile, Sir Toby Belch in *Twelfth Night.*[29] Harris played the more charming rôles, like that of Romeo,[30] and some admired him more than Betterton, "he being," said Pepys, "a more ayery man."[31] Underhill, the famous first grave-digger in *Hamlet,* was the all-around funny man, and years later Colley Cibber remembered him as having been unexcelled for "boobily heviness" and as altogether "the most lumpish, moping mortal, that ever made beholders merry."[32] Nokes was usually cast as a silly fop or a heavy husband, and was one of a number in the company who specialized. The fame of stage villains rarely survives their own age, but Sam Sandford was a fiend *par excellence;* "he acted strongly with his face,—and (as King Charles said) was the best Villain in the world."[33]

Other important actors were Thomas Sheppey, Robert Nokes, Thomas Lovell, John Mosely, Robert Turner, and Thomas Lilleston, all of whom had their special abilities. We should not forget, either, John Downes, prompter and librarian of the com-

[29] John Downes, *Roscius Anglicanus, passim.*
[30] *Ibid.,* p. 22.
[31] July 22, 1663.
[32] *Apology for his Life,* cf. John Downes, *op. cit.,* p. 151 (note).
[33] John Downes, *op. cit.,* p. 169 (note).

pany, to whose memoir we owe most of our knowledge of the parts taken by the various actors. About a dozen men were sufficient for the company, but owing to replacements, etc., considerably more than that came under Davenant's supervision. To the names already mentioned may be added those of Richards, Blagden, and the famous Kynaston (before they were lured away), and also those of William Betterton, Dixon, Angel, Floid, Price, Smith, Medburn, Young, Norris, Pavy, Dacres, and Cademan.[34]   Of these less prominent figures Philip Cademan is most interesting to us as the son of Davenant's second wife by his former benefactor, Dr. Cademan.   Philip rarely rose above such parts as that of Guildenstern in *Hamlet,* and was an employee rather than an actor-sharer.   His stage career came to an end while he was acting a part in his stepfather's last play, *Man's the Master,* and was pierced in the eye by the foil of Henry Harris.[35] After that, he became a permanent pensioner of the company. Considerable vim must have marked the histrionic duels at the Duke's House, for in 1666 the actor Smith actually killed his opponent.[36]   Davenant's own plays were especially lethal, and the revival of *The Unfortunate Lovers* in the first year of the new era was the indirect cause of a death at the neighboring Fleece Tavern.   The faults of the actor-duellists were being discussed when gentlemen of the convivial company drew their own swords

. . . to shew wherein they failed; in their folly Sir Robert Gaskholl received a chance thrust in his hand, which, with the ebullition of blood, caused a pass, in which Sir Robert Gaskholl his heels flew up, and the Scotchman unfortunately followed home his thrust, and ran him, sitting in his chair, through the body; within half an hour he died, and the Scotchman is taken.[37]

[34] John Downes, *op. cit.,* pp. 19–21; L. Hotson, *op. cit.,* pp. 206, 212, 213.
[35] John Downes, *op. cit.,* p. 31; A. Nicoll, *op. cit.,* p. 275.
[36] *Pepys Diary,* November 14, 1666.
[37] *Historical Manuscripts Commission,* IV, 201.

It is hard to say what happened exactly, except that *The Unfortunate Lovers* had proved especially unfortunate for Sir Robert Gaskholl and one unpredictable Scotchman.

Teaching and controlling his numerous actors was the least of Davenant's tasks; as a *Restoration* theatre manager, he had the more delicate problem of governing actresses. In view of the notorious careers of so many of these first English actresses, and of the fact that they were ultimately cast in male rôles to add piquance to especially scabrous plays, it is surprising to learn that they were first brought to the stage as a reform measure. One of Davenant's patents stipulates that actresses be employed because formerly the female parts "have been acted by men in the habits of women, at which some have taken offence." [38] It is true that one of the most trenchant accusations in Prynne's *Histriomastix* had been that play-acting was an offense to Biblical law because it forced men to don the raiment of the opposite sex. Such abuses were not to smudge the escutcheon of the Restoration stage, and at the time he had moved into Lisle's Tennis Court, Davenant had enrolled eight women as regular employees.

Where these women were found, the English stage never having provided any tradition or training for their sex in the profession, is a problem. From what is known of the earlier lives of most of them, they came from obscure but respectable families. One of them seems to have been the daughter of the publisher of Davenant's *Gondibert*, John Holden,[39] the same man to whom Betterton is supposed to have served an apprenticeship, and she certainly could have had no theatrical experience before the poet took her into his company. Probably all that was required was youth, beauty, and a good speaking and singing voice; the manager himself essayed to teach the art of acting. That Davenant was a judge of feminine charm is suggested by

[38] January 15, 1662; cf. A. Nicoll, *op. cit.,* p. 286.
[39] John Downes, *Roscius Anglicanus,* p. 175 (note).

the careers of those he selected, and that he could teach acting is proved by Pepys's note in 1666, "Mrs. Williams says, the Duke's house will now be much the better of the two, because of their women, which I am glad to hear."[40]   Of the original group of eight, the four principal ones, Miss Davenport, Miss Saunderson, Miss Davis, and Miss Long, were boarded right in Davenant's home, where they could remain under the astute eye of the poet's wife, and could occupy their idle moments by amusing his numerous infants. The other four, Miss Jennings, Miss Holden, Miss Gibbs, and Miss Norris (or Mrs. Norris, since she may have been the wife of the actor by that name), were regularly employed, but were not boarded on the premises.[41]

It is more difficult to make discoveries about the acting of the women of the company than about that of the men, for in their case records have survived of actions off the stage rather than upon it. One should hasten to add, however, that half of them at least lived blameless lives. No scandal attached to Miss Holden or to Miss Norris; Miss Ann Gibbs became the wife of one of Davenant's authors, Thomas Shadwell, future poet laureate, and played Emilia in his *Sullen Lovers;* Miss Saunderson played Ophelia to Betterton's Hamlet, and in December 1662 she married him and proved a constant and devoted wife.[42] The other four, however, to use Downes's brisk phrase, "by force of Love were Erept the Stage."[43]

This was not Davenant's fault certainly, nor in every case was it their own. Miss Davenport achieved such fame as the creator of a rôle in Davenant's *Siege of Rhodes* that she became known by the character name, Roxalana, rather than by her own. Aubrey de Vere, Earl of Oxford, twentieth of a line which had already survived too long, fell in love with her and made himself a nuisance at Lisle's Tennis Court with his persecutions. The actress (one of those, by the way, who resided with Davenant)

[40] October 25.
[41] John Downes, *op. cit.,* p. 20.
[42] John Downes, *op. cit.,* pp. 21, 29, 172.
[43] *Ibid.,* p. 35.

would have none of him, and he finally proposed marriage.
The story goes that the poor woman consented, only to find,
several weeks after the wedding ceremony had been performed,
that the officiating clergyman had been the Earl of Oxford's
trumpeter.[44]   The misfortune was the theatre manager's as well
as hers; on May 20, 1662, Pepys went "to the Opera, and there
saw the 2nd part of 'The Siege of Rhodes,' but it not so well
done as when Roxalana was there, who, it is said, is now owned
by my Lord of Oxford." Either Davenant used his skill to good
effect with Miss Davenport's successor, or Pepys changed his
mind, for a half year later he saw the play again, "done with the
new Roxalana, which do it rather better in all respects for person, voice, and judgement, than the first Roxalana." [45]

It was another of Davenant's plays which spelled the professional demise of a second of his talented boarders. The sweet-
voiced Mary Davis, cast as Celania in *The Rivals,* was very
alluring, "especially in Singing several Wild and Mad Songs.
My Lodging is on the Cold Ground, &c. She perform'd that so
Charmingly, that not long after, it Rais'd her from her Bed on
the Cold Ground, to a Bed Royal." [46]   There is nothing doubtful about this story; the actress actually became one in the in-
numerable throng of Charles's mistresses,[47] the notorious "Moll
Davis," Nell Gwyn's hapless rival at Whitehall. On May 31 of
the year she fell from grace; Pepys recorded that Miss Davis "is
quite gone from the Duke of York's house, and Gosnell [48] comes
in her room." There is no need to chronicle the gilded downfall
of Miss Long and Miss Jennings.

One point must be made before we leave the subject of the

[44] *Memoirs of Count Grammont,* II, 53–55. Several versions of the story
exist; cf. *Evelyn's Diary,* Jan. 9, 1662.
[45] December 27, 1662.
[46] John Downes, *op. cit.,* p. 23.
[47] *Pepys Diary,* January 11, 1668.
[48] December 26, 1666. Gosnell can scarcely be said to have taken the place
of Mary Davis; Pepys was apt to be partisan when speaking of the career of
his wife's maid. Once he expressed his disappointment upon going to the
theatre to find "Gosnell not singing, but a new wench that sings naughtily."

personnel of the company at Lisle's Tennis Court. Unlike the more abrasive Killigrew, Davenant won the respect and affection of his actors. The only one with whom he ever had any trouble was the perfect lover, Henry Harris, whose popularity made him so "very high and proud" that his demands for money became extortionate.[49] The rest espoused their manager's interests so heartily that on one occasion they made a mass attack on an agent of Sir Henry Herbert who had come with one of his master's warrants to worry Davenant.[50] When the poet died, the players attended his funeral in a body. Their loyalty even extended to his memory. Richard Flecknoe, the classical bore of English letters, after showing the bad taste to satirize Davenant just after his death, felt the weight of their disapproval to such an extent that he indited a Postscript

> To the Actors of the Theatre in Lincoln's Inn Fields.
> I promised you a sight of what I had written of Sir William D'avenant, and now behold it here: by it you will perceive how much they abused you, who told you it was an abusive thing. If you like it not, take heed hereafter how you disoblige him, who can not onely write for you, but against you too.
>
> Rich. Flecknoe.[51]

Flecknoe did not care for Davenant: When his play *Love's Kingdom*, "full of Excellent Morality," had been presented at the Duke's House, it had "Expir'd the third Day," whereupon the author, having missed his benefit, published it, "not as it was Acted at the Theatre near Lincoln's-Inn, but as it was written. . . ."[52]

The plays in which Davenant cast his actors—happily they were not then called "vehicles"—formed an interesting assortment. Early in the game, on December 12, 1660, he had peti-

[49] *Pepys Diary,* July 22 and October 24, 1663.
[50] L. Hotson, *op. cit.,* p. 212.
[51] Richard Flecknoe, *Sir William D'avenant's Voyage to the other World,* 1668.
[52] John Downes, *op. cit.,* pp. 31, 201.

tioned for exclusive rights to present his own works and nine old plays formerly belonging to the King's Company: *The Tempest, Measure for Measure, Much Ado about Nothing, Henry VIII, King Lear, Macbeth, Hamlet, The Duchess of Malfi,* and *The Sophy. Romeo and Juliet* and *Twelfth Night* he managed to add to the list later. In addition he salvaged a number of plays once belonging to the boy companies, notably to that at the Cockpit which he had managed after 1639.[53] He died before the Restoration produced a full tide of new dramatic authors, so old plays formed the staple of his company; however, he produced also two extremely important social comedies of Sir George Etherege, several plays of Dryden and Shadwell, and such isolated specialties as Tuke's *Adventures of Five Hours.*[54] He was loyal enough to old friends to stage certain doubtful quantities such as *Cutter of Coleman Street* by Abraham Cowley and *The Villain* and other plays by Thomas Porter, son of Endymion, insuring their success with elaborate costumes and scenes; another friend, the Earl of Orrery, entrusted his heroic plays, *Mustapha,* etc., to Davenant's company.[55] Samuel Pepys, although he felt a certain partisanship for the Duke's House, went oftener to the King's, possibly because of its greater social brilliance, and his diary supplements the testimony of other records [56] that Killigrew had the more distinguished repertory. Jonson, Beaumont and Fletcher, and even Shakespeare were more richly represented there, not through any fault of Davenant, but because Killigrew had the inner track with the authorities and had become the deputy of the master of the revels.

The Duke's House opened with a judicious alternation of Davenant and Shakespeare, individually and in combination. *Hamlet* seems to have been the third play given, *The Siege of*

---

[53] A. Nicoll, "Rights of Beeston and Davenant in Elizabethan Plays," *R. E. S.,* I, 84.
[54] John Downes, *op. cit., passim.*
[55] *Ibid.,* pp. 23, 25 *et passim.*
[56] A. Nicoll, *op. cit., passim.*

Rhodes and *The Wits* coming first with jubilee accoutrements, the former having the phenomenal run (for that day) of two weeks.[57] Davenant showed enough restraint to revive only those of his own plays which were keyed to the tastes of the day. *Love and Honour* was such a play, and when it was produced, King Charles, the Duke of York, and the Earl of Oxford gave Betterton, Harris, and Price their coronation suits so that Alvaro, Prospero, and Lionel might shine with true sartorial majesty.[58] Another of the early productions was *The Law Against Lovers,* Davenant's unhappy attempt to combine *Measure for Measure* and *Much Ado About Nothing.* Similar Shakespeare adaptations followed: [59] *The Rivals* based upon *The Two Noble Kinsmen,* and sophisticated versions of *Macbeth* and *The Tempest.* In the second of these Davenant had John Dryden as his collaborator, and the adaptations, whatever violence they did the originals, accomplished through their supplementary music a further step toward the development of opera.

It is easy to grow harsh with Davenant for altering Shakespeare. We should remember, though, that this was not lese majesty in his day, and that he was the manager of a commercial organization whose business was to please a Restoration audience. These things are a matter of degree. We ourselves still applaud Cibber's version of *Richard III,* and few of us have ever witnessed a play of Shakespeare presented exactly as he wrote it, certainly not exactly as he staged it. Not all of the plays were tampered with. *Twelfth Night,* and perhaps *Romeo and Juliet* and *Hamlet,* were presented unaltered. Although Pepys, before he had been to the theatre to see it, spoke of the play of "Henry the Eighth with all his wives," [60] and although it must have been tempting to add the parade of Queens to the pageantry of that drama, we know from Downes's list of characters that no such additions were made. Davenant was satisfied that it be acted

[57] John Downes, *op. cit.,* pp. 20–21.
[58] *Ibid.,* p. 21.
[59] See below.
[60] December 11, 1663.

"all new cloath'd in proper Habits." *Lear* also was performed "as Mr Shakespear Wrote it." [61]

Sir William was truly a lover of Shakespeare, and no doubt he considered it a service to make the master's works palatable to an audience. That he had the zeal of a disciple is proved by Dryden's confession that Shakespeare was a poet whom Davenant held in *"particularly high veneration, and whom he first taught me to admire."* [62] He may have performed a like service for Shadwell and other youthful dramatists. [63] There is no question that Davenant was the chief conduit through which Shakespearean stage tradition has reached us today. In describing the production of *Henry VIII,* Downes says: "The part of the King was so right and justly done by Mr. Betterton, he being Instructed in it by Sir William, who had it from Old Mr. Lowen, that had his Instructions from Mr Shakespear himself, that I dare and will aver, none can, or will come near him in this Age. . . ." [64] Lowin, incidentally, was the Elizabethan tragedian who had spoken the prologue to Davenant's *Platonic Lovers* at Blackfriars in 1635. On another occasion Downes, speaking of Betterton's famous Hamlet, says, "Sir William (having seen Mr. Taylor at the Black-Fryars Company Act it, who being Instructed by the Author Mr Shaksepeur) taught Mr. Betterton in every Particle of it . . ." [65] This is vital information, considering that Betterton became the fountain head of acting tradition in the eighteenth century. Betterton also became the source of anecdotes concerning Shakespeare's life, and these too he had from his manager. It is worth mentioning that the stories of Southampton's active patronage of Shakespeare, and of the latter's youthful expedients in holding horses outside the theatre, have as their oldest source Sir William Davenant. [66]

[61] John Downes, *op. cit.,* pp. 24, 26, 33.
[62] *Preface to The Tempest* (Scott's edition of Dryden), III, 106–07.
[63] John Aubrey, *op. cit.,* II, 226.
[64] John Downes, *op. cit.,* p. 24.
[65] John Downes, *op. cit.,* p. 21.
[66] J. Q. Adams, *Life of Shakespeare,* pp. 128, 154, 377.

It is pleasant to realize that during Davenant's life the Restoration theatre had not yet become a center of ribaldry and ruffianism. Some of the plays were spicy, but so had they been long before the Civil Wars. It was no easy task to get auditors inside the theatre, and most of those who came were fashionable idlers with dull palates. A week was a long run. As a kind of bribe, lackeys were admitted free to the pit, and everyone was offered reduced rates at the beginning of the third act.[67]   Davenant had to resort to the expedient of granting concessions to sell oranges through the house. Gentlemen could remain free through one act to see how they liked the play, and some of the young sparks utilized the limitless emptiness of their time by coming on five successive days, thus seeing an entire play for nothing.[68]   It was the difficulty in getting an audience that finally led to the competitive obscenity of the two houses. In view of this well-known feature of late seventeenth-century dramatics, it is interesting to observe with what pellucid ideals the era began. Davenant's patent of January 1662, the terms of which he himself probably worded, insisted that "no new plays shall be acted . . . containing any passages offensive to piety and good manners," and that old plays "shall be corrected and purged," with the result that the theatre shall provide "not only harmless delights, but useful and instructive representations of human life."[69]   A warrant which he had drawn up in 1660 might almost have been designed for the perusal of Cromwell and the Council of State.[70]

Davenant took his business seriously, and we can see in many directions the badge of his professional conscience. He strove to give his audience the best, sometimes incurring unnecessary expense in doing so, and the prologues and epilogues to his own plays express how earnestly he desired to please. Moreover he strove to preserve order and decency in his house. In February

[67] A. Nicoll, *op. cit.*, p. 13 *et passim*.
[68] See the epilogue to Davenant's *Man's the Master*, etc.
[69] A. Nicoll, *op. cit.*, p. 286.
[70] L. Hotson, *op. cit.*, p. 201.

1665, he obtained a government order "that no person, of what quality soever, do presume to enter at the door of the attiring-house, but such as do belong to the Company and are employed by them." [71] He protected his actors, treated them generously, and encouraged the efforts of those who were learning their trade.[72] But he held them with a firm rein. A commentator on the lax practices of the later theatres observed: "I have often heard Mr. Betterton say, that when he first played under Sir William D'Avenant, the Company was much better regulated, and they were obliged to make their study their business." [73] The poet had long wanted to hold the puppet strings in his own little world of illusion, and when the closing years of his life brought him the opportunity, he summoned the energy to do his work well.

4

Davenant never lived to see the apotheosis of his dreams in that last word in theatrical elegance—the new Duke's House in Dorset Garden. After his death in 1668, his widow with the aid of Betterton and the others managed Lisle's Tennis Court. She was a remarkable woman, and deserves a place beside her husband in the history of the London stage. Four years after Sir William's death, she erected a subsidiary theatre for young actors in the Barbican, and at the same time coöperated in the building of the Dorset Garden Theatre, financed at £9000! [74] The care of the playhouse industry and of the seven children left her by her husband occupied her for the twenty-two years she survived him, and she remained a widow until her death on February 24, 1691.[75]

Since the Duke's House held the fate of most of Davenant's children, we may, while we are still on the subject, sketch their

[71] W. J. Lawrence, *op. cit.*, II, 168.
[72] *Pepys Diary*, March 21, 1667.
[73] E. Curll, *Betterton's History of the Stage*, p. 28.
[74] L. Hotson, *op. cit.*, pp. 190–94, 232.
[75] *Gentleman's Magazine*, 1850, p. 367.

careers before turning to the last days of the poet himself. Charles,[76] the eldest, was twelve when his father died. At seventeen, he received the reins of theatre management from his mother, and continued in the activity for several years. At twenty-one, he wrote *Circe a Tragedy* presented with a (necessarily) apologetic prologue by John Dryden. A year later he married an heiress, the daughter of Sir Leoline Walden. Notwithstanding all these preoccupations, he managed to work in a career at Cheam School, and at Oxford and Cambridge, attaining finally to a dubious LL.D. His subsequent career as a commissioner in the Excise, a Parliamentarian, and a voluminous writer on political economy has earned him a permanent place in English annals, but it lies somewhat outside our province. He was laid beside his mother in the vault of St. Bride's, Fleet Street, in 1714, leaving behind one son, Henry Molins. It was also at about the age of seventeen that Charles's brother Alexander [77] was initiated into playhouse economy, for in 1675 he supplanted his stepbrother, Thomas Crosse, as treasurer of the Duke's House. Like Charles again, he married an heiress, Allett Brome, who brought him £3000. Instead of taking his brother's cue and buying his way into government service, he invested in a wood-wharf next to Dorset Garden, and not succeeding in business, began to swindle with his interests in the theatrical company. In 1693 he found it convenient to exit in haste to the Canary Islands, whither the curious must follow him if they would seek in the archives for his subsequent fate. Ralph,[78] a third brother, succeeded Alexander as treasurer of the company in 1683 when the latter married and went into the wood business. The handling of money was an increasingly hazardous occupation in these disorderly times, and on the eighteenth of May, 1698, Ralph's career ended decisively when he was "murthered by 3 soldiers, as he was goeing into his own lodgings in Gray's Inn

[76] Anthony à Wood, *Athenae Oxonienses,* IV, 476; *Fasti Oxonienses,* II, 73; L. Hotson, *op. cit.,* p. 236 *et passim; Alumni Oxonienses,* I, 375.

[77] L. Hotson, *op. cit.,* pp. 284–86, 293.

[78] *Ibid.,* pp. 285, 304.

Lane, who designed to have robbed the house." Less is discoverable about Nicholas and Thomas Davenant,[79] although both were connected with the theatre enterprise, the latter becoming nominal manager of the company in 1688 and retaining some small interest in it until as late as 1704. It is curious that all of these sons should have been interested in the commercial rather than the artistic side of the theatre. Perhaps Sir William's Merchant Taylors' blood flowed strong within them yet.

The only sons who seem to have had no connection with the theatre were William and Richard. These two divided their father's opposite talents, the one taking to books, the other to arms. William [80] entered Oxford and received a B.A. degree in 1677, and an M.A. degree in 1680. He occupied part of his time at the University in translating La Mothe Le Vayer's *Notitia Historicorum: or Animadversions upon the famous Greek and Latin Historians*—no doubt an excellent work, but one which those interested in this prodigy's father need not feel constrained to read. William apparently took orders, but he seems also to have been interested in the law. He was cut off from either profession in 1681 at the age of twenty-four, when, having gone to France as a traveling tutor, he was drowned while swimming in the Seine. Richard,[81] the youngest son, born in the year of Sir William's death, became a page to the Duke of Monmouth. Despite the ancient Stuart allegiance and supposed Catholicism of his father, he fought with Monmouth, stood beside him on his scaffold, and then became a Colonel in the service of William of Orange. He died in 1745 leaving two daughters as his heirs. Few sons seem to have been vouchsafed the poet's children. This is true also of their distant cousins, a numerous clan of clerical Davenants descended from the brother

[79] *Ibid.*, pp. 229, 232, 286–301 *passim.* It has been suggested by A. Nicoll that Thomas and Nicholas may have been the same person. Isolated facts about the Davenant children appear in *H. M. C.*, XXIII, pts. 1, 2, 3; XLV, pt. 2; *Calendar S. P. D.*, N. Luttrel, *Brief Historical Narration,* etc.

[80] *Alumni Oxonienses,* I, 376; A. à Wood, *Fasti Oxonienses,* II, 360; *H. M. C.*, XXXVI, pt. 4, 617; *Hearne's Collections,* I, 320.

[81] See the obituary notice, *Gentleman's Magazine,* 1745, p. 332.

of the Bishop of Salisbury and settled at Gillingham in Dorset. The last of Sir William's descendants to achieve even a moiety of distinction was his grandson, Henry Molins, who was sent by George I as envoy extraordinary to an Italian princess.[82] For the rest, the Davenants of the eighteenth century dwindled into obscurity, becoming nothing more martial than town-majors of Portsmouth, nothing more artistic than sugar-bakers of Twickenham.[83]

Sir William's progeny were so numerous that they have called for a considerable digression. It has been distinctly out of chronological order, but we will plead an excuse similar to that of Davenant when he wrote *The Cruelty of the Spaniards* and placed an English army in Peru years before England had explored the region— "It may pass as a vision discerned by the Priest of the Sun, before the matter was extant, in order to his prophecy." Let us return now to the poet himself.

Sir William had not been established long at Lisle's Tennis Court when he began to feel the weight of years upon him. He wrote only one laureate work during the Restoration, "Poem to the King's most Sacred Majesty," published in 1663; and in this he explained that he now lacked "that Dexterity of Thought" to be truly productive. The poem must have been written in a time of depression, for it contains the passage:

> Now methinks, I hear my Pinnace hal'd!
> Which boldly in a Mist too far has sail'd;
> And I discover, through the Glass of Fear,
> That the whole world's High-Admirall is near.
> Too long my wither'd Lawrel I have worne,
> The Poet's Flag, by Grief's foul weather torn:
> Grief which is taught by Reason to complain,
> That I, when all are better'd by your Reign,
> Should seem unworthy, in my faded Bays
> To carry Fame a Present of your Praise.[84]

[82] *Alumni Oxonienses,* I, 375.
[83] *Musgrave's Obituary,* II, 146.
[84] *Folio,* 1673, p. 269.

It was true enough that his old fertility had gone; his only plays now were adaptations of the works of others, and it was impossible for him to accustom himself to the changing Restoration tastes. Even during the later Caroline period he had regretted the loss of the "good easie judging souls" of the less finical Elizabethan audience,[85] and the new plays made him feel completely behind the times. It seems strange that a dramatist so popular about 1660–62 should be growing obsolete by 1667–68, but such was the case. Davenant could not produce the sparkling social comedy coming into vogue, his idea of comic novelty being such a dramatic harlequin as his *Playhouse to be Let,* a piece compounded of his Commonwealth entertainments and short adaptations from the French, the whole thing farcical and homespun. The best of his pre-Commonwealth plays upon which he had depended in lieu of fresh inspiration were themselves falling from favor. In 1661 *Love and Honour* had appeared so enticing to Samuel Pepys that it broke his resolution to stick to business—". . . against my judgement and conscience (which God forgive, for my very heart knows that I offend God in breaking my vows herein) to the Opera. . . ."[86] Yet by 1667 a much better play than *Love and Honour* had lost its allure. On April 18, he wrote: ". . . saw 'The Wits,' a play I formerly loved, and is now corrected and enlarged: but, though I like the acting, yet I like not much in the play now."

Davenant's last effort was *Man's the Master,* a comedy adapted from a foreign play, and one in which he tried to meet the requirements of the day:

> . . . old Poets, like old Ladies, may
> Be more afraid to venture the survay
> Of many apt to censure their decay.

> Both know they have been out of fashion long;
> And, e're they come before a shining throng,
> Would dress themselves by Patterns of the Young.

[85] Prologue to *The Unfortunate Lovers.*
[86] October 21.

Well, our old Poet hopes this Comedie
Will somewhat in the fine new fashion be;
But, if all gay, 'twould not with Age agree.

A little he was fain to moralize
That he might serve your minds as well as eyes:
The Proverb says, Be merry and be wise. . . .[87]

Proverb! One can see Buckingham and Lady Shrewsbury shudder. On March 26, 1688, only a little over a week before the author died, Pepys went to see it:

I alone to the Duke of York's house, to see the new play, called "The Man is the Master," where the house was, it being not above one oclock, very full. But my wife and Deb, being there before, with Mrs. Pierce and Corbet and Betty Turner, whom my wife carried with her, they made me room; and there I sat, it costing me 8 s. upon them in oranges, at 6 d. a-piece. By and by the King came, and we sat just under him, so that I durst not turn my back all the play. The play is a translation out of the French, and the plot Spanish, but not anything at all extraordinary in it, though translated by Sir W. Davenant, and so I found the King and his company did think meanly of it, though there was here and there something pretty: but the most of the mirth was sorry, poor stuffe, of eating sack posset and slabbering themselves, and mirth fit for clownes; the prologue but poor, and the epilogue little in it. . . .

Pepys saw the play again several months later, and being less worked upon by the high cost of oranges and the example of the courtier gallants in the King's box, he decided on this second occasion that it was "a very good play."[88] However, there is little doubt that it continued to displease the less ingenuous critics.

Davenant was afflicted by financial troubles until the end, but in this direction misfortune was no novelty. His theatre was

[87] The prologue.
[88] May 7, 1668.

closed by the plague from June 1665 to October 1666, and in the midst of this period the Lord Chamberlain wrote on behalf of a creditor who had brought suit several years before: "Mr. Creed hath beene a petition[r] soe long against you & I have given you soe often notice. . . . I shall therefore desire that you take some speedy course for his satisfaction." [89] There had been many such reminders, and in order to satisfy the demands upon him, Davenant had for some time been liquidating his shares in the company.[90] Since shares were salable at upwards of £600 each, and since he had held ten of them, he was able by leaning upon his principal in this way to keep well afloat during the last few years of his life. It is pleasant to discover that of the 7.7 shares he disposed of, one half-share was given to his old friend Abraham Cowley, and another half-share was put in trust for the necessitous widow of his old patron Endymion Porter. Perhaps he was too open handed, for when the end came he was still a debtor and he had, including one additional share which had reverted to him, only 3.3 shares of his theatrical stock to pass on to his wife and his brood of children.

Since even these 3.3 shares would be at the mercy of his creditors if he willed them to his family, he and Lady Mary resorted to a device which saved the children but sent the father into the other world with the weight of fraud on his back. He made no will, and at his death his widow renounced administration of his estate in favor of one John Alway, "Principal Creditor." But Alway in reality was no creditor at all, but a stalking horse "of no residence" whom the real creditors could never find.[91] Sir William's personal property and his theatrical stock found their way intact into the hands of his heirs. When we remember how John Davenant had prepared for death by sitting in his Oxford tavern reckoning up his debts so that every penny might be paid immediately, we must regret that his son occupied his last

[89] A. Nicoll, *op. cit.*, p. 275.
[90] L. Hotson, *op. cit.*, pp. 220–21.
[91] *Camden Society*, "A selection from the Wills of Eminent Persons," p. 160; "Davenant v. Crosse Bill and Answer," L. Hotson, *op. cit.*, p. 374.

moments with such different calculations. Yet any man's virtue
is an armed force of limited muster; had William Davenant lived
in his father's small sphere, his integrity also might have withstood the assaults of temptation. His children were very young,
and the world had not been generous.

There are more intimate details about the poet's funeral than
about any episode in his life. On April 7, 1668, Samuel Pepys
was spending the afternoon at His Majesty's Theatre, absorbing
drama and the news of the town: "Here I hear," said he, "that
Sir W. Davenant is just now dead." Two days later he left the
office early,

. . . and up and down to the Duke of York's playhouse there to see.
which I did, Sir W. Davenant's corpse carried out toward Westminster, there to be buried. Here were many coaches and six
horses, and many hacknies that made it look, methought, as if it
were the buriall of a poor poet. He seemed to have many children,
by five or six in the first mourning-coach, all boys.[92]

John Aubrey can take us on into the Abbey, for he was an invited guest:

I was at his funerall. He had a coffin of Walnutt-tree; Sir John
Denham sayd 'twas the finest coffin that ever he saw. His body
was carried in a herse from the play-house to Westminster-Abbey,
where, at the great west dore, he was received by the sing[ing] men
and choristers, who sang the service of the church ('I am the Resur-
rection &c') to his grave, which is in the south crosse aisle, on which,
on a paving stone of marble, is writt, in imitation of that on Ben
Johnson, 'O rare Sir Will. Davenant.' [93]

The usual crop of elegies was forthcoming. These were of
mixed tone. The cruel satire already quoted [94] from the flyleaf
of a copy of Denham's poems concludes in softer vein:

[92] April 9, 1668.
[93] John Aubrey, *op. cit.,* I, 208.
[94] See above, Chap. I, note 28.

And yet I feare thy want of breath
Will prove the Inglish stages death.
Could I to thee new life bequeath,
No other head should were y[e] wreath.

Even Flecknoe's prose satire describing Davenant's adventures in the "Poet's Elizium" interrupts its maunderings about his poor technique, his vanity, his commercialism, etc., to quote an elegy by a contemporary poet "more humane than the rest"—

Great was his wit, his fancy great
As e'er was any poet's yet;
And more advantage none e'er made
O' th' wit and fancy which he had . . .[95]

The longest and most elaborate of the elegies [96] is purest eulogy until it comes to the last line, and then the author was inspired to devise a smutty pun upon Davenant's *contretemps* in youthful dalliance. In general these light-hearted funeral choristers set the tone for the world's future treatment of the poet—they patronized him.

It is well to depend for an intimate insight into the nature of a man upon the characterizations of those who knew him; there is such a characterization of Davenant, and one written by no less a person than John Dryden. But it is not yet time to grow valedictory. Before we can come to a full understanding of Davenant's character, we must consider his literary works, and his contemporary and subsequent reputation. However, judging him at this point solely on the basis of the *actions* of his life, we must realize that he comes off well: He has displayed weaknesses of which many of us might be guilty, qualities of which any of us might be proud.

Anthony à Wood recognized that a notable had died, and in the month following the poet's burial he sent for the details of

[95] Richard Flecknoe, *op. cit.*
[96] Printed entire by L. Hotson, *op. cit.*, pp. 224–26.

the event so that he might add them to his collections. Aubrey wrote in response to his request:

That sweet swan of Isis, Sir William Davenant, dyed the seaventh day of April last, and lyes buried among the poets in Westminster Abbey, by his antagonist, Mr. Thomas May,[97] whose inscription of whose marble was taken away by order since the king came in. Sir William was Poet Laureate and Mr. John Dryden hath his place. But me thought it had been proper that a laurell should have been sett on his coffin—which was not done.[98]

Sweet swan of Isis! How un-swanlike had been his existence! Nearly a half century of his sixty-three years had been packed with danger, action, change, and enterprise. We are proudly concerned about the harrowing speed of modern life—deceived apparently by the difficult names the psychologists have given our nervous responses to mild stimuli. Compared with Davenant, even adventurous men of our times are as sedentary as mollusks. The rest of us are rarely even sued for debt.

[97] It was the Royalist contention that Thomas May became a Parliamentarian because Davenant rather than he had been selected as poet laureate; cf. Dr. A. G. Chester, *Thomas May, Man of Letters.*
[98] John Aubrey, *op. cit.,* I, 208.

INTERCHAPTER

WHEN we think of Davenant's harassed and crowded life, we wonder how he found leisure to write anything at all. He was, in fact, one of the most prolific writers of his century. In the years 1672 and 1673 his widow, Mary Davenant, and his friend and publisher, Henry Herringman, combined to bring out his works in folio. This collection, even though incomplete, contains a thousand folio pages, many of them closely printed in double columns. Lady Mary selected Prince James as the dedicatee, and she reminded him of Sir William's devotion to the Stuarts:

I have often heard (and I have some reason to believe) that your Royal Father, of Ever Blessed Memory, was not displeased with his Writings; That your most Excellent Mother did Graciously take him into her Family, That she was often diverted by him, and as often smil'd upon his Endevors.

To the Reader, Henry Herringman explained:

I here present you with A Collection of all those Pieces Sir William D'avenant ever design'd for the Press. In his Life-time he often express'd to me his great Desire to see them in One Volume, which (in Honor to his Memory) with a great deal of Care and Pains, I have now accomplished. . . . My Author was Poet Laureat to two Great Kings, which certainly bespeaks his Merits; besides I could say much in Honor of this Excellent Person, but I intend not his Panegyrick. He was my Worthy Friend, let his Works, that are now before you, speak his Praise. . . .

Considering the bulk of the material placed in his hands, Herringman cannot be condemned for his failings as an editor, or for his omission of some of the dramatic pieces. The volume contains *Gondibert,* half the length of *Paradise Lost* although only half finished, besides a host of miscellaneous poems.[1] Its dramatic pieces, supplemented by the few omitted, occupy in a modern edition five thick octavo volumes. It is this body of work that we are now to describe and evaluate.

Writing as he did in a period of literary transition, and being essentially a venturer, which in the realm of authorship took the form of innovation, Davenant produced no single work which does not invite the student into avenues of speculation and inquiry; hence an exhaustive study of his plays and poems would swell to inordinate proportions. The best that can be done in limited space is to indicate the historical significance of these works and to dwell upon their most neglected aspect, which, strangely enough, is their intrinsic interest.

Gondibert, which Davenant considered his masterpiece and which will therefore engage us first, can be conveniently considered along with his other non-dramatic poems; but the twenty-seven dramatic pieces, scattered through the forty years between 1627 and 1667 defy systematic approach. Their bewildering diversity, and the fact that some of them are so unique that they would tax the resourcefulness of a Polonius, make any strict grouping according to types impracticable. A grouping according to chronology would be still more pointless, because the outside pressure applied by the specialized demands of his age and by Parliamentary prohibitions prevented Davenant from developing individually as a playwright. He had no "periods," and some of his early plays are his best. Yet a division must be made somehow. Now despite the sporadic and incoherent nature of his dramatic output, Davenant always brought to his work two fairly definable creative impulses, and a rough cleavage can be made between the plays on the basis of these creative

---

[1] The volume is in three sections, each separately paginated. Page references in the present study are to the first section. Quotations from plays are taken from the edition of Maidment and Logan.

impulses, or kinds of inspiration, better than in any other way.

Davenant began to write too late to escape the schematic tendencies of Stuart drama; and the flattening-out process, evidenced in the gradual disappearance of romantic comedy and realistic tragedy, forbade him a rich and free artistic transmutation of materials. As a result, native or realistic elements appeared in his plays, or parts of plays, only in combination with the comic spirit. More to be regretted, exotic, fanciful, and ornate elements were the almost inevitable concomitants of his serious vein. He wrote plays shading from farce to melodrama, and in some of the intermediate types his creative impulses seem to have been mixed, so that the tone is sadly jumbled; however, the plays can be divided into two groups according to whether each is more interesting for its light and realistic, or for its serious and fanciful, ingredients. *The Just Italian,* although almost a tragicomedy, has been grouped with *The Wits* because its comic underplot is the best thing about it. Conversely, *The Platonic Lovers,* although never tragic in tone, has been grouped with *Love and Honour* because it is serious and exotic upon the whole. In his lighter vein Davenant merely perpetuated an Elizabethan tradition, so this phase will be treated first. His serious vein culminated in *The Siege of Rhodes* and foreshadowed the heroic plays of the Restoration. A separate chapter will be devoted to Davenant's adaptations of the plays of Shakespeare and others; and our survey will conclude with an account of the impression made by his works as a whole upon his own and subsequent generations.

Since this digression has taken the form of a bill of fare, it may be concluded with the assurance that Davenant's works, while they offer few epicurean delicacies, do offer abundant, varied, and—lest anyone be fearful—prevailingly wholesome fare.

VII

GONDIBERT

My Poem will, I hope, appear as pleasant as a summer Passage on a crooked River, where going about and turning back is as delightful as the Delays of parting Lovers.—PREFACE TO GONDIBERT.

I

MUCH of Davenant's non-dramatic verse has never been reprinted, and none of it has been edited or published in an attractive form. Although some of this verse is pedestrian in tone and infra-literary in degree, there remains when this is culled out a worthwhile sheaf no thinner than that of the average Cavalier poet. Davenant achieved excellence as often as Suckling and Lovelace, and his failures to achieve excellence were never so utterly dismal as some of theirs. He lacked the virtuosity, the graceful brilliance, of these twain at their best; therefore, and because the very bulk of his work has militated against him, he has been relegated to a lower order. The production upon which he himself staked his chances for undying fame was none of his plays, but *Gondibert: an Heroick Poem*. This child of his heart, although it has been less neglected than the other poems, deserves extended discussion, so there is space only to indicate the general nature of what remains.

His products in one lowly category, commendatory verses written for fellow poets, and prologues and epilogues written for fellow playwrights, must be dismissed with the statement that they are always gracious, and adequate according to the standards of their kind.[1] The remainder of his shorter poems, except for certain laureate works separately published,[2] and a few pieces still in manuscript or in seventeenth-century anthologies,[3] are to be found in *Madagascar with Other Poems,* 1638, and—the best of them—in *Poems on Several Occasions, never before Printed,* dated 1672 but first issued in the folio of 1673. Here, bulking largest, is a group of occasional poems such as "Madagascar" itself, and of verse epistles and personal tributes—to Henrietta Maria, to Charles, father and son, to various lords and ladies, and to Endymion and Olivia Porter and other intimate friends. Such verse was as characteristic of the day as the embroidered court costume of white and carnation silk, and we must not be too much offended at the authors if they could not claim, with Burns, that they had never paid a compliment at the expense of truth. Davenant's complimentary verse varies greatly in quality. There is the trite eulogy, ornamented at times with tortuous conceits. The conceit (against which Davenant himself was to open the fire of criticism), is most apparent in the *Madagascar* volume, and in commending this volume Suckling unguardedly proclaimed its author the true successor of John Donne. Davenant's later poems in this class are apt to be discursive and philosophical rather than ingenious, and one of them, the excessively laudatory "Poem to the Earl of Orrery," is so long as to be monumental. By no means, however, are all these poems such as any courtly versifier might have produced. Mixed with the rest is the adroit *jeu d'esprit,* and the glowing

[1] A number of these are reprinted in the folio. See also Henry Carey's translations, *Romulus and Tarquin,* 2nd ed., 1638, and *History of the Wars of Flanders,* 1654. Others are cited in Hazlitt's *Handbook,* and in Corser's *Collectanea, passim.*

[2] See the poems to Charles II in the appended bibliography.

[3] The anthologies are listed in the bibliography. For pieces still in manuscript, see Ashmole MS, 36, 22v; MSS of St. John's College, Camb., 416, 38; *Historical MSS Commission,* III, 303; and Add. MSS in the British Museum. Among the latter, "Reason" (Sloan MSS, 2230) is not an unprinted poem, but a non-autograph copy of "The Philosopher's Disquisition," *Folio,* 1673, p. 326, with a last stanza proving the latter to have been planned as a part of *Gondibert.*

tribute expressive of sincere and ardent feeling. Examples of both of these have already been quoted.[4] Allied with the occasional and complimentary poems is a series of elegies and epitaphs, appropriate in sentiment, and achieving at times a genuine tenderness. Davenant, as well as Dryden, was of that Restoration chorus which lamented the death of the "incomparable Virgin," Anne Killigrew—as though she were the last of her kind that the times could be expected to produce.[5]

Among the shorter poems is a second group composed of comic and descriptive pieces sometimes semi-autobiographical in nature. Several of these deserving to be better known have already been quoted, or will be mentioned later on.[6] Such pieces as "A Journey into Worcestershire" and "The Long Vacation in London" throw light on Davenant's life, "Jeffereidos" and "The Plots" upon the life of his times. These verses are pleasant, if unpoetical, and possess the excellent quality of concreteness. This group is commendable also for its omissions; contrary to the custom of his day, Davenant in comic vein eschewed the ribald and the abusive.

Finally there is a group of ballads, songs, and philosophical poems, and while Davenant was not preëminently a lyrical poet, his well-known aubade is not his only achievement in this class. There are songs in boisterous vein such as the Plutonian "Song to a Dreadful Tune," beginning:

> You Fiends and Furies come along
> With iron Crow and massie Prong;
>   Come drag your shackles and draw near,
> To stirre a huge old Sea-coal Cake,
> Which in our hollow Hell did bake,
>   Many a thousand thousand year.[7]

[4] See above, pp. 49, 70.
[5] *Folio*, 1673, p. 324.
[6] See pp. 50, 285.
[7] *Folio*, 1673, p. 302.

In contrast there are lyrics celebrating the quiet joys of domestic love and of religious reflection—for instance the duet, "Endymion Porter and Olivia," ending:

Olivia

When at the Bowers in the Elizian shade
I first arrive, I shall examine where
    They dwel, who love the highest Vertue made,
For I am sure to find Endimion there.

Endimion

From this vext World when we shall both retire,
Where all are Lovers, and where all rejoyce,
    I need not seek thee in the Heavenly Quire,
For I shall know Olivia by her Voice.[8]

An excellent illustration of the religious poems is "The Christian's Reply," ending:

Fraile Life! in which through Mists of humane breath,
    We grope for Truth, and make our Progress slow,
Because by Passion blinded, till by Death,
    Our Passions ending, we begin to know.

O rev'rend Death! whose looks can soon advise
    Even scornfull Youth, whilst Priests their Doctrine wast;
Yet mocks us too, for he does make us wise,
    When by his coming our Affaires are past.

O harmless Death! whom still the valiant brave,
    The wise expect, the Sorrowfull invite,
And all the Good embrace, who know the Grave,
    A short dark passage to Eternal Light.[9]

Better than either of these are the songs "Your Beauty, ripe, and calm, and fresh" and "The Lark now leaves his wat'ry Nest," [10]

[8] *Ibid.*, p. 321.
[9] *Ibid.*, p. 335.
[10] See above p. 29.   This song has been set to music by Horatio Parker.

one of which has already been quoted, and both of which appear in that eminently accessible volume, *The Oxford Book of English Verse.*

Some of Davenant's songs are polite, formal, even satirical, and such examples as "The Dream," "The Mistress," "To Clelia," and "Against Women's Pride" reflect the rising vogue of *verse de société.* One such song was set to music by Berkenshaw and Samuel Pepys.[11] Another is interesting for its similarity in form and subject, but utter dissimilarity in point of view, to Lovelace's "To Lucasta, going to the Wars." Lovelace's,

> Yet this inconstancy is such
> As you too shall adore;
> I could not love thee, Dear, so much,
> Loved I not Honour more.

presents an odd contrast with Davenant's,

> For I must go where lazy Peace,
> Will hide her drouzy head;
> And, for the sport of Kings, encrease
> The number of the Dead.[12]

Considering the time at which these verses were written, Davenant's stanza is infinitely the more original; yet it helps to explain why its author made few notable contributions to lyrical poetry: Davenant was rarely spontaneous, rarely able to deliver himself from the pale cast of thought.

It may be incautious to introduce the subject of technique just after bringing some of our author's verses into juxtaposition with a stanza considered by Professor Saintsbury to epitomize literary excellence. Lovelace, like Suckling, had the good fortune to concentrate the best of his talent into a few songs of inimitable verve and polish. Both Lovelace and Suckling are "anthology

---

[11] "This cursed Jealousy" from *The Siege of Rhodes;* cf. the *Diary,* Feb. 26, 1662.

[12] "The Souldier going to the Field," *Folio,* 1673, p. 321.

poets" while Davenant is not. He deployed his talent over a wider field and achieved a higher general level of competence. Much of his verse, produced rapidly and under pressure, is rough or mechanical, but it never sinks (except intentionally) to the grade of the doggerel too common among the Cavaliers. He had a good ear, albeit an impatient hand and a too flexible standard; and in his better work he produced many single lines, if not whole poems, which are felicitous and musical. His rimed verses at least scan, and this cannot always be said for the verses of most of his contemporaries. One would not, of course, care to be assigned the task of scanning some of the blank verse in Davenant's plays; like that in most plays of their time it often tends to disintegrate into rhythmic prose. On the other hand, Davenant's blank verse is at times as regular and strong as that of Beaumont. Certain of the courtier dramatists, Thomas Killigrew for instance, wrote in cadences because this was the only technique they had mastered, but Davenant could write any type of verse he cared to. At fifty he essayed the distich popularized by Waller and Denham, and achieved as much technical proficiency as his masters.[13] To summarize briefly we may say that in technique, as in spirit and content, the miscellaneous poems just reviewed are not to Davenant's discredit. They should be judged after a comprehensive reading. They contain many good things that the critics have missed, but their average is only a creditable mediocrity. As a non-dramatic poet, Davenant's reputation must rest chiefly upon *Gondibert*.

2

The circumstances under which Davenant produced his *chef d'œuvre*, which he called a "Heroick Poem," have already been described.[14] The first two books were written in Paris, and the first half of the third at Cowes Castle on the Isle of Wight. In

[13] In *The Siege of Rhodes*.
[14] See above, pp. 109–10, 114–15.

this Royalist prison the poet indited his *Postscript* on October 22, 1650. The poem was published in two editions in London, 1651, while its author awaited trial in the Tower.[15] It might be logical to begin a discussion of the poem with an account of its sources, but *Gondibert* is not so frequently read in these days, and comment of any kind will be more intelligible after we have reviewed its story—its story of

> . . . old, unhappy, far-off things
> And battles long ago.

King Aribert, glorious in peace and war, is the aged ruler of Lombardy; and Princess Rhodalind, compound of every excellence, is his only child. The brilliant but ambitious Prince Oswald aspires to the hand of Rhodalind and thereby to the throne, but both the Princess and her royal father favor another. This other is Duke Gondibert, the unclouded mirror of all perfection. Untouched even by such a noble stain as ambition, Gondibert never suspects the peculiar favor he enjoys in the eyes of Rhodalind and the King. Both lords have been conquerors for Lombardy, and as the tale opens, Oswald is encamped at Brescia with an army of scarred veterans, and Gondibert is encamped at Bergamo with an army of valiant youths—all warriors and all lovers.

Perceiving who is the chief obstacle to his advancement, Oswald lays ambush to Gondibert one day as the latter is returning from a stag hunt with a small band of followers; too chivalrous, however, to profit by superior numbers, he agrees to fight his rival in single combat. The higher lieutenants in each faction plead for the privilege of engaging each other. They take place by their leaders, and the fight begins. Blow by blow, wound by wound, and finally death by death, it progresses before our eyes. When the din of conflict ends, Gondibert lives, splendid in victory, and Oswald dies, splendid in defeat. Of the seconds only

---

[15] For discussion of the editions, see the appended bibliography.

one on each side remains alive: Hubert, the brother of Oswald; and Hurgonil, suitor to Orna, the lovely sister of Gondibert. The outraged forces of the fallen champion now rally under Hubert and attack the small band of huntsmen, but Gondibert's gallantry and tactical wisdom outweigh the strength of numbers, and the young men win the day. As magnanimous as valiant, the victor permits Hubert to go off with his defeated Brescians, while he dispatches messengers to Verona and then leads the remnant of his followers to Bergamo. Fainting of his wounds along the way, he is succored by Ulfin, a warrior aged in the service of his family, and is borne to the palace of Astragon.

We leave Gondibert at this point, and follow his envoys to Verona. One of these is Hurgonil, who travels in fear that the wounds of battle upon his face will weaken his cause with Orna, and the other is one Tybalt, who travels in hope, for he has long nourished a secret passion for Gondibert's niece Laura, and Laura's professed lover has just died a soldier's death. We see Verona as it awakens at dawn and pulses to the first distorted rumors of the civil conflict. Then Hurgonil and Tybalt arrive, and we see the effect of their authentic intelligence—upon the populace, upon the court, and finally upon Rhodalind and her train. Rhodalind and Orna are rejoiced that Gondibert and Hurgonil still live, while Laura, to Tybalt's private misgiving, is prostrated with sorrow at the death of her lover, Arnold. The effect of the news is most striking upon a fourth lady, Oswald's sister, the imperiously beautiful Gartha. She upbraids the Princess as the cause of her brother's death, and then mounts her chariot and drives in a fury to Brescia.

For the time Gartha holds the center of the stage. At Brescia she finds Hubert preparing the army for an attack upon Bergamo. She adds fuel to the fire, and diverts the attack to Verona itself. But at this juncture, as war clouds cover the sun, a King's minister arrives from the capital. This is the crafty Hermegild, and he comes in the cause not of the King but of himself. He has long admired Gartha, and he promises that if she will be his in spite of his years, he will so use his power and cunning that Rhodalind and the crown will fall to the lot of Hubert. His counsels prevail, and when he returns to Verona with Gartha, Lombardy rejoices over an apparent pacification.

The tale returns us now to Gondibert and the sanctuary whither Ulfin has carried him. Astragon is a philosopher, and his Palace is a spacious retreat consecrated to religio-philosophical devotion and, above all, to scientific inquiry. Part cathedral and part research laboratory, the Palace is still delightfully bucolic; and its complicated organization and teeming workers make it none the less a perfect place for Gondibert's recovery. But he is nursed back to health—here entereth *dilemma*—by Astragon's daughter, Birtha. Birtha! Compared with her innocent charm, her pure perfection of mind and body, even the graces of Rhodalind are obscured. Gondibert has never been ambitious, has never aspired to Rhodalind and the crown, and he is certain now that in Birtha and this peaceful retreat he has found his destiny. Birtha requites his passion, and when Astragon is convinced that the Duke's condescension to his daughter is no mere whim, he blesses their exchange of vows.

Alas for true love, two of Gondibert's lieutenants, Goltho and Ulfinore, have also succumbed to the charms of Birtha, who, to be sure, is more nearly of their station. Much worse, news arrives that King Aribert has openly proclaimed Gondibert his successor and the future husband of his daughter! The court itself visits the Palace of Astragon to notify Gondibert officially of his glorious fate, and it requires all of his skill to reassure the drooping Birtha, and to be noncommittal and yet courteous to gracious majesty. He follows the court to Verona, leaving Birtha as a betrothal stone a miraculous emerald which will lose brilliance if ever he breaks his faith. Astragon resolves to send Birtha herself to the court to wait upon Rhodalind and thus test her powers of patience and restraint. The action is now centering at Verona. We follow none of the principal characters hence, but instead the youthful and naïve Goltho and Ulfinore.

Comic relief enters the story with their arrival at the capital, and with the narrow escape of Goltho from the wiles of Dalga, a professional enchantress. Upon this pleasant but minor note, the story ends—just half way towards its conclusion.

Whether there is war between Brescia and Bergamo, whether the machinations of Hermegild succeed, whether he wins Gartha, Hurgonil weds Orna, Tybalt wins Laura, Hubert wins Rhodalind, or Gondibert weds Birtha, we shall never know. "And I beseech you," pleads the author, "if thou art so civill to be pleas'd with what is written, not to take ill that I run not on till my last gasp." *Last gasp* has a sinister ring, considering that the poet was interrupted by nothing less than a Parliamentary trial for high treason, and we must concede that for him to go on with his tale of love and valor would have been "to beget a Poem in an unseasonable time." There is no hint in the Postscript, which we have been quoting, of what the conclusion was to be. Davenant hoped to finish the poem and did not wish to spoil the effect; he had an ingenuous faith in the efficacy of suspense, and even in his Arguments to the various cantos never gave away anything essential. At intervals in the poem the reader is darkly threatened with a tragedy:

> And thou (what ere thou art, who doth perchance,
>   With a hot Reader's haste, this Song pursue)
> Mayst finde, too soon, thou dost too far advance,
>   And wish it all unread, or else untrue.[16]

Nevertheless, one suspects that the poem, designed as we shall see as a drama in narration, would have proved a tragicomedy, and that however thorny their path Gondibert and either Rhodalind or Birtha (which one is baffling!) would have been united at the end. The sources offer no clue of the intended conclusion, but these sources are interesting and will aid us in analysis.

Davenant felt that the dignity of such a poem as this de-

[16] Book III, Canto 2, Stanza 44. See also II, 8, 91.

manded a basis among scrolls thick with the dust of antiquity, so he pictured such scrolls before him:

> By what bold passion am I rudely led,
>   Like Fame's too curious and officious Spie,
> Where I these Rolls in her dark Closet read,
>   Where Worthies wrapped in Time's disguises lie?

These rolls in Fame's dark closet are the work of a "Lombard author," an engagingly mysterious figure (like Chaucer's *Lollius*) who is referred to constantly and is even held partly accountable for the structure of the poem:

> Let none our Lombard Author rudely blame
>   Who from the Story has thus long disgrest. . . .

The incidents told by this Lombard author belong, by Davenant's seventeenth-century reckoning, roughly to the eighth century:

> Nine hasty Centuries are now fulfull'd
>   Since Opticks first were known to Astragon;
> By whom the Moderns are become so skill'd,
>   They dream of seeing to the Maker's Throne.[17]

With our ratiocinative faculties thus challenged, we think of Paulus Diaconus, c. 725–c. 795, chief preserver of Lombard history of his own and preceding centuries. In the *De Gestis Longobardorum* there appears an actual King Aripertus, the succession to whose throne caused civil turmoil involving a Prince Godepertus and a Princess Rodelinda.[18] Since Davenant's poem introduces us to a Gondibert, a Rhodalind, and internecine broils over the throne of a King Aribert, we are apt to conclude that Paulus was Davenant's Lombard author. Upon Paulus this honor has actually been thrust.[19]

---

[17] For the above quotations, see I, 4, 1; II, 7, 1; and II, 5, 17.

[18] Book II, chaps. 28–30, pp. 81–86 in the English edition of W. D. Foulke.

[19] Georg Gronauer, *Gondibert, Eine literarhistorische Untersuchung*, pp. 57–64; see note below.

It is disturbing, however, to discover that Paulus has been saddled with events he never recorded. Except for the similarity in a few names and in the fact of a civil war (epidemic alike among Lombards and the nations of fiction), nothing could be more unlike than Davenant's story and the career of Aripertus or, indeed, anyone else in the *De Gestis Longobardorum.* Of the score of characters in *Gondibert* only five appear anywhere in Paulus. These five appear, significantly enough, in two tales based upon the Lombard historian by Bandello and retold by Belleforest—the Alboinus-Rosemunda story (previously used by Davenant in his *Albovine*), and the Godepertus-Grimualdus story just mentioned.[20] In the popular tale as told by Belleforest Godepertus appears as Gundebert (Davenant's Gondibert) and Aripertus as Aribert (Davenant's Aribert). It is fairly obvious that the slender wisps of historical material appearing in the poem came from that quite unrecondite work, *Histoires Tragiques,* and that the whole business of the "Lombard author" is a harmless convention. In his preface Davenant asserted the Poet's superiority to mere fact, and he probably never looked into the *De Gestis Longobardorum* or any other Latin (and therefore formidable) work.[21]

Davenant must, in fact, plead guilty to inventing his story—an act somewhat less culpable to be sure in a "heroick poem" than in an avowed epic. Details have been traced with more or less justice to various works. The relations of King Aribert and his daughter Rhodalind have suggested to one scholar those of Latinus and his daughter Lavinia in Book VII of the *Æneid;*[22] and the relations of Astragon and his daughter Birtha have suggested to another those of Prospero and Miranda in *The Tem-*

---

[20] *Histoires Tragiques,* Tome IV, Hist. 19 and Hist. 20.

[21] G. Gronauer (cf. note 19), who makes Paulus Davenant's chief source, recognized Belleforest as a possible intermediate, but was misled (like K. Campbell in tracing the source of *Albovine;* see below pp. 225–26) by his failure to consider that material from Paulus appears in several instances in the *Histoires Tragiques,* as well as in other popular works, such as Machiavelli's *History.*

[22] G. Gronauer, *op. cit.,* p. 64.

pest.[23]   Such devices as that of the magic emerald are constant quantities in the literature of the romance. The stag hunt in Book I, Canto 2 may have derived from the stag hunt in Denham's *Cooper's Hill;* and Astragon's Palace, the paradise of scientific research, unquestionably derived from Salomon's House in Bacon's *New Atlantis.*[24] However the real source of *Gondibert*—that which explains its spirit and kind rather than mere details of its content—is the wave of "neo-romantic" themes and ideals which inundated Europe, especially France, during the seventeenth century. *Gondibert* should be viewed in relation not to historical and epic literature but to Davenant's own *Siege of Rhodes* and the heroic romances of Scudéry and her kind. The possible influence on Davenant of *Ibrahim ou l'Illustre Bassa* (published with a critical preface in 1641) will be noted later on,[25] and it has been pointed out that when *Gondibert* was being written, Chapelain was at work on his *Pucelle,* Lemoyne on his *Saint Louis.*[26] From 1651 on, many heroic poems appeared in France (each with its critical preface) to take their place beside the prose romances. It was not unusual for Davenant to be in the vanguard of a literary movement.

3

It is impossible to lavish on *Gondibert* unqualified praise, and it will be the kindlier policy to dispose of its defects before turning to its indubitable merits. The dissatisfaction of many readers will arise from a distaste for its class and for the mid-seventeenth century conception of the heroic. *Gondibert* is anything but epic in tone. It is superlatively elevated; the characters are conventional, and their emotions stilted. The virtues of the protagonists are mainly, beauty and unearthliness in the women,

23 A. W. Ward, *op. cit.,* II, 200, III, 168–69.   Ward's statement that Davenant "plagiarized characters and situations from *The Tempest"* is far too strong.

24 Isaac Disraeli, *op. cit.,* suggested this source, and G. Gronauer, *op. cit.,* pp. 72–79, quotes excellent parallels.

25 See below, p. 245.

26 J. E. Spingarn, *Critical Essays of the Seventeenth Century,* I, xxxiv, II, 331.

valor and chivalry in the men, and magnanimity or an abstract
variety of general excellence in both. Their vices are no meaner,
as the author tells us in his preface, than such as arise from the
"distempers of love and ambition." Even the villains, if they
may be called such, possess grandeur in excess, while Gondibert,
Rhodalind, and Birtha are paragons unalloyed. When Gondibert makes even the most temporary retreat in battle, the poet
hastens to excuse it; and when Birtha is described (in what is
one of the most tender and poetic cantos of the poem), she proves
not only innocent but unimaginably, almost ridiculously, so:

> She thinks that Babes proceed from mingling Eyes, . . .
> Or they are got by close exchanging vows.[27]

The effort to exalt valor results in a glorification of mere wounds,
and the effort to exalt and dignify physical love results sometimes
in bathos. There is the case of the stag:

> His Rivals that his fury us'd to fear
>   For his lov'd Female, now his faintness shun;
> But were his season hot, and she but neer,
>   (O mighty Love!) his Hunters were undone.[28]

This, we must hasten to add, is the worst stanza in the poem;
usually the author is nothing if not decorous. In fact decorum—
politesse—weaves a sheen of unreality into the very texture of
the poem. There is—although not to the same extent as in the
French romances of the period—the solemn gallantry of the
salon. Yet strangely enough, the characters—although figures
in tapestry—occasionally come to life and astonish us with a
robust humanity. Certainly they become more and more real as
the poem proceeds.

Davenant wished to do more than write a romance in rime,
and his method of dignifying his poem results in another of its

[27] II, 7, 45.
[28] I, 2, 42. Love arms the young men of Bergamo. For disquisitions on
love, see I, 2, 15–19; III, 3, 1 ff.

possible defects. The narrative is interlarded with philosophy, and the author choruses some of its most minute details. Besides long didactic speeches, of the poet to the reader, of Ulfin to his son, of Astragon to Birtha and Gondibert, there is a tendency to define and enlarge upon "power," "care," "jealousy," "humility," "honor," "marriage," or indeed any abstraction which may be mentioned. The stanzaic form, wherein every four lines was designed to contain a full period, encouraged this practice. It is true that the philosophical comment is well expressed and often profound; the worldly wisdom is shrewd and arresting:

> Since wrongs must be, Complaints must shew the Griev'd
> And Favorites should walk still open Ear'd,
> For of the suing Croud half are reliev'd,
> With the innate Delight of being heard.[29]

Some, Isaac Disraeli for instance, have considered *Gondibert* a philosophical or ethical poem, and the quality we are discussing its greatest excellence; [30] but in narrative poetry a reader expects action, characterization, and a portrayal of the physical world (which, when he chose, Davenant could well provide); the extraneous matter in *Gondibert* clogs its movement and partially defeats its interest as story.

The stanzaic form may be another source of discomfort to some readers. Davenant considered the couplet breath-taking in a long narrative, and employed the stanza of four alternately rimed decasyllabic lines, used most conspicuously before in Sir John Davies' *Nosce Teipsum,* and afterwards in Dryden's *Astræa Redux* and *Annus Mirabilis,* and in Gray's *Elegy.* Dryden frankly confessed that he imitated the prosody of *Gondibert,* and praised Davenant's use and prefatory defense of the interwoven stanza.[31] Sir Walter Scott considered that this stanza had the disciplinary effect of simplifying and condensing

[29] III, 6, 8.
[30] See below, p. 278.
[31] *Preface to Annus Mirabilis,* 1669.

the Caroline style.[32]   The poet was, in fact consciously striving
to simplify style. He was experimenting in every way. It is
interesting to notice that although he rejected the distich, he
imitated at times its balanced line:

> These were my Merits, my reward is Pow'r,
>   An outward Trifle, bought with inward Peace;
> Got in an Age, and rifled in an How'r,
>   When feav'rish Love, the People's Fit, shall cease.[33]

The usual objection has been that the stanza is more fitted for
elegiac than for narrative poetry, but such matters must rest with
the taste of individual readers; in Davenant's words, "Numbers
in Verse must, like distinct kinds of Musick, be exposed to the
uncertain and different taste of several Ears."

Last in our toll of weakness, and this I believe is a weakness
only because the poem comes to us as a fragment, *Gondibert* is
constructed upon quasi-dramatic principles. Genuinely devoted
to the stage, Davenant conceived the design to write five books,
each equivalent to an act,[34] and to divide the books into cantos,
each equivalent to a scene. Although Dryden considered this
"rather a play in narration . . . than an heroic poem," [35] the
scheme was brave and ingenious, and had the poem been completed might have proved entirely successful. The drawback is,
that to finish reading *Gondibert* as we have it is to leave the
theatre in the middle of the play. We have had exposition,
entanglement, and an initial climax, but not the continued action
and dénouement which give these things force. An insubstantial
memory is the result, and the characters and their predicament
soon fade from our minds.

After dwelling so long upon the deficiencies of the poem, we

---

[32] See below, pp. 277–78.
[33] II, 2, 26.
[34] Thomas May in his Character of Henry II had previously borrowed from
drama the five-part principle of construction; cf. A. Chester, *op. cit.* The device
was not unfamiliar on the Continent.
[35] Essay of Heroic Plays, 1672.

must hasten to insist upon its compensating merits. *Gondibert*
is thoroughly worth reading. It is worth while for its details.
While the versification is often rugged, it is sometimes delightful. At the very beginning we come upon a description of
King Aribert and "Recorded Rhodalind"!

> Her father (in the winter of his age)
>   Was like that stormy Season froward grown,
> Whom so her youthful presence did asswage,
>   That he her sweetness tasted as his own.[36]

The gentle Princess—

> Her speech, like Lovers watch'd, was kind and low—

pines quietly for Gondibert:

> Yet sadly it is sung that she in Shades,
>   Mildly as mourning Doves love's sorrows felt;
> Whilst in her secret Tears her Freshness fades,
>   As Roses silently in Lymbecks melt.[37]

This harmony and pathos is not spent alone upon Rhodalind,
but inspires nearly all of a very lovely description of Birtha and
her awakening womanhood in Book II, Canto 7. In contrast—
and the poem has astonishing variety—there is the macabre humor of the description of Ulfin's maimed veterans:

> In whom such Death and want of Limbs they find,
>   As each were lately call'd out of his Tombe,
> And left some Members hastily behind.
> .   .   .   .
>
> And Ulfin might be thought (when the rude Wind,
>   Lifting their Curtains, left their ruines bare)
> A formal Antiquary, fondly kind
>   To Statues, which he now drew out to aire.[38]

[36] I, 1, 14.
[37] I, 1, 43.
[38] I, 6, 15–18.

Many individual episodes are adroitly turned, and, in spite of the decorative nature of the poem as a whole, are not only vividly but realistically presented. Such details as Gartha's frenzied ride to Brescia, Birtha's timid spying upon the grand dames of the visiting court, and Goltho and Ulfinore's arrival in the wicked city of Verona, have genuine dramatic as well as pictorial qualities. Ulfinore and Goltho have spent their boyhood and youth at the wars, and are easy prey for the seductive Dalga standing at her window:

This Beauty gaz'd on both, and Ulfinore
   Hung down his Head, but yet did lift his Eyes,
As if he fain would see a little more;
   For much, though bashful, he did beauty prise.

Goltho did like a blushless Statue stare,
   Boldly her practic'd Boldness did out-look;
And even for fear she would mistrust her Snare,
   Was ready to cry out that he was took!

She, with a wicked Woman's prosp'rous Art,
   A seeming Modesty, the Window clos'd;
Wisely delay'd his Eyes since of his Heart
   She thought she had sufficiently dispos'd.

And he thus strait complain'd! Ah Ulfinore,
   How vainly Glory has our Youth misled!
The Winde which blowes us from the happy Shore,
   And drives us from the Living to the Dead.

To bloody Slaughters, and perhaps of those
   Who might beget such Beauties as this Maid;
The Sleepy here are never wak'd with Foes,
   Nor are of ought but Ladies Frowns afraid.

Ere he could more lament, a little Page,
   Clean and perfum'd (one whom this Dame did breed

To guess at Ills too manly for his age)
   Steps swiftly to him and arrests his Steed.

.   .   .   .

And when his Friend advis'd him to take care,
   He gravely, as a Man new potent grown,
Protests he shall in all his Fortunes share,
   And to the House invites him as his own.[39]

Poor Goltho soon learns that it is not a great lady who has become enamoured of him, and his rescue from the Circe rounds
out the incident. This is scarcely a typical portion of the narrative, but many of the romantic actions are turned with the
same dexterity as this realistic one.

At the end of each canto there is usually a graceful peroration,
and these can be more readily excerpted than the more organic
passages. At the end of Book I, for instance, we have an apos-
trophe to sleep:

And now the weary World's great Med'cin, Sleep,
   This learned Host dispenc'd to ev'ry Guest;
Which shuts those Wounds where injur'd Lovers weep,
   And flies Oppressors to relieve th' Opprest.

It loves the Cotage, and from Court abstains,
   It stills the Sea-man though the Storm be high,
Frees the griev'd Captive in his closest Chaines,
   Stops Wants loud Mouth, and blinds the treach'rous Spie!

Kind Sleep, Nights welcome Officer, does cease
   All whom this House containes till Day return;
And me, Grief's Chronicler, does gently ease,
   Who have behind so great a Task to mourn.

When one begins to quote the poem, a score of passages occur
to him. The stag hunt in Book I, Canto 2, drew a word of

[39] III, 6, 32–39.

praise even from Edmund Gosse, Davenant's most savage critic.[40] Thomas Hobbes considered this hunt, and "The Battaile, The City Morning, The Funeral, The House of Astragon, The Library and the Temples" equal to the descriptive accessories of Homer and Virgil.[41] This is to damn with loud praise, but it is undeniable that the details mentioned are excellent. "The City Morning" is a reference to a description of the night life of Verona giving place at cold dawn to the business of the day:

> There from sick Mirth neglected Feasters reel,
>   Who cares of Want in Wine's false Lethe steep;
> There anxious empty Gamsters homeward steal,
>   And fear to wake, ere they begin to sleep.
>
> Here stooping Lab'rors slowly moving are,
>   Beasts to the Rich, whose Strength grows rude with Ease;
> And would usurp, did not their Rulers care,
>   With Toile and Tax their furious Strength appease.[42]

Most interesting of all, and most rich in curious lore, is the description of Astragon's Palace. Here is GREAT NATURE'S OFFICE where NATURE'S REGISTERS (scientists) organize data collected by INTELLIGENCERS (field workers) who have at their disposal NATURE'S NURSERY (a botanical and zoölogical garden). Here, too, is THE CABINET OF DEATH (an anatomical museum) and A MONUMENT OF VANISH'D MINDES (a library). Lest anyone suspect that science and religion are antithetical, there dominate all, three richly ornamented fanes, consecrated severally to Praise, Prayer, and Penitence. The poet's tone, whether he is treating of learning or worship, is sincerely devout. He discusses the books in the library, among them the commentaries on the Bible:

[40] From Shakespeare to Pope, p. 139.
[41] The Answer to the Preface. For the parts indicated see I, 5; II, 1; II, 4; II, 5, and 6.
[42] II, 1, 19–20.

About this sacred little Book did stand
Unweildly Volumes, and in number great;
And long it was since any Readers hand
Had reach'd them from their unfrequented Seat.

For a deep Dust (which Time doth softly shed
Where only Time does come) their Covers beare,
On which grave Spyders streets of Webbs had spread,
Subtle, and slight, as the grave Writers were.

In these, Heav'ns holy Fire does vainly burn,
Nor warms nor lights, but is in Sparkles spent,
Where froward Authors with Disputes have torn
The Garment seamless as the Firmament.[43]

These are splendid lines. The only stanzas which Davenant
quoted in his prefatory essay expound the belief that praise of
the Almighty is more fitting devotion than prayer or penitence:

Praise is Devotion fit for mighty Minds!
The diff'ring World's agreeing Sacrifice,
Where Heav'n divided Faiths united findes;
But Pray'r in various discord upward flies.

For Pray'r the Ocean is, where diverslie
Men steer their Course, each to a sev'ral Coast,
Where all our Int'rests so discordant be,
That Half beg Windes by which the Rest are lost.

By Penitence, when we ourselves forsake,
'Tis but in wise design on pitious Heav'n;
In Praise we nobly give what God may take,
And are without a Beggers Blush forgiv'n.[44]

At many points it is possible to gauge Davenant's religious convictions. He was an earnest if confused seeker after enlighten-

[43] II, 5, 48–50.
[44] II, 6, 84–86.

ment, and he strove bravely to pour old wine into new bottles. His beliefs represent a curious mingling of primitive Christianity and the new rationalism, and approach Quakerism much more nearly than Catholicism or the Anglicanism of his day. There is a note of unfriendliness toward sects of any kind, especially, of course, toward Calvinistic sects. The seventeenth-century mind, Davenant's in particular, is often curiously revealed. The poet was a soldier by class and political affiliations, but a pacifist by instinct. In precept and example he glorifies war in this poem; yet he inserts the stanza:

> How vain is Custom, and how guilty Pow'r!
>   Slaughter is lawful made by the Excess;
> Earth's partial Laws, just Heav'n must needs abhor,
>   Which greater Crimes allow, and damn the less.[45]

Davenant, like his age, was often self-contradictory.

Gondibert is rich in rewards for the seeker after the quaint and the characteristic. In view of the lip-worship of Homer and his race common in the poet's circle, here is an amazing sentiment:

> Behinde this Throng, the talking Greeks had place,
>   Who Nature turn to Art, and Truth disguise,
> As Skill does native Beauty oft deface,
>   With Termes they charm the Weak and pose the Wise.[46]

It is amusing to compare the lusciousness of the picture of Eve in the Garden composed by Milton the Puritan, with the excessive modesty of a similar picture composed by Davenant the Cavalier:

> From thence breaks lov'ly forth the World's first Maid,
>   Her Breast, Love's Cradle, where Love quiet lies;
> Naught yet had seen so foule to grow afraid,
>   Nor gay, to make it cry with longing Eyes.

[45] II, 1, 75. A pacifist speech in Davenant's *Siege*, cf. folio 64, is repeated almost verbatim in Shirley's *Young Admiral*, III, 2.
[46] II, 5, 44.

And thence, from stupid Sleep, her Monarch steals;
    She wonders, till so vain his Wonder growes,
That it his feeble Sov'raignty reveales;
    Her Beauty, then, his Manhood does depose.

Deep into Shades the Painter leads them now,
    To hide their future Deeds; then stormes does raise
O're Heav'n's smooth Face, because their life does grow
    Too black a Story for the House of Praise.[47]

4

Whatever the merits of his poem, Davenant's performance
fell short of his intentions. How admirable these intentions were
is illustrated in *The Preface to Gondibert,* one of the most important critical essays of the seventeenth century. The auspices
under which this preface appeared were unfortunate. It was
published, together with a reply by Thomas Hobbes and commendatory verses by Cowley and Waller, in Paris, 1650, while
the poem itself, or as much as was finished, was withheld. The
unusualness of this procedure made perfect game for the satirists:

Room for the best of Poets heroick,
If you'l believe two Wits and a Stoick;
Down go the Iliads, down go the Aeneidos,
All must give place to the Gondiberteiados.

.   .   .   .

A Preface to no Book, a Porch to no house:
Here is the Mountain, but where is the Mouse?
But, oh, America must breed up the Brat,
From whence 't will return a West-Indy Brat.
For Will to Virgina is gone from among us,
With thirty two Slaves, to plant Mundungus.[48]

[47] II, 6, 63–65.
[48] *Certain Verses Written By severall of the Authors Friends . . .,* p. 1.

Davenant's catalogue and criticism of the epic poets has already been mentioned, with the misconstruction put upon it by the wits, who had apparently ignored the poet's surmise that those worthies, from Homer to Spenser, "will in worthy memory outlast even Makers of Laws and Founders of Empires."

The preface, in fact, casts no aspersion on older narrative poetry, nor for that matter does it discuss it at any length; rather it offers a prospectus of *Gondibert,* and expounds the author's ideals of poetic composition. These ideals represent at some points a revolt against the practice of the so-called metaphysical school, and this revolt, enforced by parallel sentiments expressed by Hobbes, Cowley, and Waller, has led to the 1650 publication being called the manifesto of neo-classicism.[49] If we think only of the best in neo-classicism, the designation is fairly accurate. The sources of the essay have been suggested as Chapelain's preface to Marino's *Adone,* Scaliger's *Poetice,* and Tasso's discourses on the epic; [50] but most of its important matter could have been suggested by the thought of Sidney, Bacon, Greville, and Jonson, and by eternal artistic verities never completely forgotten. We can imagine its genesis in long conversations among Davenant, Hobbes, Cowley, Waller, and, perhaps, some of their French contemporaries, when the canons of criticism would have been discussed and sifted. In this connection, note the strange reluctance of posterity to take Davenant seriously: "Davenant's long preface to *Gondibert,*" observes the modern commentator, "is a dilution of the æsthetic theory of Hobbes." [51] We may say with as much justice that Hobbes's æsthetic theory is a concentration of Davenant's; it was formulated in his *Reply* to the preface. To Davenant's acknowledgment of indebtedness to himself and their two fellow exiles, Hobbes replied, "I have used your Judgement no less in many things of mine, which coming to light will thereby appear the better." If not the leading spirit in the

---

49 Edmund Gosse, *From Shakespeare to Pope,* p. 131.
50 J. E. Spingarn, *op. cit.,* II, 331.
51 *Ibid.,* I, xxxiii.

group, Davenant was something more than an attendant echo.

Briefly the important contributions of the Preface are as follows. There is a plea for originality, the author contending that the example of Homer and Virgil need not be so sedulously followed that pagan themes, supernatural machinery, invocations to the gods, and a division into twenty-four books become desiderata in all heroic poems. There is a definition of the material of art, and an interesting distinction between truth and fact. "Truth narrative and past is the Idol of Historians (who worship a dead thing) and truth operative, and by effects continually alive, is the mistress of Poets." Furthermore ". . . wise Poets think it more worthy to seek out truth in the Passions than to record the truth of Actions." In his present poem, the author's aim is to give us "an easy and familiar view of ourselves" and "to bring truth, too often absent, home to mens bosomes, to lead her through unfrequented and new ways, and from the most remote Shades; by representing Nature though not in an affected, yet in an unusual dress." Then there is a discussion of the "ornaments" of poetry, an attempt to define the coeval conception of such a word as "wit," and, most important, there is an attack upon the conceit and such abuses as had become common among the Caroline poets, including the affectation that the writer who expends time and labor upon his verses betrays a "want of natural force." "Inspiration," says the author sagely, "is a dangerous Word." Finally there is a whole-hearted effort to convince the reader of the dignity of poetry—not only as a source of perpetual joy, but also as a shaping influence upon the lives of men. This theme occupies the major portion of the essay.

Everywhere, and especially when he comments upon life as he has found it, there is evidence of Davenant's native shrewdness, of his mastery of the telling phrase:

. . . the world is onely ill govern'd, because the wicked take more pains to get authority then the vertuous, for the vertuous are often preach'd into retirement. . . .

Learning is not Knowledge, but a continu'd Sayling by fantastick
and uncertain winds toward it.

Old Men, that have forgot their first Childhood and are returning
to their second, think it [wit] lyes in a kinde of tinkling of words;
or else in a grave telling of wonderful things; or in a comparing of
times without a discover'd partiality; which they perform so ill by
favoring the past that, as 'tis observ'd, if the bodies of men should
grow less, though but an unmeasurable proportion in seven years,
yet, reckoning from the Flood, they would not remain in the stature
of Froggs; so if States and particular persons had impair'd in
Government, and increas'd in Wickedness, proportionably to what
old men affirm they have done from their own infancy to their
age, all publick Policy had been long since Confussion, and the
Congregated World would not suffice now to people a Village.

To this, Hobbes, who was himself past his prime, replied, "The
dotage and childishness they ascribe to Age, is never the effect
of Time, but sometimes of the excesses of Youth, and not a
returning to, but a continual stay with Childhood." Not so much
in this rejoinder as in his reply as a whole, Hobbes's style, with
its dry didacticism and eternal categories, contrasts strongly with
the more imaginative, discursive, and easy style of Davenant.
Simply as a piece of prose Davenant's preface has not been
enough attended. The fact that he was composing his essay as
an epistle to a friend lent him an ease and freedom of manner.
The combination of dignity and familiarity he achieved is significant in view of the fact that John Dryden knew this preface so
well. In Dryden's critical prefaces, with their profound effect
upon English prose style, I am certain that we can trace a decided
influence of William Davenant. For this reason, as for its original thought and its expression of a loving devotion to poesy, *The
Preface to Gondibert* should be more widely read.

  It would be a tainted compliment to conclude a discussion of
a poem with praise of its preface. Yet there is little more to be
said about *Gondibert* itself. A careful reading of it leads to a
genuine respect for its author. Considering the nature of the

Cavalier spirit, considering how each poet was so incapable of sustained effort, how their works seem to rise from withered roots, this poem, so often uninspired and so often imbued with false standards of taste, is still a remarkable achievement—for its competence, for its frequent directness and simplicity, for the fact that it contains scarcely a single shoddy or wholly trivial stanza. The serious-minded lover of literature, disposing of minor authors with efficient haste, will find little virtue in it. It does not stir the emotions, or make the spirit soar. Yet in its mazy corridors glimmer the parti-colored lights of chivalry and romance; if one is not too busy, he may find charm in the quaint old patterns. Not the least of its appeal lies in the way it reflects its author's ingenuous conviction that his words will be delightful to generations yet unborn, that he himself will be remembered as a prophet of valor and of love:

> Thou, who perhaps, proudly thy bloomy Bride
>   Lead'st to some Temple, where I wither'd lie;
> Proudly, as if the Age's Frosts defy'd,
>   And that thy springing self could never die.
>
> Thou, to whom then the cheerful Quire will sing,
>   Whilst hallow'd Lamps and Tapers brave the Sun
> As a Lay-Light, and Bells in triumph ring,
>   As when from sallies the Besiegers run.
>
> That when the Priest has ended, if thine Eies
>   Can but a little space her Eies forbear,
> To shew her where my Marble Coffin lies,
>   Her Virgin Garlands she will offer there.[52]

We smile at this, as at the poet's optimistic hope that his cantos will be sung like Homeric lays; yet when we turn again to the quips of the Cavalier satirists, or to the more calculated witticisms of modern academics, they seem a trifle less apt than we had thought.

[52] III, 3, 3-5.

VIII

THE COMIC

*This leads us to observe the craftiness of the Comicks, who
are only willing when they describe humor (and humor is
the drunkenness of a Nation which no sleep can cure) to lay the
Scæne in their own Country . . . : yet when they would set
forth greatness and excellent vertue, which is the theme of
Tragedy . . . they wisely, to avoid the quarrels of neighbourly
envy, remove the Scene from home.*—PREFACE TO GONDIBERT.

I

ALTHOUGH Davenant did not always lay the scene of comedy in his own country, at least he laid it in his own
world. The scene of his serious plays he laid in some
other world, and since as a dramatist he is known chiefly by his
Siege of Rhodes, it is not always recognized how often the
workaday world, treated concretely and amusingly, appears in
his plays. The workaday world treated concretely and amusingly cannot give us such glorious comedies as *Twelfth Night*
and *Old Fortunatus,* but it can give us something worthwhile
and legitimate; in his lighter vein Davenant, dealing with actual
life rather than with fads and fashions, created passages of abiding artistic worth. The literary ancestry of his comedy may be
found in the colorful *genre* pictures common in English drama
from the time of the miracle plays, and in the new method of
characterization perfected in the comedy of humours of Ben
Jonson. In his choice of themes Davenant sometimes fore-

shadows the comedy of the Restoration, but his plays are definitely in the old tradition.

It may tend to repair the violence we are doing to chronology if we note that his earliest plays (which are serious and will therefore be treated later on) contain scenes in which most of the elements of his comedy appear. In *The Cruel Brother* there are relief episodes dealing with the "humours" of a country nobleman, Lothario, who has ridiculous ambitions to become a court favorite, and of his retainer, Borachio, a kind of Sancho Panza, full of wise saws and modern instances. In *Albovine* the underplot features the importunities of Grimold, the familiar type of bluff old soldier, who desires his rightful pay and who is fearless enough to make shrewdly caustic comments upon the major characters and their difficulties. In *The Siege* there is a group of "irregular humorists" reminding us of Pistol's crew in *Henry V;* it consists of two seasoned soldiers who tyrannize over two timid volunteers (young gentlemen taking a postgraduate course in war) until one of them reveals himself to be a coward and is in turn tyrannized over. This is the most fully developed of these early underplots, occupying nearly half the extant version of the play; the agreement between the inexperienced volunteers to advertise each other's prowess [1] produces dialogues which are highly amusing. There is little point in lingering over these early underplots, for Davenant's comedy appears in more perfection later on. It is interesting, however, to observe that in these first essays the conflicts are among men; we shall notice that hereafter Davenant illustrates the tendencies of his age by finding the material of comedy chiefly in frays between men and women.

In the fourth of his early plays, licensed for the stage on October 2, 1629,[2] and thereupon performed at Blackfriars, Davenant first exploited the comedy of manners. The play is

---

[1] Cf. Jonson's *Every Man in his Humour;* A. W. Ward, *op. cit.,* III, 329, suggests a source in Fletcher's *Humourous Lieutenant.*

[2] *Dramatic Records of Sir Henry Herbert,* p. 32.

titled *The Just Italian,* and its story, divested of complexities, is as follows. Altamont, the just Italian, tries to tame Alteza, his arrogant and wayward wife, by introducing into their house his sister, Scoperta, to parade as his mistress. But instead of succumbing to jealousy, Alteza counters by inviting an aggressive young gallant, Sciolto, into the house to be her paramour. The two cat's-paws, Scoperta and Sciolto, succumb to propinquity and fall in love. When Altamont has been convinced of the purity of their intentions, and of the reformation of his wife (resulting from the salutary effect of Sciolto's behavior, when he upbraids her for the contrast she presents to the pure Scoperta), imminent bloodshed is averted and the play ends happily. This main plot is comedy only in the technical sense; it is quite serious, and in its threats of impending disaster, in its abundance of disguisings, quarrels, and alarms, lapses at times into the mode of tragicomedy. Although there is the usual extravagance of its author's serious vein, certain scenes are not lacking in reflections of actual life. At the end of Act III an interesting speech by Altamont epitomizes the old theme of human frustration, of the sad truth that whereas youth does not know, age cannot do,

> . . . life is like the span
> Forc'd from a gouty hand, which, as it gains
> Extent and active length, the more it pains.

There are a number of excellent passages, remarkably penetrating in thought considering the fact that the writer had only lately reached his majority. The theme of the play is in undeniably bad taste, and Alteza and Sciolto, in their speech and intentions if not in their deeds, bemire themselves too thoroughly for us to be quite reconciled to their reformation; yet there is a singularly purifying last act, and a very graceful conclusion.

The truly redeeming feature, however, is the underplot. Altamont's brother, Florello, a high-spirited but necessitous "cast soldier," arrives home from the wars and, unperturbed by the fact that Altamont has not found happiness by marrying wealth, conceives a scheme to win Alteza's sister, Charintha. He borrows a thousand ducats from his brother, and poses as Dandolo, a Milanese count who has been wooing Charintha by correspondence. He copes with the inopportune arrival of the real Dandolo by greeting him as a bastard brother and outfacing both him and his two burlesque bravoes, Stoccato and Punto. When he is finally exposed, Charintha finds him a charming fellow in his own right and accepts him as her husband. The scenes in which Florello appears are delightful; the dialogue is bright and nimble, and the situations delectably absurd. There is a Petruccio-like buoyancy about the impostor that makes us understand the lady's final willingness to forgive him. While in the rôle of a wealthy nobleman he cuts a magnificent figure, distributing diamonds and rubies to all and sundry with a brusque, "I have enow. Wear 'em." Meanwhile he commissions one of his servants to remember for him his hosts' names. The discreet ferocity displayed by the amiable poltroons, Staccoto and Punto, both Jonsonian characters, is also very funny. Florello is the enemy of their master, but, since he is young, they resolve to "carve him gently up"; however, when he shows the bad breeding to carry the quarrel out of the realm of words into that of actual physical violence, they chide him for ignorance of "the rudiments of wrath," "the quiet and courteous ways of spleen," and with unimpeachable dignity let themselves be kicked from the house. In view of the excellence of these comic scenes, it is curious that *The Just Italian* was not revived at the Restoration, and that there is record of no later performance than that indicated on its title-page.

The basic situation in the main plot of *The Just Italian* reappeared several years later in Shirley's *Lady of Pleasure,* just as it had already appeared several years before in Fletcher's *Rule a Wife and Have a Wife.* We can go further back and find parallels for Davenant's handling of this theme of worthy hus-

band and unruly wife (especially in his characterization of Altamont) in Heywood's *Woman Killed with Kindness,* and
Kyd's (?) *Arden of Feversham.* In Davenant's next play, *The
Wits,* we shall find a new combination of episodes which had
appeared (to mention plays only by the four dramatists who
had the most immediate influence on his comedy) in Shakespeare's *Merry Wives of Windsor,* Jonson's *Volpone,* Middleton's
Blurt Master Constable, and Fletcher's *Wit Without Money.*
Thus it is with nearly all of Davenant's plays. Space does not
permit that we enumerate, much less discuss, what might be
called the sources of each play. Perhaps it is just as well, for this
type of analysis would only prove something which is already
generally recognized about Caroline drama. When Davenant
began to write, the profusion of antecedent drama denied him
virgin themes and situations. Fresh material comes when
changing times bring a new social tissue and a new philosophical outlook; and even then literature of conduct (in contrast
with literature of thought) will often lag a generation behind
life. Davenant lived in a period of social and intellectual upheaval, but in the realm of the drama this period was a continuation and attenuation of that which had gone before. The Elizabethans had been tremendous reapers, and a Carolinian had
either to forage in their harvest or to find his crop (as some did)
along hedgerows and in ditches. Sometimes through accident,
sometimes through frank imitation, Davenant repeated his predecessors; but if the fabric of his plots is theirs, the patterns are his
own—considered in a just light they are original.

2

Between *The Just Italian* and *The Wits,* licensed January 28,
1634, intervened the years of Davenant's illness; and the new
play, his first homogeneous comedy, gave proof to the world that
the young dramatist had come up smiling. Our version of the

play, little impaired, as we have seen, by the rigors of Sir Henry Herbert's censorship,[3] tells the following story. Two country gentlemen, a skittish oldster named Sir Morglay Thwack, and his companion, Pallatine, leave their estates and come up to London with the amiable intention of playing havoc with feminine virtue. Their holiday is to cost them nothing, for they are resolved to live by their wits—that is, by their ingenuity. But the city contains more practised artists both at love making and at living by one's wits than themselves. Pallatine's younger brother, the brother's sweetheart, Lucy, and her friend, Lady Ample, the wealthy ward of one Sir Tyrant Thrift, subject the country invaders to a series of farcical misadventures until they are at last forced to sue for a costly peace. At the end, the younger Pallatine is in a financial position to wed Lucy; and Lady Ample, who has incidentally revenged herself on her usurious guardian, is in a position to be magnanimous to the elder Pallatine, whom she has transformed from a predatory gallant into a humble lover with intentions superbly honorable.

The process of humiliating the country victims, by decoying them into supposed houses of assignation, into church crypts, by robbing them, bundling them into chests, and throwing them on the mercies of the town-watch, involves a great deal of horseplay; but this, while it gives us a succession of lively and, in their kind, entertaining scenes, is not the chief appeal of the play. Nor is the appeal in the characterization. Lucy is interesting as representing the *beau idéal* in town gallants' sweethearts; she is virtuous herself, but generous, and her hearty spirit of cameraderie makes her—somewhat distressingly—tolerant of her suitor's licentiousness. Sir Morglay Thwack and several of the minor characters reveal the pervading influence of Jonson's comedy of humours; and the constable and his crew remind us of Dogberry's band in presenting a burlesque picture of the populace.[4]

---

[3] For the opposition to this play by the licenser and the Blackfriars audience, see above, p. 53.

[4] The part of the watch was expanded in 1667 (cf. Pepys, April 18), and it is the augmented version that appears in the folio.

Upon the whole there is little emphasis on character, and none of the personages are new to the drama of the time.

The chief virtue of *The Wits* is that, however improbable the plot, the author has given us the authentic London scene conveyed through the medium of unflaggingly vivacious dialogue. The first recorded estimate of this play came from his critical Majesty, Charles I, who "commended the language, but dislikt the plott and characters," [5] and the opinion was reëchoed many years later by Samuel Pepys, who, after seeing the play many times, with diminishing enthusiasm, pronounced it "a medley of things, but some similes mighty good." [6] Davenant's knack at creating metaphors, his chief stylistic distinction, frequently took the form in comedy of emphasizing diminutives. The younger Pallatine informs one of his impoverished henchmen,

> . . . a mouse yok'd to a peascod may draw,
> With the frail cordage of one hair, your goods
> About the world.

Later, he himself is threatened with,

> . . . not a single turf for a jointure;
> Not so much land as will allow a grasshopper
> A salad. . . .

The device, used here for comic effect, may have been suggested by the verbal cameo-cutting which Shakespeare perfected in depicting the train of Queen Mab and other details of the fairy world. The readiness of the characters at repartee, their mutual resourcefulness in abuse, as well as the similes so "mighty good," must have led Davenant's contemporaries to commend his language. To us, this language is chiefly remarkable for the concreteness and aptness with which it reflects Davenant's world. Not only does this quality of the dialogue constitute the chief virtue of *The Wits,* but of the author's comedy in general.

[5] *Dramatic Records of Sir Henry Herbert*, p. 54.
[6] Jan. 18, 1669.

We may take for illustration from the present play certain passages which anticipate a Restoration usage by depicting the horrors of country life. The hard fate of the county dame is the theme: Husbands can escape to the festivities of the London term, but their wives must remain at home "to knit socks for their cloven feet," or to

> . . . talk
> Of painful child-birth, servants' wages and
> Their husband's good complexion, and his leg.

Here is a typical dialogue in this vein:

Lucy

And then the evenings, warrant ye, they [country wives]
Spend with Mother Spectacle, the curate's wife,
Who does inveigh 'gainst curling and dyed cheeks;
Heaves her devout impatient nose at oil
Of Jessamine, and thinks powder of Paris more
Prophane than th' ashes of a Romish martyr.

Lady Ample

And in the days of joy and triumph, sir,
Which come as seldom to them as new gowns,
Then, humble wretches! they do frisk and dance
In narrow parlours to a single fiddle,
That squeaks forth tunes like a departing pig.

Lucy

Whilst the mad hinds shake from their feet more dirt
Than did the cedar roots, that danc'd to Orpheus.

Lady Ample

Do they not pour their wine too from an
Ewer, or small gilt cruce, like orange water kept
To sprinkle holiday beards?

Lucy

And when a stranger comes, send seven
Miles post by moon-shine for another pint!

Elder Pallatine

All these indeed are heavy truths. . . .[7]

The very fact that the dramatist's language is so graphic makes
certain passages painful; Sir Morglay Thwack is the chief offender in coarse speeches, and at times we feel like crying with
Lucy, "Rose vinegar to wash that ruffian's mouth!" Yet the
play as a whole is not offensive, and remains at its broadest a
hearty and wholesome comedy.

Unlike Davenant's previous plays, *The Wits* enjoyed a long
life on the stage. Although more cordially received at court
than on the public stage in 1634, its popularity grew, and when
revived at the Restoration among the plays with which Davenant
opened Lisle's Tennis Court, it prospered for the unusual run
of eight days.[8] Betterton played the elder Pallatine, Underhill
played Sir Morglay Thwack, and Miss Davenport played Lady
Ample. King Charles, Prince James, and Samuel Pepys were at
the opening, August 15, 1661, and Pepys returned two days later
and again on the eighth day of the run, this time taking his wife
—ample proof that at this time he found it "a most excellent
play," which he liked "exceedingly." It remained a stock piece
with the Duke's Company, and Pepys continued to go to see it.[9]
Although it began to pall on the taste of him and no doubt of
other seasoned playgoers toward the end, it was acted both at
court [10] and on the public stage for many years. It was the last
of Davenant's original plays to be revived, its final appearance
being at Lincoln's Inn Fields on August 19, 1726, when Ogden,
Milward, Norris, Miss Vincent, and Miss Grace played the lead-

---

[7] Act II, Scene 1.
[8] John Downes, *Roscius Anglicanus,* p. 21.
[9] Upon April 18, and 20, 1667, January 18, 1669.
[10] May 2, 1667, August 21, 1672; cf. A. Nicoll, *op. cit.,* pp. 308–09.

ing rôles.[11] The eighteenth century found it likewise the one original play of the author worth reprinting.

In view of the popularity of *The Wits* it is remarkable that Davenant's next comedy, *News from Plymouth*, was, so far as is discoverable, never acted after its première at the Globe,[12] which must have followed closely upon its licensing on August 1, 1635.[13] It is an excellent play, even though its plot is even more a "medley of things" than that of *The Wits*. The plot may be briefly described as follows. Three captains of the fleet, Seawit, Cable, and Topsail, are in port at Plymouth. Like Davenant's comic characters in general, they are rich in the joy of life but poor in everything else. Seawit's case is typical; after cudgeling his brains, he remembers that he does have some expectations:

> After the death of an old aunt, I have
> The toll of a wharf near Rotherithe will
> Yield me about four marks a year.

We must agree with his confidant that these are "narrow blessings." To make matters worse, Plymouth is expensive:

> . . . If you walk but three turns
> In the High-street, they will ask you money
> For wearing out the pebbles.

Worst of all, the port has presented a dearth of female companionships, and the Captains have found

> . . . none but a few matrons of Biscay,
> That the Spaniards left here
> In eighty eight.[14]

---

[11] Announced at this revival as "not acted 16 years"; cf. J. Genest, *op. cit.*, III, 183.

[12] See above, p. 59.

[13] *Dramatic Records of Sir Henry Herbert*, p. 36.

[14] Davenant must also have known Portsmouth well, for it was Buckingham's port of embarkation during the campaign of the Isle of Rhé. On the strength of no better evidence than that "Portsmouth" is once referred to as the scene instead of "Plymouth" (Act I, Scene 2), Fleay (*Biog. Chron.*, I, 102) concluded that Davenant's play was an adaptation of one by a "superior author."

From these extremities they are relieved by the hospitality of the wealthy Widow Carrack and her two guests, the attractive and well-endowed Lady Loveright, and Mrs. Joynture. The men rival each other to laying siege to the ladies, Lady Loveright seeming such a prize as to make them contemplate in her case even the extreme step of marriage. In the series of intrigues and mock quarrels which follows, Seawit's superior cleverness gains advantage over Topsail and Cable, and.Cable is also outplayed by Widow Carrack, who is determined to convert his incidental love-making to her into honorable courtship. When it becomes evident that Lady Loveright is to fall to the lot of none of the Captains but to her former suitor, the deserving Studious War-well, a kind of conditional engagement is patched up between Seawit and Mrs. Joynture, and between Cable and Widow Car-rack, whereupon the chastened mariners put out to sea and the play ends.

That we have here no very remarkable story is obvious. What the play offers is a war between the sexes and a series of interesting episodes growing out of this war rather than a care-fully developed central plot. Although there is again a minor emphasis upon character, several of the personages are interest-ing. Widow Carrack, who greets Cable's boisterous philander-ing with an equally boisterous defense, has the sanguineous tem-perament of the Wife of Bath, and the cheery insensitiveness of the Wives of Windsor. Lady Loveright prefigures a type of heroine common in later days, in her insistence that her lover's excellences derive not from wealth or birth but from himself— that he be "self-made." In the main, however, she is a dupli-cate of Lady Ample of *The Wits,* just as Seawit is a duplicate of the younger Pallatine. Two characters, designed to provide incidental mirth, owe their inspiration to Ben Jonson. These are the silly and pedantic Sir Solemn Trifle; and the terrifying fire-eater, Sir Furious Inland. The first displays his conceit by cir-culating inside international news—to the effect that the Spanish fleet at Gibraltar has been sunk by the French horse, and that

> . . . Rome is taken
> By the ships of Amsterdam, and the pope himself,
> To save his life, turned Brownist . . .

—so that in his rôle as in his character Sir Solemn derives from
Jonson.[15] Sir Furious Inland, however, although in the line of
Bobadill and the *Miles Gloriosus* type, differs from these in that
his courage is genuine and his exploits in the future rather than
in the past:

> Shew me the King's enemies, and I'm satisfied!
> If not, let's subjects look to it, for I must fight.

After venting his belligerence on one Captain Bumble, an inoffensive Dutch skipper, and upon the more prominent characters in the play, he is finally turned upon by the joint company
lest with a two-handed sword he might "depopulate the island."
We expect to see him humbled, but instead of turning tail in
the manner of his comic prototypes, he rejoices in the affray and
offers to fight his aggressors and the rest of the world besides.
It is refreshing to find such a character remaining terrific to
the end.

The chief merit of *News from Plymouth* like that of *The Wits*
lies neither in plot nor in characters but in the dexterity with
which the author has given us sketches of seventeenth-century
life. Owing to a background of reality, there is not the shallowness we should expect in such a play. When Cable warns young
Sir Furious:

> You are not now amongst your tenants' sons,
> Swaggering at a wake, in your own village,

we glimpse the past of this frightful blade. Cable is himself
warned by Widow Carrack, and when she pictures those aged
seamen who, for a dinner, talk of monsters they have seen in
the deeps, we glimpse *his* probable future. A speech or two may

[15] F. E. Schelling, *op. cit.*, II, 301, notes the resemblance to *Staple of News*.

be quoted at length to illustrate Davenant's charming particularity. On one occasion Seawit upbraids the mischievous heiresses:

> Were you never beaten? never for stealing
> Conserves? Never swaddled for losing your
> Sleeve silk, or making your work foul at tent-stitch?
> Never for picking plums out of mince-pies,
> Or breaking o' your lutes for negligence?
> Had neither of you an old grandmother
> With a short ebon staff, that us'd to beat you
> For these faults? Sure, had you been ever beaten,
> You would not dare to use me thus.[16]

In a speech in which Topsail pretends to deplore the follies of youth, we have another colorful illustration:

> Tis true, to these unpleasant hazards
> Riot and youth must bring us:
> The gallant humour of the age, no remedy.
> Whilst yet the mother's blessing quarrels and chimes
> I' th' pocket thus: the thrift of thirty years
> Sav'd out of mince pies, butter, and dry'd hops.
> It must away; but where? In the metropolis,
> London! the sphere of light and harmony,
> Where still your tavern bush is green and flourishing.[17]

The contacts he enables us to establish with the homely realities of his day make Davenant, in this vein, delightful. And while satire abounds, it is always whimsical, never malicious, and does not detract from the prevailing pleasantness of tone. *News from Plymouth,* like Davenant's comedy in general, deserves to be better known.

When *News from Plymouth* was written, Davenant had already produced *Love and Honour,* his first successful tragicomedy. In spite of its ultra-romantic atmosphere, this play

[16] Act IV.
[17] Act I.

contains a comic underplot exploiting Davenant's favorite theme: the expedients of men of action who wish to marry money but whose ears are blasted by that "odd heathen word, call'd join-ture." In this instance we meet one Colonel Vasco who marries an old widow hoping soon to inherit her dowry; when he finds his wife amazingly vital for all her hundred and ten years, and what he thought were the last throes of infirmity only a slight indisposition with which she is afflicted "about every fifty years," he repents his bargain and manages to secure a divorce. In this play the underplot is rather fully developed; in his subsequent tragicomedies the comic element is apt to consist merely of a few light scenes featuring the dialogue of the minor characters. The audience of 1635 and thereafter preferred sentiment to humor, and Davenant's subsequent plays were in the vein of *Love and Honor* rather than that of *News from Plymouth*. When he returned to comedy again after several years devoted to tragicomedies, masques, and occasional poems, it was, unfortunately, to the serious comedy of manners such as he had experimented with in *The Just Italian*.

   This play, *The Distresses*, licensed November 30, 1639,[18] and acted then, though apparently never thereafter, concerns the vicissitudes of two beautiful señoritas, Claramante and Amiana, who escape the rigors of Spanish home life and over-officious relatives by fleeing to the protection of their lovers.[19] The acquaintances of their lovers mistake them for light women, and make their attempts at disguise, concealment, and flight highly perilous. Catastrophes are averted, relatives are reconciled, and the play ends happily. This in barest outline is the story. Its complexities are unending. Orgemon, the lover of Claramante, and Dorando, her new admirer, are at first allies against her quarrelsome brother, Leonte; but when they discover that they

---

   [18] *Dramatic Records of Sir Henry Herbert*, p. 38. The play was licensed as *The Spanish Lovers*.

   [19] The play may be placed in a line of those with a similar theme, Middleton's *Blurt Master Constable* (1601), T. Killigrew's *Thomaso or the Wanderer* (1654), and Aphra Behn's adaptation of this last, *The Rovers* (1667).

are rivals, they arrange a duel, whereupon they are reconciled by
Claramante, and finally proven to be brothers—sons of the eccentric Basilonte, who is also the father of the second señorita,
Amiana! Curiously too, Amiana's lover, Androlio, is the chief
of those unchivalrous gallants who make Claramante's venture
from home so full of distresses—one more of the oddities in this
astonishing plot.

The plot of *News from Plymouth* represents a mosaic of situations from older native dramas, the same in several instances as
those which had contributed to *The Wits*. This later play, on
the other hand, with its setting in Cordova, its theme of family
domination and of delicate señoritas jeopardizing themselves by
entering the apartments of men, its intrigue and dueling, seems
almost certainly to owe its ultimate source to the *Capa y Espada*
drama of Spain. In Lope de Vega's *La Noche de San Juan*
(1631) most of the plot materials of *The Distresses* may be
found. The play also shows the influence of contemporary
French fiction, in its method of revealing unsuspected identities,
and of complicating love affairs among sets of blood relations.
Coming as it did after Davenant had given himself over to the
writing of fanciful tragicomedy, its tone is unhappily mixed; it
is so plotty, so crowded with intrigue and improbable action, that
it can scarcely be read with pleasure, while its characters indulge
in heroics of speech and behavior quite out of tune with the spirit
of comedy of manners. Although on the whole the least worthy
of Davenant's plays, it is not without interesting scenes and passages of witty dialogue. "Patience," says Orco, the wag of the
play, "is one of the seven deadly virtues"—a line in the epigram-
matic mode of Oscar Wilde.

3

The Distresses was the last of Davenant's plays written before
the Parliamentary edict closed the theatres. While it contains few
of those lively pictorial transcripts from seventeenth-century life

such as make his other comedies notable, it does not indicate that the dramatist's sojourn in the luxuriant land of tragicomedy had lost him permanently the seeing eye and portraying hand. Works scattered through his later period prove that he had retained the old knack. *The First Day's Entertainment at Rutland House,* the piece with which he inaugurated his Commonwealth Opera on May 23, 1656, has actually served as source material for historians of London. The entertainment as a whole has already been sufficiently described,[20] but in the present connection passages may be quoted from that half of it which depicts humorously the rival capitals of France and England. Says the observant Parisian:

Before I leave you in your houses (where your estates are managed by your servants, and your persons educated by your wives), I will take a short survey of your children; to whom you are so terrible, that you seem to make use of authority whilst they are young, as if you knew it would not continue till their manhood. You begin with them in such rough discipline, as if they were born mad, and you meant to fright them into their wits again before they had any to lose. When they encrease in years, you make them strangers; keeping them at such distance, out of jealousie they should presume to be your companions, that when they reach manhood, they use you as if they were none of your acquaintance. But we submit to be familiar with ours, that we may beget their affection before 'tis too late to expect it.

Davenant apparently had learned something which Englishmen as a whole have not learned during the several centuries since. The following is more particularly about London itself:

Oh the goodly landskip of old Fish-street! which, had it not the ill luck to be crooked, was narrow enough to have been your founders perspective: and where your garrets (perhaps not for want of architecture, but through abundance of amity) are so made that opposite neighbours may shake hands without stirring from home.

[20] See above, pp. 121–23.

Is unanimity of inhabitants of wise cities better exprest then by their coherence and uniformity of building? Where streets begin, continue, and end in a like stature and shape: but yours (as if they were rais'd in a general insurrection, where every man hath a several design) differ in all things that can make distinction. Here stands one that aimes to be a palace, and, next to it, another that professes to be a hovel. Here a giant, there a dwarf, here slender, there broad; and all most admirably different in their faces as well as in their height and bulk. . . . 'Tis your custom, where men vary often the mode of their habits, to terme the nation fantastical; but where streets continually change fashion, you should make haste to chain up the city, for 'tis certainly mad. . . .

I have now left your houses, and am passing through your streets, but not in a coach, for they are uneasily hung, and so narrow that I took them for sedans upon wheels: Nor is it safe for a stranger to use them till the quarrel be decided, whether six of your nobles, sitting together, shall stop and give place to as many barrels of beer. Your city is the only metropolis of Europe, where there is a wonderful dignity belonging to carts.

Davenant was still harder on Paris than on London—pardonable in an Englishmen even though he had recently taken a French wife. Some years later Pepys, another Englishman with a French wife, found these descriptions vastly entertaining. On February 7, 1664, Madame Pepys was ill, so the diarist sat up with her "and with great mirth read Sir W. Davenant's two speeches in dispraise of London and Paris, by way of reproach one to another, and so to prayers and to bed." The world owes something to a man who helped Pepys in keeping his wife amused.

Homely reality reappears also in *The Playhouse to be Let,* Davenant's only original comedy written during the Restoration. This play, which Langbaine defined as "several Pieces of different Kinds handsomely tackt together," [21] pictures a London playhouse in disuse during the long vacation. The playhouse

21 *Op. cit.,* p. 109.

keeper, the tirewoman, and one actor are the only occupants besides a few menials, and these are receiving applications for the use of the building. Throughout the first (and most interesting) act, there is revealing comment upon London public entertainment, from acrobatic shows to "opera"; then for the succeeding acts we overhear a kind of dress rehearsal by the successful applicants. A French company presents *Sganarelle ou le Cocu Imaginaire* (actually an adaptation of Molière's farce written by Davenant in perseveringly broken English); a music master and a dancing master present companies respectively in Davenant's two short Commonwealth pieces, *The History of Sir Francis Drake,* and *The Cruelty of the Spaniards in Peru;* finally a group of strolling actors performs a burlesque playlet featuring the principals in the Antony and Cleopatra story. The idea for the structure of this dramatic anomaly probably came from Fletcher's *Four Plays in One,* although such composite bills seem at one time to have been rather common on the English stage.[22]

The concluding skit was the only part of *The Playhouse to be Let* to find much favor with the Restoration audience; whereas the play as a whole was not revived after 1663,[23] Langbaine mentions that he had seen what he calls the *tragedie travestie* acted by itself at the end of "Orinda's" translation of *Pompey* at Dorset Garden.[24] Davenant must be given credit for introducing burlesque to the Restoration stage, and for occupying an important place in the tradition of this literary mode in England. He was among the first of English writers to use the word *burlesque* itself,[25] an excellent comic poem of his, written about 1635, having the title "The Long Vacation in London, in Verse Bur-

[22] F. E. Schelling, *op. cit.,* I, 401.

[23] Edward Browne mentions it in his notebook as acting during the long vacation (W. J. Lawrence, *op. cit.,* I, 140), and the license fee is mentioned among accounts of Nov. 3, 1663 (*Dramatic Records of Sir Henry Herbert,* p. 138).

[24] *Op. cit.,* p. 109.

[25] The earliest citation of the word in the *N. E. D.* is dated 1656; the date of composition of Davenant's poem is fixed by internal evidence, but the poem was not printed until 1673 (in the folio) and the title may have been altered in the interim.

lesque, or Mock Verse." Here the word applies only to the quality of the versification, and, of course, mock verse and parody had long been common in English literature. But actual burlesque, as distinct from parody, also appears early in Davenant. In 1630 [26] he had written "Jeffereidos, on the Captivity of Jeffrey," a mock epic in two cantos, celebrating the capture of Jeffrey Hudson, the Queen's dwarf, who ran afoul Flemish pirates while fetching his royal mistress a midwife from France. The poem is written in heroic verse (of the older type), contains epic similes, and amusing references to the poet's "authorities." It is interesting that Pope should have had an English predecessor in the form he made so famous. Davenant also perpetuated the custom exercised by Peele and Beaumont of using drama to jibe at the romances. In his masque, *Britannia Triumphans* (1638), appears a *mock romanza* in place of an antimasque. The *dramatis personæ* consists of Giant, Dwarf, Squire, Knight, and Damsel. The giant, having just caught a whale,

> . . . nimbly home did pack
> With ten cart load of dinner on his back:
> Thus homeward bent, his eye too rude and cunning,
> Spies knight and lady by an hedge a funning.

Laying down his "modicum of meat," he cries,

> Bold recreant wight! what fate did hither call thee
> To tempt his strength that hath such power to maul thee?

Whereupon the damsel intervenes,

> Patience, sweet man of might! alas heaven knows
> We only hither came to gather sloes.

The giant and the knight hurl defiances, and then fall into a fight, which is rapidly converted into a comic dance. This,

[26] For the episode (which dates the poem) see *D. N. B.*, XXVIII, 150.

while a slight thing, is true burlesque, and a very amusing example of the type. The Antony and Cleopatra playlet which concludes *The Playhouse to be Let* is also true burlesque, and, although utterly pointless in plot if the truth be told, it is remarkable for the vigor with which august tragic figures are pushed from their pedestals. It is curious that Davenant in his last original play should have introduced to the restored stage the comic type which Buckingham was to use so effectively in *The Rehearsal,* to lampoon him and the other dramatists of his school.

Although an innovator, to a certain extent, even in the field of the comic, Davenant is here chiefly interesting for the intrinsic merit of his work. If his themes and character types display little variety, it is because he wrote comedy only at scattered intervals. He had the keen eye, the sense of the ridiculous, and the verbal dexterity requisite in a comic author. It is unfortunate that the tastes of his courtly audience did not concur with his particular talent, which, more fully exercised, might have given us the best comedy between Jonson and Etherege. As it is, he must yield place to James Shirley. Davenant, because he possessed less innate poetry, could not equal James Shirley in romantic drama, but he might easily have been Shirley's counterpart in the field of Caroline comedy. He had more talent, I am convinced, than Richard Brome, himself too frequently underestimated, although unlike Brome, he never had Ben Jonson, the best of all possible mentors, to guide his apprentice hand. Unlike Brome again, he loved to don the buskin; and on such occasions, "to set forth greatness and excellent vertue," he was unfortunately impelled "to remove the Scene from home."

IX

WIT AND FANCY

Wit is not onely the luck and labor, but also the dexterity of thought, rounding the world, like the Sun, with unimaginable motion; and bringing swiftly home to the memory universal surveys.—PREFACE TO GONDIBERT.

I

EDWARD PHILLIPS, the drama-loving nephew of Milton, praised Davenant, for the "fluency of his wit and fancy." [1] He was thinking primarily of our dramatist's serious plays, for it was by these that he was chiefly known to the Restoration. In Phillips's day the word "wit" had not the restricted application it has today. A colloquialist such as John Aubrey was using it to indicate any kind of perspicacity, whether that of a minor divine who had done great things in his Commentary on the Epistle to the Colossians or to a tavern-drawer who could lie convincingly about the reckoning. As used in literary criticism the word was almost a synonym for "fancy," and connoted fertility in invention and ingenuity in ornamenting language with new and original metaphors. In this sense the word was applied to the "wit-writings" of the Cavalier lyricists. Emphasis upon sheer ingenuity converts literature into an acrobatic art, and unfortunately, although he ultimately rebelled against "wit" as it had crystallized into the conceit, Davenant was enough a part of his era to believe that mere "dexterity of

[1] *Theatrum Poetarum Anglicanorum,* p. 20.

221

thought" could evoke in the mind "universal surveys." It is always to be regretted when a fad imposes itself upon the literature of an entire period; yet no weakness, however general and basic, should be allowed to absorb our whole attention, and when we find the Truth and Beauty of the Elizabethan play supplanted by their diminutives, the Wit and Fancy of the Caroline play, we should not quarrel with the fact but seek the best in what we have.

Davenant's first plays, *The Cruel Brother* and *Albovine, King of the Lombards,* although prophetic of his fanciful vein, stand in some isolation; they were not, as we shall see, inspired by contemporary taste. *Albovine* is usually reckoned the earlier of the two, apparently because it was the first in print. However, an author would more likely prefer to come before the reading public with his second play, especially if it had been refused a hearing in the theatre. *Albovine* was published in 1629, but *The Cruel Brother* was licensed for the stage January 12, 1627,[2] the earliest date on which we have mention of any of Davenant's works. A comparison of the two plays also suggests that *The Cruel Brother* was the earlier. Both are romantic tragedies.

Fletcher, Middleton, and Massinger had preserved the tradition of romantic tragedy up until Davenant's day, and such plays as *Thierry and Theodoret* and *The Bloody Brother,* although they contributed nothing of story, have been suggested as the inspiration of *The Cruel Brother.*[3] Davenant's first essays in tragedy, more primitive, bloodier, and less subtle than those immediately preceding them, represent a reversion to a type dominant during the first years of the century. In this respect they contrast oddly, and not to their disadvantage insofar as kind as distinct from quality is concerned, with the tragedies of Ford, who, in *'Tis Pity She's a Whore* and *Love's Sacrifice* (produced concurrently with Davenant's two tragedies), achieved originality by reaching toward forbidden, and somewhat spotted,

[2] *Dramatic Records of Sir Henry Herbert,* p. 31.
[3] F. E. Schelling, *op, cit.,* II, 341.

fruit. In his initial attempts Davenant could almost be called a bookish dramatist. The blank verse of *The Cruel Brother* illustrates the fact. Witness the following passage selected purely at random:

> . . . How can it choose
> But choke the very soul, and bruise the heart,
> To think that such a giddy snipe: a fool,
> That merely lives to disparage nature,
> Should creep to this ambitious Government.
> Still he rules the Ruler. The Duke is ward
> Unto a page; whose eyebrows wear more beard
> Than doth his chin. And there's his instrument,
> A dark fellow; that with disguised looks
> Could cheat an hypocrite, older than time.[4]

This is much more strong and regular than typical dramatic verse of the late twenties. The blank verse of *Albovine* is less regular, and it becomes even more remiss in some of the later plays. The influence of Fletcher upon Davenant from the very beginning is undeniable, and the theme of *The Cruel Brother*— a ruler's lust after the wife of his favorite, with the resulting contrast between pure and sensual love—is distinctly Fletcherian, but in the treatment of this theme there are reminiscences in language, characterization, and tone, as well as in versification, of Shakespeare and Webster.

The story of *The Cruel Brother* is, briefly, as follows. Count Lucio, the youthful favorite of the Duke of Sienna, is the patron of the humbly born but high-minded Foreste. He falls in love with Foreste's sister Corsa, and to his friend's misgiving secretly weds her. The Duke is informed of the marriage, and his initial anger at his favorite's dereliction quickly subsides into a guilty passion for his bride. Since Corsa is invincibly virtuous, the Duke, detesting the while his own turpitude, suborns a servant to admit him to her chamber, where he satisfies his lust by violence.

[4] Act I.

When Foreste learns of the event, he confronts his sister, and although convinced of her lack of moral guilt, expunges the stain upon his blood and upon his friend's honor by slashing her wrists and bleeding her to death. Lucio, an ineffectual pawn in the game, joins Foreste, and together they confront the Duke. They spare his life, as that of their anointed sovereign, and inflict the allegedly harsher punishment of excoriating him with his guilt. As they depart, the repentant sinner remembers that he has arranged for Foreste's assassination in the event that he come to the palace, and, hastening to countermand his orders, he falls into his own trap. Foreste and Lucio, returning to attack the murderers, are also pierced; and they and the Duke expire together, collectively repentant, mutually forgiving.

We have here the old concatenation of broken commandments and a stage strewn with the dead, but with the newer Fletcherian motif of the terrestrial immunity of kings. Davenant is not so guilty of subscribing to the latter doctrine as a bare synopsis of his plot might lead one to suspect. The theory, specious but sincerely intended, is that it will be more cruel to spare the Duke than to slay him; moroever, not Foreste, the protagonist of the play, but Lucio makes the decision against letting the ravisher share the fate of his innocent victim, Corsa. The play is not unsound, and pleads strongly, almost oppressively, for moral rectitude. Foreste is its most original and interesting character: He is a man of middle years, something of a philosopher, with a passion for personal honor and ideal justice, and with a curious consciousness of the force of public opinion. His sister is the pathetic and sentimental heroine of the school of Fletcher, but she is tenderly depicted and is often appealing, especially in one scene where she is protected from the salacious insinuations of the Duke by her failure to understand them. Crudities and lapses of taste are not wholly absent from the play, but they are not the rule. Even the horrors of that scene in which Foreste slays his sister are somewhat alleviated by the elevated, almost sacramental, atmosphere which the dramatist strove for. The play is compact, and illustrates the tendency toward a simplified structure. Unity, if not artistic appropriateness, is achieved by letting several characters who have been little more than buffoons in the earlier scenes become involved in the serious action and to act as instruments of tragic justice.

As a first play, and one by a twenty-one year old author, not long resident in the dramatic center, *The Cruel Brother* is genuinely praiseworthy. That it is the most regular in versification of Davenant's plays has been pointed out; it is also more dignified and less extravagant in its language than *Albovine* and other later plays. There are many excellent speeches, and though they lack the color which the playwright afterwards achieved, they are vigorous and display a turn of phrase obviously inspired by Shakespeare. Echoes from *Hamlet* and *Othello* have been noted in its language.[5] *Othello,* as well as Webster's *Duchess of Malfi,* may be listed among the sources of its composite plot. The Duke reminds us in some respects of Angelo in *Measure for Measure* (a play which exerted a potent influence on subsequent drama), and Lucio reminds us of Amintor in Fletcher's *The Maid's Tragedy.* To the latter, insofar as its plot is concerned, *The Cruel Brother* owes more than to any other one play.

Shakespeare served along with Davenant's immediate predecessors also as the model for his second tragedy, *Albovine, King of the Lombards,* and Iago was unquestionably the prototype of the villain Hermegild in this blood-curdling drama.[6] In *Albovine,* however, Davenant forsook his usual custom of fabricating an original plot from those of several older plays, and dramatized an historical episode—the skull-goblet story of King Alboinus and Queen Rosemunda originally told by Paulus Diaconus in Book I, Chapters 28–30 of his *De Gestis Longobardorum.*[7] Davenant's immediate source was not Paulus, as has been lately claimed, but the story as it had been adapted by Bandello and

---

[5] J. D. E. Williams, *op. cit.,* pp. 12–15. It is worth noting that Davenant, while he followed suggestions of phrasing, never borrowed whole phrases.

[6] *Ibid.,* pp. 1–12.

[7] Edition of W. D. Foulke, pp. 49–52, 81–86.

then retold by Belleforest in Tome IV, Histoire 19, of *Histoires Tragiques*.[8] The names of several of the characters, Rhodalind, Grimold, and Gondibert, were adapted from names in another of Belleforest's tales deriving originally from Paulus, *Histoires Tragiques, IV,* 20, the source of elements in the heroic poem *Gondibert*.[9] The plot of *Albovine*, which departs considerably from Belleforest's and every other version of the tale, is as follows.

King Albovine, the Lombard conqueror of Italy, incenses his wife, Rhodalind, by inviting her to drink from the skull of her father whom he has defeated and slain. The affront transforms her into a tigress. At the suggestion of her ambitious admirer, Hermegild, she victimizes the court favorite, Paradine, by substituting herself in the bed of his bride, Valdaura, and by threatening to declare a rape unless he help her murder the King. In order that Paradine be disposed of after the deed is done, Hermegild, who fears (with good reason) that Rhodalind will transfer her affections to her unwilling paramour, tells Valdaura that her husband has been unfaithful and adjures her to poison him. Then this arch plotter completes his web of deception by telling Paradine that the King knows he has lain with Rhodalind and has himself seduced Valdaura. From this point on the complications become endless. Valdaura pretends to Paradine that she has poisoned him, in order to win the boon of death at his hands, and the King likewise throws himself on the sword of his deluded favorite. By this time Paradine has discovered the extent to which he has been deceived, and when Rhodalind comes to him to suggest that he slay Hermegild and then become

---

[8] The keen-eyed Gerard Langhaine enumerated versions of the Alboinus story, *op. cit.*, p. 107; and A. W. Ward, *op. cit.*, III, 170, chose Belleforest as Davenant's immediate source. K. Campbell, *Journal of Germanic Philology*, IV, 20–24, evidently unaware that names resembling Rhodalind, Grimold, and Gondibert, appear not only in Paulus Diaconus but also in a later story by Belleforest, concluded that Davenant must have gone directly to *De Gestis Longobardorum*. Since the appearance of this article, an elaborate thesis has been published (H. Morgenroth, *Quellenstudien zu William Davenants Albovine*) to *prove* that Paulus and not Belleforest was Davenant's source!

[9] See above, p. 185.

her royal husband, he makes her his third victim. Then he makes Hermegild his fourth, just when the latter believes that all his plots have succeeded. The unfortunate but bloody dupe finally falls by the weapons of the King's guard, and Albovine's son is declared ruler of Lombardy.

Until the middle of the third act *Albovine* is an admirable play, and although later on the mixture of lust and bloodshed becomes revolting, and there is too much plot for plot's sake, the piece retains a species of crude power until the end. The lust of the King and Hermegild after Rhodalind, and of Rhodalind after Paradine, is revealed in language too rich to be digestible, and Albovine's affection for Paradine is too demonstrative after the fashion of King James. Too much capital is made of the murders, and when Paradine's successive victims are seated behind an arras so that they may strike terror in the aggregate, the play becomes a dramatic chamber of horrors. Let us write this down to the excesses of creative youth.

The language, strong, vivid, and marvelously ingenious in hyperbole, is striking throughout, and its high astounding terms remind us of earlier romantic tragedy to an even greater extent than does *The Cruel Brother*. King Albovine, although he changes in nature later on, is in the earlier acts the all-conquering barbarian, and reminds us of Tamburlaine. He cries in his pride—

> I am the broom of heaven; when the world grows foul,
> I'll sweep the nations into th' sea like dust.

In his cups—

> Fill me a bowl, where I may swim
> And bathe my head, then rise like Phoebus from
> The ocean, shaking my dewy locks.

And in his wrath—

> Howl, meagre wolves and empty tigers! Let the hoarse
> Thracian bull bellow till he rend his throat;

And the hot mountain-lion roar until
Their clamour wake the dead!

This may fit our definitions of bombast, but it is rather ingratiat-
ing. The more subtle characters inspire more subtle language.
Hermegild, of the line of Elizabethan malcontents, is

> . . . a man
> Created in the dark: he walks invisibly;
> He dwells in labyrinths; he loves silence;
> But when he talks, his language carries more
> Promiscuous sense than ancient oracles.

The sweet and gentle Valdaura, and the noble but weak and
susceptible Paradine are Fletcherian characters, and even
Rhodalind, although compounded in part of Shakespeare's Lady
Macbeth and Webster's Vittoria Corombona, has some of the
traits of Fletcher's Evadne. By very reason of her strangeness
and passionate intensity she is the most memorable of Davenant's
women.

Had Davenant written nothing other than these two early
tragedies, had he died let us say at twenty-three, literary historians would mention him regretfully as a youth of exceptional
promise. These plays, despite their excesses and lapses in taste,
and their inconsistencies in characterization, display a technical
competence, virility, and imagination which speak well for their
author's potentialities.

2

Apparently the failure of *The Cruel Brother* to be well received on the stage, and the failure of *Albovine* even to get a
hearing, awakened Davenant to the fact that sentiment, not passion, was the order of the day. The third of his serious plays,
The Siege, licensed for the stage July 22, 1629,[10] is a tragicomedy

[10] Assuming that this is the play mentioned under the title of *The Colonel;*
cf. *Dramatic Records of Sir Henry Herbert,* p. 32. A colonel appearing in the
dramatis personæ is only a minor character, but it is probable that Florello
himself was designated a colonel in the original draft of the play.

of love and honor, and strikes the note for the tone of all his subsequent serious plays. Florello, a commander in a Florentine army besieging Pisa, is in love with Bertolina, daughter of the enemy governor. He deserts to Pisa for the sake of his beloved, but she repulses him as one who has betrayed his cause. Driven desperate by the loss of both love and honor, he returns to his command and performs prodigies in storming the city. Later he conquers his own mad jealousy by magnanimously consecrating Bertolina to his friend and rival. Thereupon the high-minded damsel reveals the fact that she has never ceased to adore him, and his return to honor is rewarded by a return of love.

The Siege is very definitely in the succession of plays conducting us from Fletcher's tragicomedy to the heroic plays of the Restoration. The way it dwells upon the sensibilities of its characters in elevated language, and the way it concentrates on the theme of love, honor, friendship, and jealousy, and upon the valiant prowess inspired by these emotions, foreshadows the spirit as well as the content of Davenant's own *Siege of Rhodes,* written a quarter-century later. It is curious that Davenant should have written such a play in 1629 when his other plays of that early period are so different in spirit; and the suggestion has been made that *The Siege* was reworked at some time before its publication in the folio of 1673.[11]

Davenant's next serious play was actually called *Love and Honour,* and, first performed at Blackfriars after its licensing on

---

[11] F. E. Schelling, *op. cit.,* II, 342. The play was licensed for printing (as *The Colonel*) to Ephraim Dawson, Jan. 1, 1630, but no early publication exists, and there is evidence of no stage presentations other than that indicated by Herbert's records. It is quite probable that the play was revised, because many of Davenant's were. Several, such as *The Wits,* the author altered and amplified himself. The exigencies of publication effected changes in others. *The Unfortunate Lovers* was published in London during the Civil Wars, and the part of Fibbia, "a Precision," appears to have been expediently reduced. Herringman and Lady Davenant, too, seem to have assumed the rôle of censors. The brevity and the preponderance of comic underplot in *The Siege* as we have it indicates an acting version.

November 20, 1634,[12] it became the author's first unqualified success. The plot is amazingly complex, and can only be outlined here. In a war between Italian states, Alvaro, the son of the Duke of Savoy, aided by his friend Prospero, captures Evandra, the daughter of the Duke of Milan, along with two important members of her faction, Leonell and his sister, Melora. Alvaro's father, as a result of a blood feud between Savoy and Milan, is determined to execute Evandra, but Alvaro has fallen in love with his fair captive and refuses to give her up. She is concealed in the house of Prospero, who has also fallen in love with her, along with Leonell, a third victim of her charms, and with her devoted friend, Melora. The play now becomes a contest of chivalry, each of the three lovers being determined that his blood shall be sacrificed instead of Evandra's, while Evandra herself is determined that none but her shall suffer. The situation is complicated by jealousy between Prospero and Leonell (Alvaro is of a nobility superior to such a passion), and by Melora's scheme to save the day by palming herself off as the Princess and dying in her stead. Ingeniously, the author gives each of these five personages an opportunity to offer himself as a heroic sacrifice for the others. Just when the Duke of Savoy is deciding whether to execute both Evandra and Melora (whose conflicting claims after they have fallen into his hands prevent him from knowing which is which) or, in their place, Leonell, who has turned out to be a Prince of Parma and therefore important enough to satisfy his thirst for vengeance, a series of revelations proves that no revenge is necessary. His brother has *not* been killed by Evandra's father, but is still living. Evandra now celebrates the sudden political amity by accepting the hand of Leonell, while Alvaro, although he has displayed little previous interest in her, contents himself with Melora.

---

[12] *Dramatic Records of Sir Henry Herbert*, p. 36. Before the final title was decided upon, Herbert changed, at Davenant's request, the original title, *The Courage of Love* to *The Nonpareilles, or the Matchless Maids*. According to Mildmay's journal, the play was acting in December, 1634; cf. F. G. Fleay, *Biographical Chronicle*, I, 102.

There is no one for Prospero, so this downright youth retires to the relatively calm and simple life of the battle front.

For all the utter improbability of its story, and the unreality of its personages, *Love and Honour* was such a play as the decade loved. For a courtly audience, the graceful rhetoric of its ornate language was something to be emulated in the actual intercourse of fashionable life, while Evandra and her shining satellites provided a pattern of emotional etiquette in a glittering world which transcended their own. The social *milieu* extending outward from the immediate circle of Charles and Henrietta was genuinely preoccupied with what was considered love and honor. Love and its preliminary amenities, if not its consequences, were the absorption of the ladies; and the gentlemen, so far as they had any serious occupation at all, were soldiers. What the city audience would think of such a play it is difficult to say, but the city audience, owing largely to the influence of the drama-loving Queen, was no longer of first importance. The court was setting the taste. Moreover *Love and Honour* possessed a quality valued at the time by high and low alike—*puzzle interest*. Apparently playgoers can grow tired even of artistic inevitability, for a staled taste had led to a valuing of mere surprise. The Caroline audience loved to hang suspended by a network of cross-purposes and mixed identities until the last moment, when the showman would cut his threads and let them fall with delicious speed into the soft down of unlikely felicity.

When the plague invaded London during the winter of 1636–37, and the court drew up its skirts to retreat nimbly to the royal seat at Hampton, Charles ordered the King's Company "to keepe themselves togither neere our Court for our service," and on New Year's Day *Love and Honour* was presented.[13] In 1661 Pepys, against "judgement and conscience which God forgive," [14] went to see it when it was revived at Lisle's Tennis

[13] *Dramatic Records of Sir Henry Herbert*, pp. 57, 76.
[14] Oct. 21; he went again Feb. 23 and pronounced it "a very good play."

Court costumed in the authentic coronation suits of King Charles and his court.[15]   It held the stage for a number of years, for Langbaine mentions performances both before and after the removal of the Duke's Men to Dorset Garden.[16]   For Davenant, 1634 was a red-letter year; in *The Wits* and in *Love and Honour,* in the realm of laughter and of sighs, he had created "lasting plays."

3

After 1634 Davenant belonged definitely to the court, and masques as well as courtly dramas grew from his hand. Of the masques the graceful and amusing *Temple of Love,* thrice presented by order of the Queen in February 1635, is by far the best, and this, as well as *The Triumphs of the Prince D'Amour* (1636), *Britannia Triumphans* (1638), and *Salmacida Spolia* (1640), has already been sufficiently described.[17]   An unusual profusion of contemporary gossip survives concerning Davenant's masques [18]—estimates of the cost of costumes and of the special masquing building erected at Whitehall, official grumbling at the general expense and untimely levity, private grumbling at performances on the Sabbath, allusions to ladies who had begged off from taking part because of their lack of new jewels, down to a very specific comment by Algernon, Lord of Northumberland, when *Salmacida Spolia* was presented: "A company of worse faces did I never see assembled than the

---

[15] See above, p. 158.

[16] *Op. cit.,* p. 109. On Jan. 11, 1720, the aged Peg Fryer, who in her youth had played the aged widow of the underplot of this play, recited her lines from memory during a production of Malloy's *Half-Pay Officers;* cf. J. Genest, *op. cit.,* III, 35.

[17] See above, pp. 57–58, 75–79. For a full discussion of these masques, see R. Brotanek, *Die englischen Maskenspiele;* and P. Reyher, *Les Masques Anglais.* E. Welsford, *The Court Masque,* devotes considerable space to the Italian influence on Jones and Davenant. In my opinion Davenant's masques, as a type distinct from Jonson's, owe most, especially in their method of introducing impromptu vaudeville-like divertissement, to the French *ballet de cour.*

[18] *Calendar S. P. D.,* 1634–35, 1637–38, 1639–40, *passim; Strafford's Letters, passim.*

Queen has got together upon this occasion; not a new woman amongst them." [19]   A study of these masques is interesting also owing to the fact that some of the stage plans and many of the original designs for costumes and scenery by Inigo Jones have survived.[20]

One masque which thus far has only been mentioned, *Luminalia*, presented on Shrove Tuesday night, 1638, as the counterpart to the King's masque, *Britannia Triumphans*, will illustrate why we need not pause long to analyze Davenant's contribution in this field.   In fulfillment of the Queen's order—"to make a new subject of a Masque for herselfe, that with high and hearty invention might give occasion for variety of Scenes, strange apparitions, Songs, Musick and dancing of several kinds"—a festival of light and darkness was devised.   The piece begins with the entrance of Night "drawne by two great Owles."   After she and her attendants, Oblivion, Silence, and the Four Nocturnal Vigils, sing several songs, the antimasquers, representing such creatures of night as thieves, watchmen, coiners, and lackeys, make four entries to perform pantomimic skits and comic dances. Then—

These Antimasques being past, the Scene of night vanished; and a new and strange Prospect of Chimeras appear'd, with some trees of unusuall forme, Mountaines of gold, Towers falling, Windmils, and other extravagant edifices, and in the further part a great City sustained by a Rainbow, all which represented the City of Sleepe.

With such scenic competition as this there was little incentive to literary finesse, and we need not follow the remainder of the masque, with its customary mythological trappings, its entries of the royal and noble masquers, its eulogistic songs, down to the end when Aurora informs Hesperus that the sun *has re-*

---

[19] *Historical Manuscripts Commission,* Third Report (1872), p. 79.

[20] In the collection of the Duke of Devonshire. For reproductions of a considerable number of them, see *Designs by Inigo Jones for Masques and Plays at Court,* Oxford, 1924.

signed the power of making day to a terrestr'all beauty—
Henrietta Maria!

As a writer of masques—he never so much as claimed
Luminalia[21]—Davenant had become simply a librettist for Inigo
Jones (whose name preceded his on the title pages) and for the
court musicians. Under the circumstances it is remarkable that
he wrote as well as he did; few non-Jonsonian masques are better than Davenant's. Although *The Temple of Love* is the only
one of the five even faintly dramatic, and although for his
antimasques the author was inclined to let groups of courtier
gallants enter and perform vaudeville divertissements of their
own, these entertainments are never wholly formal and slipshod.
The dialogue in blank verse is interesting for its political allusions if for nothing else, and the songs, while not the lyrical
masterpieces of Jonson, are better than the "words" in most post-
Elizabethan matings of "words and music." The song concluding *The Temple of Love* offers a fair illustration:

Amianteros, or Chaste Love

(1)

Whilst by a mixture thus made one
Y'are th' emblem of my Deity,
And now you may, in yonder throne
The pattern of your union see.

(2)

Softly as fruitful show'rs I fall,
And th' undiscern'd increase I bring,
Is of more precious worth than all
A plenteous summer pays a spring.

---

[21] Davenant's name is not on the title-page of the first edition, and the masque
was not reprinted in the folio. R. Brotanek, "Ein Unerkanntes Werk Sir Will
Davenants," *Anglia Beiblatt*, XI, 177–81, attributed the work to him on the
basis of internal evidence; and an ascription of it to him in the Stationers'
Register, March 6, 1657–58, establishes the claim.

(3)

The benefit it doth impart
   Will not the barren earth improve,
But fructify each barren heart,
   And give eternal growth to love.

Sunesis

To Charles, the mightiest and the best,
And to the darling of his breast,
   (Who rule b' example as by power)
May youthful blessings still increase
And in their offspring never cease,
   Till time's too old to last an hour.

Masques were ordered like floral decorations, and few writers, then or since, could have filled the orders with Davenant's efficiency, grace, and good humor.

4

While the digression into the subject of his court masques has interrupted our survey of Davenant's serious plays, it may help to enforce the point that these plays were strongly affected by their author's immersion in the artificialities of Whitehall. *The Platonic Lovers,* licensed November 16, 1635,[22] actually made dramatic capital of the theme which Henrietta Maria had prescribed for *The Temple of Love.* Aptly described as "a drama of love debate . . . for and against fruition of love in marriage,"[23] it essays to set off in a series of contrasts ordinary earthly love as opposed to the etherealized and disinterested love which was the pretended admiration of the *précieuses* at court. Phylomont and Theander, the rulers of neighboring dukedoms, are each in love with the other's sister. But whereas Phylomont loves Ariola naturally and desires that their love be consum-

[22] *Dramatic Records of Sir Henry Herbert,* p. 37.
[23] J. B. Fletcher, *op. cit.,* p. 145.

mated in marriage, Theander loves Eurithea platonically, and not only is content to limit his relations with her to "soulful converse" but is determined that Phylomont shall have no different satisfaction. Friendship becomes distinctly strained. A good genius appears in the person of Buonateste, a philosopher who is indignant that they should wrong his "good old friend Plato with this court calumny," a "woman's paradox," fathering on him "a fantastic love he never knew, poor gentleman." True to his convictions, he administers Theander a love potion which makes him sympathize with Phylomont's desire to marry, and also to entertain a similar impulse himself. Buonateste is also the means of foiling Fredeline, a creature of Theander's who has plotted to compromise Eurithea so that she be forced to satisfy his own love, which is illicit as well as sensual.[24]

Throughout the play, the balance is held pretty evenly between the two kinds of love, and although Davenant is distinctly a skeptic about the platonic variety, and allows the pragmatic Phylomont to triumph in the end, he makes Theander a sympathetic, never a ridiculous, figure. Into his mouth and that of his seraphic sweetheart are put the most poetic speeches of the play. Theander is allowed to defend his convictions with some force:

Phylomont

. . . Being married, is't not lawful, sir?

Theander

I grant it may be law, but is it comely?
Reduce thy reason to a cleaner sense,
Think on't a noble way. You two may live,
And love, become your own best arguments,
And so contract all virtue, and all praise:
Be ever beauteous, fresh, and young, at least
In your belief; for who can lessen, or
Defile th' opinion which your mutual thoughts

---

[24] F. E. Schelling, *op. cit.*, II, 347, notes the influence of Massinger's *Parliament of Love* on this subsidiary plot.

Shall fervently exchange? And then you may
Beget reflections in each other's eyes;
So you increase not children but yourselves,
A better, and more guiltless progeny;
These immaterial creatures cannot sin.

Phylomont

But who shall make men, sir? shall the world cease?

Theander

I know not how th' are made, but if such deeds
Be requisite, to fill up armies, villages,
And city shops; that killing, labour, and
That coz'ning still may last, know, Phylomont,
I'd rather nature should expect such coarse
And homely drudgeries from others than
From me.[25]

Theander and Eurithea are such creatures as this earth never
knew, but their words as they innocently discourse "the sweetness of the Spring, and Summer's wealth" are full of tenderness
and delicacy. Like most topical plays, *The Platonic Lovers* had
a brief career in the theatre and there are records of no revivals;
yet it is so full of interesting things that it is amazing it is not
more often read.

Two years intervened before Davenant wrote his next play,
because 1636 and 1637 were plague years with the theatres
rarely open. Unlike its predecessor, this play prospered upon
the stage. *The Unfortunate Lovers,* licensed April 16, 1638, was
acted before the Queen and court, first at Blackfriars on April 23,
then at the Cockpit at Whitehall on May 30, and again at Hampton Court on September 30 [26]—ample testimony that it received
literally a royal welcome. It was among the plays earliest revived at the Restoration, and was staged first by the group acting

[25] Act II.
[26] *Dramatic Records of Sir Henry Herbert,* pp. 37, 76, 77.

at the Red Bull in 1660,[27] then by Killigrew's company at Gibbons's Tennis Court, November 19, 1660,[28] and finally, after Davenant had received a monopoly of his own plays, at the Duke's House. It became a stock piece, and Pepys, although he thought it "no extraordinary play," witnessed it four times before he gave up keeping his diary.[29] This success is the more remarkable considering that *The Unfortunate Lovers,* like *The Cruel Brother* and *Albovine,* is a tragedy of blood. However, Davenant had learned to please by this time, and the play is often in the sentimental and exotic mood of his tragicomedies.

Galeotto, scheming counsellor of the Prince of Verona, accuses the fair and virtuous Arthiopa of unchastity in order to secure her lover, Duke Altophil, for his own daughter, Amaranta. The ruse fails owing to Altophil's faith in his sweetheart, and the Prince of Verona strips the plotter of his powers. Still all is not well. The Prince himself now tries to force Altophil to wed Amaranta, for he has fallen in love with Arthiopa. Amaranta loves Altophil, but, as virtuous as her father is villainous, she is party to none of this persecution. A new force now enters the play in the person of the barbarian Lombard, King Heildebrand, to whom Galeotto has betrayed the city. Henceforth the action becomes the usual carnival of lust and bloodshed. Heildebrand, at Galeotto's connivance, strives to ravish Arthiopa, and then, by way of poetic justice, the panderer's own daughter who by this time has allied herself with the persecuted lovers. Altophil at last contrives to slay Galeotto, whereupon poor Amaranta, feeling guilty of parricide, runs upon his naked sword. The sacrifice is unavailing. Heildebrand finally has his will with Arthiopa, and after he has paid the penalty of death for his crime, the dishonored damsel and her avenger, Altophil—the unfortunate lovers—die in each other's arms. Of the six principal characters only the Prince of Verona remains alive.

[27] *Dramatic Records of Sir Henry Herbert,* p. 82.
[28] *Ibid.,* p. 116, and *Historical Manuscripts Commission,* IV, 201.
[29] March 7, 1664; Sept. 11, 1667; April 8, Dec. 3, 1668.

Since the action just outlined has as its background military plots and counterplots relative to the taking of Verona, the play has all the complexity of *Love and Honour* along with the multiple catastrophes of *Albovine*. It is an adroitly constructed play, and at least one character, Amaranta, is outstanding. It more nearly resembles *Love and Honour* than the early tragedies because of its character types and the tendency to dwell upon their sensibilities in highly decorative language. At one point Altophil craves an appropriate setting for his sorrow:

> . . . Would there were here
> Some flow'ry bank, shaded with cypress yew
> And sycamore, whose melancholy brow
> Hung o'er a little discontented brook,
> That ever murmurs, as it wisely knew
> It travell'd to some river that must soon
> Convey it to the sea.[30]

There is a tendency to philosophize:

> . . . we are prisoners all; all circumscrib'd
> And to our limits tied: the fortunate
> And luckless are alike; for thou art with
> As strict necessity unto thy happiness
> Confin'd, as others to their evil fate.[31]

The play abounds in Davenant's heroic metaphors, and we must not be surprised at the suggestion that

> . . . time break his glass, and throw
> The sand in the sun's eyes to make him wink
> And leave us in the dark.

Nor at Arthiopa's proliferous imagination as she conjures Heildebrand to spare her virtue:

> Be still a King, and may your sceptre grow
> Within your hand, as heaven had given it

[30] Act III.
[31] Act II.

A root; may it bud forth, increase in boughs
Till 't spread to the Platan tree, and yield
A comfortable shade, where other Kings
May sit delighted, and secure from all
The storms of war, and tyranny.[32]

This idiom is more appropriate to tragicomedy than to tragedy, and in *The Fair Favorite,* which, owing to martial and political distractions, was his last play (except for the indifferent *Distresses*) before the closing of the theatres, Davenant returned to the prevailing mode. Licensed November 17, 1638,[33] this play was favorably enough received to justify, like its predecessor, several court performances,[34] but there is no evidence that it was revived at the Restoration. The plot is rather slight, and the play resembles *The Platonic Lovers* in its structure and some elements of its theme.

Eumena is the platonic mistress and state favorite of a King who has been forced by political exigencies to take as his queen a woman he does not love. Oramont, Eumena's brother, accepts the common report that she is the King's mistress in a less theoretical sense, and when his friend, Amadore, champions her innocence, he renounces their friendship and provokes a duel. The two fight in this unnatural cause, and it is rumored that Amadore is slain. Despite the entreaties of Eumena and the Queen, the King is about to execute Oramont for his misdeed, only to discover that Amadore has not been slain after all. Reconciliations are effected, and Amadore wins the hand of Eumena, while the King, conveniently if somewhat suddenly, conceives a genuine affection for his loyal and neglected Queen.

This play, even though it tends to drag after the first two acts, is pleasing and graceful. The Queen is of the patient Griselda type, and her gentleness and staunchness of character

---

[32] Act IV.

[33] *Dramatic Records of Sir Henry Herbert,* p. 38.

[34] Acted at the Cockpit, November 20, December 11, 1638; *Dramatic Records of Sir Henry Herbert,* p. 77.

make her the peer of the peerless Eumena, an impossibility quite possible in Caroline tragicomedy. The language is felicitous throughout, and the tone is genuinely pure and idealistic. The King wavers between a platonic and a sensual love of Eumena, but Eumena is staunch always. To his heresy,

Honour's a word, the issue of the voice,

she opposes the true doctrine,

. . . Honour's a rich,
A glorious upper vestment, which we wear
To please the lookers on, as well as to
Delight our selves.

Let us not be too cynical in analyzing the terms of this definition.

5

The Fair Favorite completes the muster of Davenant's pre-war plays of "wit and fancy," and we shall be better prepared to treat of his best-known drama, *The Siege of Rhodes,* if we pause now to view these earlier works in the large. Less has been said about their characters than about their themes, their language, and their rarefied atmosphere—the reason being that character-ization is not an issue in works of prevailing unreality. There are few memorable personages in these plays, and the *dramatis personæ* of one duplicates that of the others. One finds the usual assortment of uncurbed monarchs, of villainous counsellors so deep and insidious as to be practically incomprehensible, of brilliant and brave but passionate and erring young heroes, and of lovely and etherealized young heroines. The heroes are prone not only to dilate upon their emotions, but to act, and the hero-ines are prone not only to offer a pattern of feminine charm and virtue, but to direct the action. Davenant's protagonists differ from the "lily-livered" heroes and pathetic heroines of Fletcher in being more positive if no more convincing, and to this degree prepare the way for the characters of the heroic plays. Fletcher's influence upon Davenant [35] and other precursors of the heroic playwrights was unquestionably great, but Fletcher was not the sole influence. Many elements of Davenant's plots, original and inventive as they are, may be found in Fletcher, such a play as *The Unfortunate Lovers* proving especially fertile in parallels. As a result Davenant has figured prominently in the miniature academic war between those who trace the origin of the English heroic play to Fletcher and English tragicomedy, and those who trace it to the French heroic romance.[36] There is little real reason for difference of opinion in view of the fact that Fletcherian tragicomedy, Caroline tragicomedy, the French heroic romance, and the Restoration heroic play itself are all part of one literary movement. The Greek novels, the Spanish chivalresque romances, the Spanish, French, and English pastorals, all contributed the original ingredients for the works of seventeenth-century neo-romantic writers,[37] who differ from each other mainly in their progressive complacency in pyramiding artificialities. France took the lead in developing romantic literature of the new order, and it is undeniable that Orrery and Dryden went to French fiction for some of their material; but French fiction had not been a closed book to Davenant, Carlell, Killigrew, Cartwright, and their fellows, even though it is sometimes hard to tell whether these are levying upon Fletcher, Gomberville, Saint-Sorlin, or upon that body of earlier exotic fiction which had nourished all three. Montague, Carlell, and Killigrew are chief of the Caroline playwrights in displaying French influence, but such influence is also perceptible in Davenant.

[35] J. W. Tupper in the introduction to his *Belles-Lettres* edition of *Love and Honour* and *The Siege of Rhodes* goes into this thoroughly.

[36] A few recent articles on this subject (which will point the way to others) are W. S. Clark, "The Sources of the Restoration Heroic play," *R. E. S.,* IV (1928), 49–63; and K. Lynch, "Conventions of the Platonic Drama in the Heroic Plays of Orrery and Dryden," *P. M. L. A.* (1929), 456–71.

[37] The present writer has touched upon this subject in *Thomas Killigrew, Cavalier Dramatist*, pp. 145–158, and plans to deal with it at greater length.

He was familiar with D'Urfé's *Astrée* [38] as with its Spanish predecessor, Montemayor's *Diana;* [39] and that he had dipped into the newer variety of fiction which was beginning to flow across the channel to delight Henrietta Maria and her court, is proved by the number of disguisings, the incognitos, the love affairs between sets of brothers and sisters, even in a social comedy such as *The Distresses.* Three of the plays just reviewed, *The Siege, Love and Honour,* and *The Fair Favorite,* have as their theme the conflicting stresses of love, honor, friendship, and jealousy, with an attendant sublimation of valor and magnanimity—the exclusive concern alike of the French heroic romance and the English heroic play.

Thus far we have been dealing only with such plays as were staged before Parliament closed the theatres. The claim of *The Siege of Rhodes* as a shaping influence on heroic plays, if not itself an example of the species, few are inclined to deny. The tendency has been the other way around, and to follow Dryden's lead in calling it "the first light we had of them on the English theatre." [40] And this in spite of the fact that those qualities which Dryden found wanting in the play to make it an example of the fully developed type, "the fulness of plot, and the variety of actions," the "drawing all things as far above the ordinary proportion of the stage, and that is beyond the common words and actions of human life," are conspicuously present in a whole body of dramatic work emanating from courtly and academic circles during the decade preceding the closing of the theatres. The prominence given *The Siege of Rhodes* is largely owing to the accident that it furnished the precedent of rime for the heroic plays. Conceived originally as a musical drama to be rendered in *stilo recitativo,* it may have taken the suggestion of rime from Corneille's *Andromède,* [41] or from the alexandrine of the French

---

[38] Such pieces as *The Temple of Love* and *The Platonic Lovers* prove this.
[39] Mentioned in the concluding scene of *The Distresses.*
[40] *Essay of Heroic Plays.*
[41] J. W. Tupper, *op. cit.,* p. xi.

stage in general. The English equivalent of the alexandrine had become the heroic couplet as given currency by Waller and Denham, but Davenant, for the sake of musical variety, interspersed among his couplets riming half-lines, quatrains, and an assortment of measures, in Dryden's words, after "the Pindaric way." [42] It is not absolutely necessary to assume French influence here. There was nothing very new about rime in an English play. Originally all plays had been rimed, and, to a minor degree in plays—to a major degree in court masques— rime had persisted. Moreover, blank verse had become so lax a medium that any progressive step must have resulted either in frank prose or in its opposite extreme. Denham's *The Sophy* (1641), the prosody of which represents about the last step in the disintegration of blank verse, contains one part carefully wrought in heroic couplets; [43] Davenant, by the way, seems to have admired this play. [44]

However inevitable the step to write, under the circumstances, an entire play in rime, the fact remains that it was Davenant who took the step. We may say in summary that the importance of his *Siege of Rhodes* rests upon the fact that it is rimed, that it did much to convey across the dramatic interregnum the love-honor-valor theme which the Caroline playwrights had been developing, that it tested the expediency of women actors and more elaborate scenery as adjuncts of the public stage, [45] and that it formed popular taste, thus paving the way to success for later writers who acted upon its suggestions.

The source of this play, like its place in the history of the heroic school, has provoked considerable discussion. The historical setting concerns the storming of Christian Rhodes by the Turkish monarch, Solyman the Magnificent, during the Mastership of

[42] *Essay of Dramatic Poesy.* Dryden gives Davenant credit for "the noblest use" of the heroic couplet up until his day; cf. *Epistle Dedicatory to The Rival Ladies.*

[43] Act IV, ll. 16–64.

[44] See above, p. 157.

[45] See above, pp. 124–25.

Philip de Villers L'Isle D'Adam in 1522. Langbaine [46] listed the
books in which this material would have been available to Davenant, who no doubt went to Knolles's *Historie of the Turks* published in 1603. Parallels for the romantic material of the play,
the inter-relationships of Alphonso, Ianthe, Solyman, and Roxolana have been found in the Solyman-Perseda cycle of themes,
used notably by an Englishman in Kyd's *Soliman and Perseda*
published in 1599; [47] further parallels have been found in
Scudéry's *Ibrahim, ou L'Illustre Bassa* published in 1641. [48] While
good cases have been made out for each of these works as
Davenant's source, the latter, Englished in 1652, has its accessi-
bility and freshness to recommend it. More recently, a case has
been made out for Heywood's *Fair Maid of the West,* in which
Bess, the barmaid quixote, becomes the prototype of queenly
Ianthe. [49] Space unfortunately does not permit a précis and comparison of these various arguments.

The Siege of Rhodes as we have it today is in two parts.
Part I, written to be produced as opera in the cramped quarters
of Rutland House with a cast of seven people, is short and, as
drama, rather rudimentary. Part II is more developed, and is
divided into acts instead of deprecatory "entries." We know
that Part I was produced in September 1656, [50] and thereafter
during the Commonwealth; Part II also was probably produced
during the Commonwealth, [51] but there is proof positive of no
stage performance before the play was used at the grand opening
of Lisle's Tennis Court in June 1661. The latter version's complement of music was evidently not so full as that of the former;
Dryden informs us that, after the Restoration, *Rhodes* was re-

[46] *Op. cit.,* p. 110.
[47] K. Campbell, "The Source of the Siege of Rhodes," *M. L. N.,* XIII (1898),
177–82.
[48] C. G. Child, "The Rise of the Heroic Play," *M. L. N.,* XIX (1904), 166–173.
[49] A. Thaler, "Thomas Heywood, D'Avenant, and The Siege of Rhodes,"
P. M. L. A., XXXIX (1924), 624–41.
[50] See above, p. 124.
[51] John Aubrey, *op. cit.,* I, 208; A. Nicoll, *op. cit.,* p. 93; W. J. Lawrence,
op. cit., II, 137.

vived "as a just drama." [52] Part I appeared in print in 1656, and both parts together in 1663, by which time a few new scenes had been added to Part I so that the character Roxolana might figure in the earlier action.

In spite of all the preliminaries in which the historical importance of *The Siege of Rhodes* has involved us, the play itself invites no extended discussion. For all its contribution to the vogue and the formal characteristics of the heroic plays, it contains little which is essentially new to Davenant's theatre. The plot itself is extremely simple. Rhodes is besieged by Solyman the Magnificent, and Alphonso, a visiting Sicilian duke, places his sword at the disposal of the Admiral and Villerius, the Grand Master. Alphonso's bride, Ianthe, coming to join her husband, is captured by the besieging Turks, but is freed by the magnanimity of Solyman. This very magnanimity arouses Alphonso's suspicions, and the knowledge that Ianthe has spent two nights with the Turks fans his jealousy into a distemper. However, his unjust suspicions are burned away in the heat of a battle, during which Ianthe rivals even his great prowess in repulsing the Turks. Thus ends Part I, with nothing achieved except a reconciliation between husband and wife. Part II almost repeats Part I, except that certain comic songs that punctuate Part I with grotesque inappropriateness have no counterparts, and the action is slightly more complex. Rhodes, unrelieved by the Christian world, is forced to capitulate, and sends Ianthe to make terms with Solyman. Solyman, although by no means unaffected by Ianthe's charms, is more concerned at the moment in subduing Roxolana, his restive and ambitious Queen. He detains Ianthe and disciplines his wife by making her entertain this fair Sicilian. Roxolana is fiercely jealous, and writes to pique the suspicions of Alphonso, who, poor man, is also being worked upon by the Admiral. (The Admiral's motives are hard to gauge; he seems to nourish a growing tenderness for Ianthe and, apparently, a proprietory interest in her virtue.) The Rhodians

[52] *Essay of Heroic Plays.*

sally forth to rescue their fair ambassador, but they are repulsed and Alphonso is captured. By this time Roxolana has been completely charmed by the virtues of Ianthe, and she not only allows the breach between herself and Solyman to be mended, but when the latter places the fate of Alphonso in her hands, she confers him upon his faithful wife. Solyman, magnificent to the end, then lets Ianthe make the terms of peace for Rhodes.

It is unfortunate that Davenant, the dramatist, should be chiefly known by this play. Half a dozen of his earlier ones are better; and have more spontaneity, if less dignity, than *The Siege of Rhodes*. Solyman combines augustness and generosity to a greater extent than any of the author's previous characters, and the temperamental Roxolana (as played by Miss Davenport) seemed to strike the Restoration audience as mightily diverting; but Alphonso and Ianthe are no different from the heroes and heroines of the earlier tragicomedies, and the other characters are quite undistinguished. *The Cruelty of the Spaniards in Peru* and *The History of Sir Francis Drake,* Davenant's other Commonwealth productions, have called for comment only in connection with their author's contribution to the development of opera, and Part I of *Rhodes* placed him in the same position as did these other pieces—that of the librettist. Part II is much better, but Davenant's vein of poetry was not strong enough to transcend the restrictions of the distich. The language of the play is not very attractive, and there is nothing one feels tempted to quote.

Yet, be our judgment of this play by absolute critical standards what it may, the Restoration audience found its combined attractions of heroics, music, scenes, and sentiment utterly entrancing, and vouchsafed it a phenomenal success. Its first run was of twelve days,[53] and it was pronounced an "everlasting play." [54] The second part was most frequently acted, as we know from the diary of the enthusiastic Pepys. Pepys not only went to see the play,[55] but he often read it to his wife or had her read it to him.

[53] John Downes, *op. cit.,* p. 20.
[54] L. Hotson, *op. cit.,* p. 247.
[55] July 2, Nov. 15, 1661; May 20, Dec. 27, 1662.

On one of the occasions he remarked: "We spent most of the morning talking and reading of 'The Siege of Rhodes,' which is certainly (the more I read it the more I think so) the best poem that ever was wrote." [56]   Once when the play was acting, the diarist had recently made a resolution to stay away from the theatre. He kept his vow, "but Lord! how it went against my heart to go away from the very door of the Duke's playhouse . . . I was very near making a forfeit, but I did command my- self . . ." Later in the day he seems to have found solace in work and in reading his wife "a piece of the *Grand Cyrus*." [57]

6

What can be said in conclusion for Davenant's works of wit and fancy—*The Siege of Rhodes,* the earlier serious plays, and, wherein it resembles these, *Gondibert* itself? Certainly it cannot be said, however much they may enlighten the student and de- light the lover of *belles-lettres,* that they have universality and, therefore, interest and appeal to the general reader of our day. On the other hand something may be said for the integrity and worth of these works in *their* day. The literary alienist, con- ducting a lynx-eyed search for decadence, will find much in these works triumphantly to deplore. But decadence—that abused and abusive term—should be defined every time it is used. If we mean by decadence simply the artistic frailty of works produced in autumnal periods of literary history, periods when the soil has been exhausted, let us say, by the foison of Elizabethan sum- mer so that it must lie fallow for a time, then these works are decadent. But too often this term carries with it implications of some kind of depravity; therefore I cannot insist too strongly that I have found in Davenant's school no signs of moral weak- ness, and many of sincere, if inflated, idealism. Those who say that pure and sensual love were contrasted by these playwrights, not only to glorify pure love but also to give their auditors a

[56] Oct. 1, 1665. See also Sept. 23, 1664; Jan. 22, 1667; Dec. 19, 1668.
[57] May 21, 1667.

chance to titillate at the spectacle of sensual love, are unjust,—not because the charge is false, but because particular authors should not be held cruelly accountable for their mixed motives when human motives are nearly always mixed. Another charge which may be made against these writers is that they dealt with chastity, courage, and integrity chiefly because of the *ornamental* nature of these virtues. The defense in this case is simple; morality is never more thoroughly vindicated than by those who assume that what is good is also an adornment.

Such plays as Killigrew's *Claricilla*, Cartwright's *Royal Slave,* and Davenant's *Fair Favorite* are essentially naïve. So also is *The Siege of Rhodes.* The quality of naïveté in Davenant distinguishes his heroic vein from Dryden's. Dryden knew quite well that he was practising a *coloratura* art. Davenant, on the other hand, just as he was convinced that he was recording the thoughts and actions of human life, and giving us an easy and familiar view of ourselves when he wrote *Gondibert,* so also was he convinced when he wrote *The Siege of Rhodes* that he was advancing "the characters of vertue in the shapes of valour and conjugal love." [58] And probably he was! It is hard for us to calculate the effect upon the crude manners and lax morals of an incompletely civilized society exercised by a Davenant or a Scudéry. Fictive patterns of virtue and nobility, in spite of—perhaps because of—their being fashioned in sugar would have had more influence on manners and morals than the ordinances of a Rump Parliament, or, in that era, the mighty illustrations of a *Paradise Lost.* How often must some English country wife, after measuring the excellences of an Ibrahim, have looked with new eyes upon the drunken lout who ruled at her table!

If the dictum is correct, that whatever has deeply interested mankind is of permanent significance to mankind, then Pepys' faith in *The Siege of Rhodes* as "the best poem that ever was wrote," and his wife's kindred estimate of *Le Grand Cyrus,* cannot be passed over with a smile. Literature of this kind goes into

[58] "To the Reader," *Quarto,* 1656.

solution, and its effects continue when it itself is dead. By 1711, when the *Spectator Papers* began to appear, the vogue of seventeenth-century heroic romance was passing, but had this vogue never been, England might have been less prepared for the humane and polished Addison and Steele. *Love and Honour, The Platonic Lovers, The Fair Favorite, The Siege of Rhodes,* and *Gondibert* were not decadent if we mean by the term something subversive to the health of the race. Their *othertimes* charm and occasional poetry have already been maintained, and it is not inappropriate to conclude upon the present note: These works too, in their mistaken way, have wrought in the cause of sweetness and light.

X

ADAPTATIONS OF SHAKESPEARE

Be not thou, Reader, (for thine own sake as well as mine) a common Spectator, that can never look on great Changes but with tears in his Eyes.—POSTSCRIPT TO GONDIBERT.

XCEPT when *Gondibert* or *The Siege of Rhodes* is being mentioned, Davenant is chiefly remembered as the heinous Restoration playhouse manager who had the effrontery to alter several of Shakespeare's greatest plays. Although his adaptations have already been discussed (to the point of supererogation) by Shakespearean scholars, justice as well as completeness demands a word about them here. We must concede at the beginning that, compared with the originals, these adaptations are bad. They could not be otherwise. We cannot concede any justification for the succession of essays [1] in which critics have vindicated their good taste by rediscovering and illustrating with elaborate analyses just how bad they are. Various writers have variously indulged in whimsicality, satire, cynicism, and pious denunciation on the subject. A choice anthology of anathema could be compiled from their reflections on this "panderer" whose "depraved taste" produced such "horrible mutilations." For anyone preoccupied with Shakespeare to be offended by the Restoration stage versions of his plays is natural, but quite illogical.

[1] For a bibliography of works on the adaptations of Davenant and others, see H. Spencer, *Shakespeare Improved*, p. 386. Works on Davenant's individual adaptations are cited in footnotes below.

These versions are not the province of Shakespearean scholarship
at all. Baroque villas have been erected with the stones of
demolished cathedrals, but the lover of Gothic architecture prefers
to linger among such cathedrals as remain intact; yet in his case
erudite interest might justify the self-flagellation involved in ex-
amining the baroque villas, for here the new is the sole remaining
vestige, in the particular instance, of the old. The Restoration
adapter in *using* the original plays did not *annihilate* them, and
certainly such men as Davenant and Dryden would not have
done so had it been possible. So far as these adaptations are
significant at all, they are significant to the student of the entire
sweep of literary history or, among specialists, to him who would
take the pulse and temperature of the Restoration itself—not, certainly, to the specialist in Shakespeare. They should be examined
with interest, not indignation, as illustrative of the undulations
of human progress.

His adaptations of the plays of Shakespeare (and others) were
all written while Davenant was managing his playhouse and re-
cruiting his repertory during the years following the opening
of Lisle's Tennis Court in June 1661. They were written—a
point too often forgotten—by one whose creative years were past,
by one who had been a playwright and poet, but was now a
rather weary old gentleman in the theatrical business. On December 12, 1660, Davenant's "proposition of reformeinge some of
the most ancient Playes that were playd at Blackfriers and of
makeinge them fitt" had been favorably received, and he had
been given exclusive acting rights to Shakespeare's *Tempest*,
Measure for Measure, Much Ado about Nothing, Henry VIII,
King Lear, Macbeth, and *Hamlet,* as well as to Webster's *Duchess
of Malfi*, and Denham's *The Sophy*.[2] He did not reform and
make fit all of the plays in this list, nor did he confine his activities in this kind to them. Since he showed little inclination to
claim his adaptations, it is difficult to determine the exact range of

[2] A. Nicoll, *op. cit.,* p. 314.

this twilight literary activity. We know on the authority of John
Downes, his stage prompter, that some of Shakespeare's plays
were presented unaltered,[3] but while *Hamlet* has generally been
considered one of these, a case [4] has recently been made against
Davenant as the author of the sophisticated text of that play
which appears in the quarto of 1676. In his *Preface to the
Tempest*, Dryden asserts that Davenant not only revised but
also "added whole scenes together" even in the case of new plays.
On September 12, 1667, Pepys saw *Greene's Tu Quoque* "with
some alterations of Sir W. Davenant's." As late as 1719 his
reputation as an improver caused his name to be forged with
that of Dryden upon the duodecimo of a version of *Julius Caesar,*
a play which had belonged not to him but to the rival company.
We shall confine our attention to those adaptations certainly
his, sketching the nature of the individual pieces first, and then
describing the features which the series has in common.

First in order of composition is *The Law against Lovers,*[5]
staged during the winter of 1661–62.[6] It is based upon *Measure
for Measure,* with the adventures of Mistress Overdone and her
tenderloin companions omitted, and with the Beatrice and Benedick story from *Much Ado about Nothing* substituted as an
underplot. Mariana does not appear in the play, and the last act,
almost entirely original, features an armed revolt against Angelo
instigated by Benedick. The play ends in a general amnesty and

[3] See above, pp. 158–59.

[4] H. Spencer, *op. cit.,* pp. 174–87.

[5] For an analysis see K. Elze, "Sir William Davenant," *Shakespeare Jahrbuch,*
IV, 153–59; and G. Illies, *Das Verhaeltniss von Davenant's The Law against
Lovers zu Shakespeare's Measure for Measure und Much Ado about Nothing,*
Halle, 1900. For further recriminations see the works indicated in note 1. A
very sane, if somewhat factual, discussion of this and other adaptations appears
in the dissertation by J. D. E. Williams, *Sir William Davenant's relation to
Shakespeare,* Strassburg, 1905.

[6] Pepys saw the play February 18, 1662. He approved it, but a rimester of
the same year considered it "the worst that ever you sawe" whose author "only
the Art of it had / Of two good Playes to make one bad." Cf. L. Hotson,
op. cit., p. 247. The play had not the continued success of the other adaptations.

pairing off of lovers, during which the Duke intimates his intention to enter a monastery, and bids Isabella to become the bride of Angelo! In the next of the series, *Macbeth*,[7] licensed November 3, 1663,[8] and first seen by Pepys a year and two days later, the part of Lady Macduff is considerably enlarged so that her virtue may strike a balance with the villainy of Lady Macbeth, but there are few important deviations from the plot and structure of the original tragedy, and further comment may rest until we turn to the tactics underlying all of the adaptations.

Our earliest date for the third play is September 10, 1664, when Pepys saw *The Rivals*,[9] a very free adaptation of Fletcher and Shakespeare's (?) *Two Noble Kinsmen*. The basic situation in the older play, the imprisonment and love rivalry of Chaucer's Palamon and Arcite (rechristened by Davenant Theocles and Philander) is retained; but the entire first and last acts are rewritten and extensive alterations are made throughout. For the very diffuse ending of the original play with its tournament and its approximate correspondence of events to those in the *Knight's Tale*, a new ending is invented so that both kinsmen may not only remain among the living but also be provided with satisfactory mates. This has been arranged for by substituting Celania, a lady and therefore eligible, for the Jailor's Daughter, whose love madness for one of the kinsmen forms the very extraneous sub-plot of the original play. The altered last act is theatrical but effective, and gives us a heart-warming scene in which the two rivals, bitter enemies in love but true comrades still, defend each other from the slander of outsiders. As a stage play *The Rivals* improves upon its original; it was a popular

[7] Treated in the usual vein by Nicolaus Delius, "Shakespeare's Macbeth und Davenant's Macbeth," *Shakespeare Jahrbuch*, XX, 69–84; see also Gustav Weber, *Davenant's Macbeth im Verhaeltniss zu Shakespeare's gleichnaminger Tragoedie*, Rostock, 1903.

[8] *Dramatic Records of Sir Henry Herbert*, p. 138.

[9] For analysis see A. Krusenbaum, *Das Verhaeltniss von Davenant's Drama The Rivals zu The Two Noble Kinsmen*, Halle, 1895; see also A. C. Sprague, *Beaumont and Fletcher on the Restoration Stage*, Harvard University Press, 1926.

success,[10] and was revived for the court at least as late as November 19, 1667.[11]

The best known of all stage versions of Shakespeare, *The Tempest*,[12] representing the combined effort of Davenant and Dryden, was seen by Pepys on what appears to have been its first performance, November 7, 1667. The alterations in this case are lamentably extensive: As foil to Miranda, who has never seen a man, we meet Hippolito, who has never seen a woman, and since Miranda is predestined the mate of Ferdinand, she is provided with a sister, Dorinda, so that Hippolito will not be left wanting. Each part must have its counterpart, so Caliban is provided with a sister, Sycorax, and even Ariel is awaited in the other world by a female sprite, Milcha. The Antonio-Sebastian conspiracy is omitted, and in its place we find Stephano and Trincalo, now master and boatswain of the ship, involved with additional mariners in a farcical campaign for the hand of Sycorax and for mastery of the island. These comic additions, and the parts played by Davenant and Dryden in their creation, will be discussed more fully later on.

The last of Davenant's adaptations, the last in fact of all his literary efforts, was first presented on March 26, 1668, when *The Man's the Master* drew a thronged house and disappointed both King Charles as he sat jesting in his royal box, and Samuel Pepys as he sat below buying oranges for four of his wife's friends.[13] Langbaine's comment that it was a translation of Paul Scarron's *Jodelet ou le maître Valet* and (as he remembered) *L'heritier Ridicule* [14] has impelled subsequent historians to de-

[10] Downes (*op. cit.*, p. 23) says that it attracted a full house for nine consecutive days; Pepys although he considered it "no excellent play" went to see it again, December 2, 1664.

[11] A. Nicoll, *op. cit.*, p. 309.

[12] See Max Rosbund, *Dryden als Shakespeare-Bearbeiter*, Halle, 1882; Otto Witt, *The Tempest, or the Enchanted Island, a Comedy by John Dryden*, Rostock, 1899; and N. Delius, "Dryden and Shakespeare," *Shakespeare Jahrbuch*, IV, 6–40. See also note 24 below.

[13] See above, p. 166.

[14] *Op. cit.*, p. 109.

scribe it as a composite of these two plays, fashioned in the manner of *The Law against Lovers*. The fact is, that whereas a few suggestions may have been followed from *L'heritier Ridicule* and from another of Scarron's Jodelet farces, *Jodelet Duelliste* (in which one of Davenant's additional characters appears at least in name), *The Man's the Master* is not a composite adaptation at all. It is simply a redaction of *Le maître Valet,* following its original, scene by scene, almost speech by speech, with only minor alterations. Scarron's play (in turn an adaptation of *Donde hay agravios no hay zelos* by F. de Rojas) concerns the adventures of a Spanish Don who has exchanged identities with his bumptious valet so that he may better reconnoitre a household which harbors not only his prospective fiancée but also the man who has wounded his brother and wronged his sister, and is full of intrigue and puzzle interest which lose nothing in Davenant's version. The alexandrines of Scarron are reduced to English prose, and the language is enforced after the English manner:

Plûtôt mourir cent fois que fausser ma parole. . . .[15]

becomes in Davenant

I'll rather die of naked poverty than break my word.

The loquacity of the characters in the original play is considerably disciplined, and the space thus saved makes way for the addition of several original scenes featuring the adventures of people backstairs, especially of a groom, Sancho, whose frugality in speech is only more remarkable than his prodigal appetite for sackposset.

When he first saw the play Pepys found these additions "sorry poor stuffe . . . fit only for clowns," but he was better pleased on later occasions.[16] The King likewise found it sufficiently

[15] Act III, Scene iii, line 1.
[16] April 3, May 7, 1668.

tolerable to permit several later court performances.[17] The play
became a stock piece and held the stage remarkably long. It was
revived sometime in 1714, on July 15, 1726, and finally on November 3, 1775, when Woodward played Jodelet, the part originally
taken by Cave Underhill.[18] *The Man's the Master* and *The Law
against Lovers* are the only adaptations claimed by Davenant
or his first publishers, our knowledge of his connection with
the others deriving generally from Downes, Langbaine, and Dryden.[19]

We may turn now to the general principles governing Davenant's methods of revising plays for his stage. Some of these have
already been indicated above. Having become a playwright of
the school of fanciful tragicomedy and, to a certain extent, of its
natural successor, the heroic school, Davenant was apt to carry
into his Restoration workshop some of the predilections of these
schools. He tended to soften and sentimentalize parts of the
plays he adapted. Characters whom we see slain in the older
plays are slain off the stage, or else slain and restored to life, or
else saved that embarrassment altogether. The old theme of love
and honor will sometimes inoculate, unexpectedly and inappropri-
ately, speeches in the original plays. At times the motives of
characters change: Angelo's persecution of Isabella in *The Law
against Lovers* is not the result of lust as in *Measure for Measure*
but of his desire to test her virtue; therefore his real transgression
is lack of faith—a violation of the code of romantic love. Allied
with these tendencies, but much less objectionable, is the adapter's
impulse to serve neo-classical ideals of construction. Consistency
dictated in some cases the transformation of prose to blank verse
(at times blank verse became heroic couplets), and the unities
dictated a simplification of construction with a slight reduction
in the number of characters. Davenant the playwright is re-

---

[17] April 23, 1668, August 3 (or 9), 1673; cf. A. Nicoll, *op. cit.*, pp. 309–10.
[18] John Genest, *op. cit.*, III, 183; V, 513.
[19] The two plays mentioned appear in the 1673 folio as well as in separate
editions. For Davenant's authorship of *Macbeth* and *The Rivals*, see John
Downes, *op. cit.*, pp. 23, 33; and of *The Tempest*, see Dryden's *Preface*.

sponsible for these changes; Davenant the theatre manager for most of those which follow.

The avenue to the restored stage was paved with good intentions, and when the patentees were receiving their rights of monopoly, they contracted to remove "several prophane, obscene, and scurrilous passages" from old plays so that nothing should be acted "offensive to piety and good manners." [20] Davenant has been called a prude by the modern critic for the exactitude with which, according to his lights, he kept his word. In these plays anything in the nature of an oath or a reference to deity is carefully excised, and the unregenerate vocabulary of the Elizabethans, especially in matters of sex, is studiously chastened. Angelo may no longer call Juliet a "fornicatress," and graphic "lechery" makes way for our own polite Latinism "incontinence." The vocabulary in general is modernized. The fifty years separating the Restoration Age from the Elizabethan brought greater changes in the language than the two hundred and fifty years since. It did not strike Davenant's contemporaries as impious when he altered "badged" to "stained," "shard" to "borne," "seeling" to "dismal," "ravin up" to "destroy," and, in general, found them words they could understand. Gerard Langbaine, an intelligent man and a true lover of Shakespeare, said simply, "Where the Language is rough or obsolete, our Author has taken care to polish it." [21]

It is well to keep in mind the viewpoint of Davenant's contemporaries, and in turning to a second class of his deviations from the original plays, we find our text in the Diary of Samuel Pepys. On one of the occasions when he had seen the altered *Macbeth,* the diarist pronounced it "a most excellent play in all respects, but especially in divertissement, though it be a deep tragedy; which is a strange perfection in a tragedy, it being most proper here and suitable." [22] This response of one member of

[20] See above, p. 160.
[21] *Op. cit.,* p. 108.
[22] Jan. 7, 1667.

his audience, one whose taste when all is said was somewhat above its average, tends to justify Davenant's liberties with the weird sisters, in increasing their number to a quartette, and in making them operatic and acrobatic as well as merely prophetic.[23] The taste of the times, which in this respect it is true Davenant had been chief in forming, demanded something in the nature of song and dance, instrumental music and spectacle, in every play. A quartette number or a Saraband dance is apt to surprise us at any moment. For this purpose, one Viola, a character foreign to Shakespeare, is added fully equipped with "castanietos" to the *dramatis personæ* of *The Law against Lovers.* These divertissements varied from unambitious dancing and singing "in recitativo and in parts" in *The Man's the Master,* to an elaborate vocal and instrumental interlude representing a cross-country hunt in *The Rivals,* and an antimasque-like performance of devils and their aides in *The Tempest.* Later *The Tempest* was further adapted into an avowed *opera,*[24] and in general the stage career of these plays tended to bring amplification of their operatic elements so that they must be accorded an important place in the development of this *genre* in England.

Another class of additions indicative of Restoration taste, this time of its preference of sock to buskin, consists of original comic scenes scattered through the adaptations. In *Macbeth,* the one tragedy in the series, the tendency is to serve the ideal of classical unity by eliminating instead of expanding the comic elements, and the humorous lines of the Porter are deleted, but this is an isolated case. Having eschewed the impossible task of making the language of Mistress Overdone and her companions refined, by substituting the underplot of *Much Ado* for this part of *Measure for Measure,* Davenant had the fortitude to add to the

[23] The Witches enter flying (by means of wires) and offer prolonged vocal entertainment.

[24] Shadwell's opera has been printed by most editors as Davenant's and Dryden's adaptation. On this subject and others concerning the operatic features of the adaptations, see W. J. Lawrence, *op. cit.,* I, 193 ff.; M. Summers, *Shakespeare Adaptations,* Introduction; A. Nicoll, *op. cit.,* pp. 123 ff.

wit combats between Beatrice and Benedick. The result is what
we might expect, for this is to put hack work in juxtaposition
with genius. The dialogue has not nearly the merit of that in
Davenant's early comedies such as *The Wits* and *News from
Plymouth;* and the author's consciousness of his declining powers,
attested by explicit statements in his Restoration prologues, epilogues, and other poems, may account for the fact that his subsequent comic additions were in the easier and, for an old-fashioned
writer like Davenant, more congenial realm of farce. In *The
Rivals,* Cunopes, a churl in love (acted by Underhill), is substituted for comic possibilities for the very serious-minded Jailer
of *The Two Noble Kinsmen,* and in *The Man's the Master,*
Sancho, the taciturn gourmet already mentioned, is added to the
original cast of Scarron's play. These c•nic scenes are homespun and reflect, albeit faintly, Davenant's old fondness for Jonsonian humours.

The most revealing of the original comic scenes are those in
The Tempest, and these, incidentally, have been the chief in-
strument in stigmatizing Davenant's literary reputation. The
additions here are of two distinct classes. There are those passages in which the combination of a man who has never seen a
woman and of two women who have never seen a man (except
for Prospero) gives rise, owing to the innocent enthusiasm of the
principals and the facetiousness of their companions, to improprie-
ties and *double-entendres* in speech. Then there are those in
which the difficulties of the stranded sailors as they tipple, quarrel, and struggle for mastery of the island, create unobjectionable
and often quite amusing farce. We have here common varieties
of Restoration and pre-Restoration comedy side by side. The one
is witty and in several instances salacious; and the other is slap-
stick and coarse but entirely wholesome. Pepys found the business of the sailors "too tiresome," as he was apt to find Davenant's
low comedy, and no doubt the majority of his contemporaries
cared least for this which we find least unpleasant. For the other

John Dryden has cheerfully assumed the responsibility. In his preface to the adaptation he writes:

. . . Sir William Davenant, as he was a man of a quick and piercing imagination, soon found that somewhat might be added to the design of Shakespeare . . . the counterplot of Shakespeare's plot, namely, that of a man who had never seen a woman; that by this means those two characters of innocence and love might the more illustrate and commend each other. This excellent contrivance he was pleased to communicate to me, and to desire my assistance in it. I confess that from the first moment it so pleased me, that I never writ anything with more delight. I must likewise do him that justice to acknowledge that my writing received daily his amendments; and that is the reason why it is not so faulty, as the rest which I have done, without the help of so judicious a friend. The comical parts of the sailors were also of his invention, and, for the most part, his writing, as you will easily discover by the style.

On the basis of these remarks, and of the fact that Dryden, not Davenant, had a fondness for sophisticated prurience, it would be easy to hold the younger and greater of the two men entirely responsible for the Hippolito-Dorinda scenes. But this would be hardly fair. Davenant was the inventor of Hippolito, a fact which does not rest solely upon Dryden's testimony. An ingenious scholar has claimed a source for Hippolito in Calderón's *En esta vida todo es verdad y todo mentira*,[25] and while some trusting authorities have accepted this as the source whereas others have proven, as is actually the case, that it is not the source at all,[26] no one has remarked the fact that Davenant had used Hippolito in a play years before. *The Platonic Lovers,* acted in 1635 and therefore antedating Calderón's play by about five years, contains several light scenes featuring a youth, Gridonell,

[25] Hermann Grimm, "Shakespeare's Sturm in der Bearbeitung von Dryden und Davenant," *Fünfzehn Essays*, Berlin, 1875, pp. 183–224.

[26] M. Summers, *Shakespeare Adaptations*, pp. xlix–liii. Those who have been deceived by Grimm's essay are carefully enumerated by Mr. Summers.

who has never seen a woman and whose discovery of the sex
brings an enthusiastic impulse to love not one but all women.
The dialogue which results [27] is almost of the exact quality,
double-entendres included, as that in the adapted *Tempest*. The
point is made here because it throws light on the tortured question of whether Davenant or Dryden was the assistant in adapting *The Tempest*, and also because Hippolito's ancestry is interesting—interesting for the fact that this callow youth intruded
his naïveté into Shakespeare's play for over a century after
Davenant's death.

While it is impossible to absolve Davenant from complicity
in the Hippolito-Dorinda scenes, one may remark that these
scenes are not so dreadful as horrified commentators have painted
them. The humor hinges upon Hippolito's insusceptibility to
the idea that ardor toward the opposite sex must be particular
not general, and unless the collaborators be accused of thus making an insidious plea for free love, their guilt diminishes to the
writing of a few—a remarkably few—ribald speeches. Pepys
considered this "the most innocent play" that ever he saw, and
compared with many Restoration comedies, it is innocent indeed. The real cause of our distaste is not inherent in the new
scenes but the fact that they adumbrate the idealistic purity of
Shakespeare's original conception of Miranda; however, we
should not be thinking of the original play. Davenant, this
adaptation notwithstanding, was the least salacious of writers;
his single subsequent work, *The Man's the Master,* for all it
was written in 1668, by which time the Restoration stage had forgotten its resolution to be well behaved, compares well with the
prevailing cleanliness of that Spanish dramatic literature which
provided its ultimate source.

On the whole the addition of Hippolito and Dorinda to *The
Tempest* is less disconcerting than the new rôle of Prospero.
He is eclipsed along with many of his most poetic speeches.
Our revels now are ended . . . and the enchanted lines which

---

[27] See especially the dialogue in Act II, Scene I.

follow have completely disappeared—which brings us to the
final and most crucial category of Davenant's alterations. Even
those scenes least altered from Shakespeare so far as context is
concerned, those in *Macbeth* for instance, have undergone a
change in their very essence, owing to—and this is a matter quite
apart from the modernization of grammar and vocabulary—a
thoroughgoing revision of their language. Absolute clarity was
the desideratum with the adapter, and as a result the abstract
and lyrical passages, those most figurative and imaginative, in a
word most Shakespearean, were recast, abbreviated, or completely
excised. A good illustration is offered by the first lines in Act I,
Scene VII, of the original *Macbeth:*

> If it were done when 'tis done, then 't were well
> It were done quickly; if the assassination
> Could trammel up the consequence, and catch
> With his surcease success; that but this blow
> Might be the be-all and the end-all here,
> But here, upon this bank and shoal of time,
> We'd jump the life to come. But in these cases
> We still have judgement here; that we but teach
> Bloody instructions, which being taught, return
> To plague the inventor; this even handed justice
> Commends the ingredients of our poison'd chalice
> To our own lips.

These lines, with their obscurity but infinite suggestiveness, are
transformed by Davenant into:

> If it were well when done, then it were well
> It were done quickly; if his death might be
> Without the death of nature in myself,
> And killing my own rest, it would suffice,
> But deeds of this complexion still return
> To plague the doer, and destroy his peace.

In which the only virtue is lucidity. When there was not the
most remote chance of the original language being misunder-

stood, Davenant was apt to retain it.   Note where the alterations
cease in the following redaction:

> To-morrow, to-morrow, and to-morrow
> Creeps in a stealing pace from day to day,
> To the last minute of recorded time,
> And all our yesterdays have lighted fools
> To their eternal homes: out, out, that candle!
> Life's but a walking shadow, a poor player
> That struts and frets his hour upon the stage,
> And then is heard no more. It is a tale
> Told by an idiot, full of sound and fury
> Signifying nothing.

To present one more illustration, this time from the adaptation
of *Measure for Measure,* Davenant was dubious of the perspicuity
of

> . . . make the angels weep; who, with our spleens,
> Would all themselves laugh mortal.

so he wrote,

> . . . make angels laugh
> If they were mortal, and had spleens like us.

Which is clear, but distressingly flat. We must confess, too,
that in these illustrations we do not see the process of revision
at its very worst.

It may seem an impeachment of Davenant's judgment that he
put himself to such pains to make things easy for what is popu-
larly conceived to have been a brilliant audience. We must remind ourselves, however, that there is a difference between social
and intellectual brilliance, and that Shakespeare today would have
to suffer drastic revision were he to be presented for the exclusive
edification of the season's débutantes and their escorts. The
Restoration audience was in all ways different from the Eliza-

bethan. In the first place the Elizabethan audience was *en rapport* with the Elizabethan playwright. An age can inspire those who receive as well as those who give. And just as Shakespeare, for all he used them so adventurously, never used words not current in his day, so we may be sure he never wrote lines which could not be apprehended by the vast majority of his auditors. Even if that bit of intellectual snobbery holds true—and I very much doubt that it does—that clowning and word plays were interpolated to placate the groundlings, who could not understand the finer passages of the plays (directed at the balconies), the fact remains that the Elizabethan groundlings, rowdy though they may have been, had a capacity for wonder, and a reverence born of their simplicity, which gave the playwrights latitude. The Restoration pit aped the ennui of the boxes; the minority of good minds in the boxes were enervated by their own cleverness. Shakespeare's audience was a sifted one, and high and low alike came to the Globe because they preferred good plays to bear-baiting; we must not let our conception of the Elizabethan audience be shaped too exclusively by satirical pamphlets written by dramatists who were embittered by the peonage forced upon them by Henslowe. The Restoration audience was also a sifted one, but in an entirely different way. People came to Lisle's Tennis Court because the theatre had become fashionable; they came to pass the time, to display themselves, to gape at the King, to ogle the ladies—at best, passively to suffer themselves to be amused. As a group their capacity to understand or to admire (in the literal sense) was small. By the lines

> . . . that but this blow
> Might be the be-all and the end-all here,
> But here, upon this bank and shoal of time,
> We'd jump the life to come. . . .

they would have been neither enlightened nor impressed. The manager of the Duke's House knew his audience better than we do.

Once Davenant had embarked upon the task of revising Shakespeare's language, he did not know where to stop, and at times seemed to prefer jejune lines of his own even when the original was clear. It may be argued that a true literary artist should have been too sensible of lyrical perfection to alter or delete some of Shakespeare's finest passages. What then of John Dryden, certainly a true literary artist, and of all Restoration authors the one best equipped to perceive the poetic delicacy of *The Tempest,* who not only obliterated the Ferdinand-Miranda idyll, but in so doing "never writ anything with more delight?" And Dryden's creative star was ascending, Davenant's had set. The most recent and most voluble writer on the adaptations says,

How this Laureate [Davenant], whose technique could change "After Lifes fitful Feuer, he sleepes well" into "He, after life's short feavor, now sleeps: Well," ever managed to achieve "The lark now leaves his watery [sic] nest," one of the finest aubades in English, is a question I confess still troubles me.[28]

If there were anything truly puzzling in such discrepancies, an admirer of "The Solitary Reaper" would find in some of Wordsworth's *Ecclesiastical Sonnets* matter for eternal bewilderment. Different times of life and different occasions bring changes in a man's work.

It is the occasion, after all, which explains and condones Davenant's adaptations. Not himself *of* the Restoration, he was living *in* the Restoration, and was now first and always a playhouse manager. He was grappling financial disaster by pleasing one of the most difficult audiences the theatre has ever known. Any poet would become (or soon wish he had become) a mechanic under the circumstances. There has been a singular reluctance to concede Davenant *excellence in the quality he professed.* Whatever their losses in other respects, the plays he adapted lost nothing in theatrical effectiveness, a fact proved by their con-

[28] H. Spencer, *op. cit.,* p. 174.

temporary and subsequent success. Those who in 1775 [29] considered *The Man's the Master* the only one of Davenant's plays
that had been acted for many years did not realize how much
of Davenant they had been applauding while witnessing Shakespeare. Some of his additions to *Macbeth* and *The Tempest*
actually penetrated into the acting versions of the nineteenth
century.[30]   Of course this is to be deplored, but we should not
hold one individual responsible for the delinquencies of an age.

Davenant had not the sacerdotal reverence for Shakespeare
which is the unfortunate concomitant of modern enlightenment.
We are schooled to appreciate Shakespeare; then, after adding
cubits unto our stature by achieving, in part, that appreciation,
we become very pharisaical about the whole business.   Davenant
had a spontaneous love for Shakespeare.   No learned commentator of our day has given more incontestable proof of esteem for
the greatest of poets than the man who in 1660 petitioned the
Lord Chamberlain that some of his greatest plays might be presented by the Duke's Men.

[29] John Genest, *op. cit.,* V, 513.

[30] I am not, as in other instances, giving the extensive stage histories of
these two plays. These may be found in Professor Odell's *Shakespeare from
Betterton to Irving,* and in similar works.

XI

FAME

Fame, like Time, only gets a reverence by long running, and like a River, 'tis narrowest where 'tis bred, and broadest afarr off.—POSTSCRIPT TO GONDIBERT.

"THE desire of Fame," confessed William Davenant, "made me a Writer." It was an honest avowal dictated by his personal observation that "Men are chiefly provok'd to the toyl of compiling books, by love of Fame, and often by officiousness of Conscience, but seldom with expectation of Riches." [1] His largest measure of fame, his *little taste of Eternity,* to use his own keen phrase, came during his lifetime, and when he compared this thing he desired so much to a river," narrowest where 'tis bred, broadest afarr off," he never thought of those rivers which dwindle as they flow across thirsty sands. The river of his fame has trickled on, widening here and there in shallow basins, but finding its course through the years to lie usually across hot and hostile deserts. As time passes, the truly great are taken on trust, and the insignificant are accorded the immunity of silence. But Davenant was neither great nor insignificant, and he has remained unaffirmed but unforgotten. Each age has viewed him through its own spectacles, distorted, diminished, in a few cases even enlarged, but very rarely as he really was. No writer has been more indulged by the patronizing, none more often haled to the bar of the inquisitorial. His reputation,

---

[1] *Preface to Gondibert,* Folio, 1673, p. 12.

contemporary and ensuing, forms a spectacle of the vagaries of critical opinion.

To those for whom poets, even poets of centuries past, are still human beings, it will be pleasing to notice how highly he was esteemed while he still lived. The decade preceding the Civil Wars was the period of his ascent. Nearly every year of these ten saw a new Davenant quarto upon the bookstalls, a new Davenant play at Blackfriars, the Cockpit, or the Globe, a new or revived Davenant masque or play in the royal quarters at Whitehall and Hampton Court. During the wars, publication of his works, piratical or otherwise, continued to appear in London. During the Interregnum, *Gondibert* and the presentation and publication of his "operas" kept his name before the public. At the Restoration, his theatre, the early vogue of his revived plays and dramatic adaptations, and a new tide of publications kept his reputation fresh. For part of this last period, some of his plays were still popular at court, and viewing the Caroline and early Restoration periods as a whole, we make the interesting discovery that supremacy in entertaining royalty belonged, first, to Ben Jonson, second, to Beaumont and Fletcher, third, to William Shakespeare, and fourth, to Sir William Davenant.[2] In 1643 the custom of the court to view plays on Sunday provoked a Roundhead jibe linking the names of Jonson and Davenant as a pair of comical divinities.[3]

The official recognition of Davenant as Jonson's successor as court poet toward the end of the pre-war period awakened some criticism,[4] but the majority recognized that there was none better qualified than he to perform the specialized duties of the post. However, since the appointment offers no proof of esteem outside the narrow circle of Whitehall, we must ignore it in determining his wider popularity. We must also ignore the eulogistic verses of such talented friends as Habington, Carew, Suckling, Cowley, and Waller, for those acquainted with the

---

[2] Computed from the lists in M. S. Steele, *Plays and Masques at Court.*
[3] *Mercurius Britanicus,* No. 12, p. 89; cf. *Calendar S. P. D.,* 1641–43, p. 566.
[4] Corser, *Collectanea,* Part 8, p. 288.

commendatory poems of the era realize how much good nature and how little honest opinion often went into the making of them. There still remains a body of impartial evidence of esteem too large to exhaust. Davenant won the voluntary praise of savants such as Richard Whitelock,[5] of poets such as Henry Vaughan,[6] of lovers of *belles-lettres* such as John Eliot.[7] In 1645 the author of *The Great Assises Holden in Parnassus* extolled "His raptures brave, and laur'ate worthiness."[8] Samuel Sheppard was of the opinion that if Shakespeare's *Othello* or Jonson's *Catiline* were placed beside Davenant's *Albovine,* they "would lose their luster."[9] We could scarcely demand more enthusiasm than that.

There is a mistaken notion somewhat hard to dislodge that the nineteenth century really discovered Shakespeare; actually the middle seventeenth century was quite aware of his superiority and of that of Jonson and Fletcher. It became more and more the custom to number Davenant among the select few worthy to be listed with this great triumvirate. He was so dignified in the prologue to *The Famous Tragedy of King Charles I,* 1649; in Edmund Gayton's *Festivous Notes upon Don Quixot,* 1654; in Sir Aston Cokaine's *Præludium to Mr Richard Brome's Plays,* 1653–58; and in other works composed before and after the Restoration.[10] In the 1660 edition of Sir Richard Baker's *Chronicle of the Kings of England,* Davenant is mentioned as one of the fifteen literary men who adorned the reign of Charles I and "not only far excelled their own Countreymen, but the whole World besides." In the 1674 edition of the work the group is cut down to eight members, but Davenant's name not only was allowed to remain, but was prominently featured.[11]

[5] *Observations on the present manners of the English;* cf. Maidment & Logan's edition of Davenant, I, xix.

[6] *Vaughan's Works,* I, pp. 64–65.

[7] *Poems or Epigrams . . .,* 1658; cf. Corser, *Collectanea,* Part 6, p. 340.

[8] *Spenser Society Publications,* XL, 20.

[9] *Epigrams . . .,* 1651; cf. *Jonson Allusion Book,* p. 295.

[10] *Jonson Allusion Book, passim.*

[11] *Ibid.,* p. 321.

It is true that many who professed the greatest admiration for the poet also jested about his nose, but that was the *humour* of the century. It is also true that *Gondibert* was greeted with an outburst of ridicule, but this came from an unusually vocal few. With the majority the poem found favor, and while the two editions of 1651 were sufficient for the buying demand until the Davenant folio appeared, there were many readers, with some of whom it rivaled the vogue of the new French *romans de longue haleine.*[12] The wits who attacked *Gondibert* were the very ones whose spirit came to dominate the court of Charles II. It was the royal circle which first took Davenant up as a poet, and it was the royal circle which first dropped him. The declining popularity of his plays during the last few years of his life was a result of the fact that the Restoration stage was becoming almost purely a court diversion, and not a result of a universal attitude.

The poet's literary prestige endured with a wide circle well into the Restoration. In 1675 Edward Phillips, nephew of Milton, wrote that Davenant was "a very large sharer in the poetic fame of the present age . . . and of no less a memory for the future, for the great fluency of his wit and fancy; especially for what he wrote for the English stage." About *Gondibert* Phillips was more equivocal, remarking that it was "the best of heroic poems, either ancient or modern, in the judgement of Mr. Hobbs; a learned man indeed, but in some other of his opinions supposed to have been proved fallible" [13]—skilful *obiter dictum* from one who had a family interest in that other narrative poem, *Paradise Lost*. Still *Gondibert* retained many admirers; in 1683 *The Grecian Story* was written, avowedly in imitation of it.[14] In 1691 a correspondent to *The Athenian Mercury,* shyly inquiring "Who in your opinion deserves the Title of the best Poet that ever was?" was referred to Chaucer, Jonson, Shakespeare, Milton,

---

[12] Edmund Gosse, *From Shakespeare to Pope,* p. 142n.
[13] *Theatrum Poetarum Anglicanorum,* p. 20.
[14] *Term Catalogues,* II, 47.

Cowley, Waller, and finally Davenant who "had a great genius" and whose *Gondibert,* in the opinion of the editor, should be read by everyone.[15] William Winstanley considered Davenant "one of the Chiefest of Apollo's sons," [16] and Gerard Langbaine, first of the really helpful students of drama, spoke of his "eternal fame" and vouched for the great success of his plays upon the stage and in print.[17] As late as 1694 he was once more listed in the royal succession of Shakespeare, Jonson, etc., and by as responsible a commentator as James Wright.[18]

Of course there is nothing in all of this that can be reckoned as genuine literary criticism. Davenant's admirers simply praised him, and his disapprovers, relatively few in number, simply condemned him. Among the satirists Flecknoe came nearest to supporting his attack with reasons, and he gave only a sentence or two, to the effect that the poet's style was over-parenthetical and too figurative.[19] As the century approached its end, however, the new critical methods coincident with the neo-classical impulse which Davenant himself had helped to foster were turned in his direction. The two leading critics of their day, John Dryden and Thomas Rymer, both considered him.

Dryden's criticism, which cannot properly be termed neo-classical, was analytical and concrete. His opinions of *The Siege of Rhodes, Gondibert,* and their versification have already been mentioned. The point remains to be made that this great man, curiously enough, always spoke of his predecessor in the tone of a humble disciple. In describing his part in revising *The Tempest,* he says, "I am satisfied I could never have received so much honour, in being thought the authour of any poem, how excellent soever, as I shall from the joining of my imperfections with the merit and name of Shakespeare and Sir William Davenant." [20] When forced to express a theory of heroic poetry

---

[15] *Jonson Allusion Book,* p. 423.
[16] *Lives of the Most Famous Poets,* 1687, p. 185.
[17] *Account of the English Dramatick Poets,* 1691, p. 115.
[18] *Country Conversations,* pp. 3, 16.
[19] *Sir William D'Avenant's Voyage to the Other World,* 1668.
[20] *Preface to The Tempest,* 1669, III, 107 (Scott's edition of Dryden).

contrary to Davenant's, he says, "I am sorry I cannot discover my opinion of this kind of writing, without dissenting much from his, whose memory I love and honour. But I will do it with the same respect of him, as if he were now alive, and overlooking my paper while I write." [21] Langbaine considered this respectful attitude on Dryden's part very remarkable, and a final proof of Davenant's greatness, for with Dryden, as he maliciously put it, "the Commendation of his Predecessors is seldome the Subject of his Pen." [22]

There is so much in Davenant that must have appeared ill from Dryden's point of view that it is probable he allowed his personal affection for a deceased friend to curb his critical impulses. It was left to Thomas Rymer to wield over Davenant the bludgeon of "Common Sense." Rymer did not concern himself with the plays, for in criticizing the older drama he went for larger game, and bagged and trussed up Shakespeare. It was the epic in the Davenant folio which he condescended to touch upon, and his discussion of it has the delightful particularity which makes Rymer so much more interesting than much better critics. A dozen details offend him. "His heroes are all Foreigners," he exclaims; "He cultivates a Countrey that is nothing akin to him; 'tis *Lombardy* that reaps the honour of all." He dislikes the way the poem begins—"with the praises of *Aribert,* when the Title had promised a *Gondibert.*" And so he continues. Finally he concludes, "After all . . . his thoughts are great, and there appears something *roughly Noble* throughout this fragment." [23] Rymer's is distinctly a dissenting voice in the seventeenth-century comment upon Davenant; yet it is well to conclude this epoch in the career of the poet's fame with him. What he says is amusing, and some of it is shrewd and just, but it is all dominated by the bigotry of the classicist. Davenant had committed the crime of departing from models. The mixture

[21] *An Essay of Heroic Plays,* 1672, I, 150 (W. P. Ker, Ed.).
[22] *Op. cit.,* p. 115.
[23] *Preface to the Translation of Rapin's Reflections* . . . , 1674, II, 168–70 (J. E. Spingarn, Ed.).

of superiority and patronage in Rymer's tone sets the key for the treatment of Davenant during the eighteenth century.

2

Fame's Twilight, if we may borrow the phrase, descended upon the works of Davenant during the Age of Pope. His plays disappeared from the stage never to return, and the repute of *Gondibert* died of inanition amidst the brilliancies of the English Augustans. This era had little time for poetry other than its own, but it cherished as an inheritance from the older poets anything in the nature of scandal. It is not surprising that the Shakespeare-Davenant legend was circulated more industriously than at any other time, before or since.

Aubrey's *Lives,* in which the story of illegitimacy seems to have had its birth, was still in manuscript, and Wood, Winstanley, Langbaine, and other authors had ignored this Restoration gossip. It was in Charles Gildon's edition of Langbaine, 1699, that there first appeared in print any innuendo concerning Shakespeare and the Davenants. Thereafter the story developed rapidly. In 1709 Hearne noted that Shakespeare was William Davenant's godfather, and "in all probability he got him." In 1719 the scandal was countenanced in Giles Jacobs' *Poetical Register,* and in 1730–44 Spence added it to his record of conversations with Pope, and to his collection of anecdotes. William Oldys was also careful to preserve the tidbit, and in 1749 Chetwood printed it in his *General History of the Stage,* having first verified it by a bit of original research: He looked at Davenant's portrait and noted that "The features seem to resemble the open countenance of Shakespeare. . . ." [24]

An anecdote linked itself to the story—to the effect that once, as a child, Davenant was asked whither he was running in such haste; when he replied that it was to greet his godfather, Shakespeare, he was cautioned not to take the name of God in vain.

[24] J. O. Halliwell-Phillipps, *Outlines,* II, 44.

The jest was actually one of some antiquity, and in its generic form had already been printed a century before, only in that case the boy was not Davenant, and the godfather was not Shakespeare but "Digland the gardiner." [25]   (So far as I know it has not yet occurred to anyone to use this as proof that a mysterious Mr. Digland was really the author of Shakespeare's plays.)   There also grew up quite a cycle of anecdotes relating to Davenant's nose, featuring an old woman who blessed his eyesight because he would never be able to wear spectacles, etc. One of these melancholy jokes penetrated into *Joe Miller's Jest-book*—let us leave it undisturbed.   In 1753 Theophilus Cibber had the grace to rebuke the scandal-mongers of his generation, remarking with pardonable sarcasm that in the days of Shakespeare and Jane Davenant "adultery was not the fashionable vice." [26]

The limited attention which the poet's works received during this half century was confined to his heroic poem.   Alexander Pope was generous enough to concede that, while it was a poor thing on the whole, there were some good things in it.[27] T. Blackwell, the younger, professor of Greek at Aberdeen, gave it a word of praise, but observed that to write an epic without employing the usual epic machinery was "like lopping off a man's limb, and then putting him upon running races." [28]   The general attitude of the neo-classicist was summed up by James Granger when he called *Gondibert* "a string of Epigrams" and maintained that its author "when he strayed from Homer deviated from Nature." [29]

The neo-classical point of view was maintained in modified form during the middle of the century.   By far the most interesting criticism that *Gondibert* evoked appeared in Bishop Hurd's

[25] In the works of John Taylor, the Water-Poet, 1630; cf. Halliwell-Phillipps, Outlines, II, 43.

[26] *Lives of the Poets of Great Britain and Ireland*, II, 64.

[27] *Library of Literary Criticism*, II, 218.

[28] *Enquiry into the Life and Writings of Homer*, 1735, p. 141.

[29] *Biographical History of England*, 1769–74, p. 43.

Dissertation on Poetical Imitation (c. 1766). In summing up a long case against the poem, the virtues of which he willingly concedes, the Bishop says,

Davenant's "studious affectation of originality" lost him the possession of what his large soul appears to have been full of, a true and permanent glory; which hath ever arisen, and can only arise, from the unambitious simplicity of nature; contemplated in her own proper form, or, by reflexion, in the faithful mirror of those very models he so much dreaded.[30]

As genuine and as closely reasoned as the essay is, it reveals the bias of a critic with rigid preconceptions, and with the fatal habit of identifying Nature with the practice of the Ancients; it belongs with Hurd's *Sermon against Enthusiasm and Bigotry* and not with his *Letters of Chivalry and Romance*. Other critics expressed their approval of Hurd's verdict. Vicesimus Knox considered the poem entirely unworthy; however, since he forestalled Macaulay by saying that the "honour of English literature" would best be served if "most of the poetical productions which were admired in the reign of Charles should now be consigned to everlasting oblivion," he can scarcely be said to have viewed *Gondibert* with an open mind.[31] Doctor Johnson gave the poem the larger reproof of never discussing it at all, although he considered Davenant to be Dryden's favorite author.[32]

Gondibert was treated as suspect, but it was at least occasionally read. Such was not the case with Davenant's plays. One of his adaptations was revived late in the century, and this, *The Wits,* and one of the masques were reprinted; all the rest were utterly neglected. Such compendiums as those published by Cibber,[33] Reed,[34] and Dibdin[35] praise the plays, but simply because they

---

[30] Richard Hurd, *Works,* II, 235–41.
[31] *Essays Moral and Literary,* III, 463.
[32] *Life of Dryden,* Napier's edition, I, 439.
[33] *Op. cit.*
[34] *Biographia Dramatica.*
[35] *Complete History of the London Stage.*

had been praised by Gerard Langbaine, and plagiarism was the habit of the times. With the possible exception of Andrew Kippis' *Biographia Britannica* (which contains as complete a biographical notice of Davenant as any that has been written since), I know of no eighteenth-century work whose author proves that he has read Davenant's plays.

At the turn of the century, and as a result of the Romantic Movement, *Gondibert* brought Davenant some faint afterglow of fame. As early as 1756 the Reverend William Thomson of Queen's College, Oxford, had paid the poem the compliment of fashioning a tragedy upon it.[36] In 1773 Doctor Aikin and Mrs. Barbauld published a series of selections from it with a running commentary of enthusiastic praise.[37] Hurd's animadversions were not suffered to go unanswered. In 1787 Henry Headley gave expression to the growing revolt against neo-classicism:

What right have we . . . to be offended at not finding the critical acts passed by Aristotle originally, and re-echoed by Bossu and the French critics, rigidly observed, when it was the author's professed intention to write without them? We may, nearly with the same propriety, accuse Shakespeare for not adhering to the unities. It was Davenant's intention to make an experiment.[38]

There is justice here, and in the author's golden sentence, "After all, it seems but candid to examine every work by those rules only which the author prescribed for himself. . . ."

Davenant found a defender in that other literary Quixote, Sir Walter Scott. In 1805, he wrote, "*Gondibert* . . . has, no doubt, great imperfections, but it intimates everywhere a mind above those laborious triflers, who called that Poetry which was only verse; and very often exhibits a majestic, dignified, and manly simplicity. . . ."[39] The author, in Scott's opinion, was

[36] *Gondibert and Bertha;* cf. Maidment and Logan, *op. cit.,* I, xlix.
[37] J. and A. L. Aiken, *Miscellaneous Pieces in Prose,* pp. 154–89.
[38] *Select Beauties of Ancient English Poetry,* I, xlviii–xlix.
[39] *Life of John Dryden* (prefaced to Scott's edition of Dryden's works), I, 40–41, 50–51.

hampered by the age in which he lived, and by the practices of the Metaphysical school, but he "abridged, if he did not explode, the quaintness of his predecessors." Another, and a more zealous, admirer of the poem was Isaac Disraeli. He hailed Davenant as a true romantic poet, and pleaded the justice of recognizing the excellences of a work, whatever its faults (of which he himself was quite aware) might be: "The critics are marshalled on each side, one against the other, while between these formidable lines stands the poet, with a few scattered readers, but what is more surprising . . . the poet is a great poet, the work imperishable!" [40] The new impetus thus given the reputation of *Gondibert* endured for several years. Several editors of selections from the British poets reprinted the poem in whole or in part, and in 1820 a review similar to that by Aikin and Barbauld was published in *The Retrospective Review*.[41] For a time Davenant emerged from utter obscurity.

The dramatic works still remained unread. The Davenant folio seems not to have fallen into the friendly hands of Charles Lamb, and the plays received no comprehensive reading until they engaged the attention of the more thorough but less inspired John Genest.[42] *Gondibert* itself was not received with unmixed cordiality during the height of the Romantic Period. Poised against Scott, Disraeli, and the rest were two such redoubtable critics as Augustus Schlegel and William Hazlitt, the first of whom lightly consigned all of the poet's works to a "merited oblivion" and the second of whom decreed that each part of *Gondibert* contained something, but the poem as a whole amounted to nothing.[43] Even in that sympathetic era Davenant could not escape, at the hands of the militant romanticists, a few critical brickbats.

[40] *Quarrels and Calamities of Authors* (1812–13), II, 237.
[41] Volume II, pp. 304–24.
[42] *Op. cit.*
[43] *Library of Literary Criticism,* II, 218.

3

The revival of interest in the older English poets had one un-calculated effect upon the dramatist's reputation later on. In the *Prolegomena* to Malone's edition of Shakespeare, and else-where, there had been printed Aubrey's manuscript account of Davenant's life, and Aubrey had been very brisk in his treat-ment of the accident to Davenant's nose. The intimacy was not destined to recommend the poet to Victorian England. In 1833 the popular Lucy Aikin pointed him out as a stigma upon the Caroline court: "A princess in any degree more delicate than Henrietta must have shrunk with loathing from affording her patronage to a man whose licentious conduct had become matter of such very peculiar notoriety." [44]

"Victorianism" has been used as a term of reproach so often by our own, in many ways less estimable, age that one hesitates to raise the old hue and cry of prudishness. It is difficult, how-ever, to evaluate a certain class of nineteenth-century criticism without reckoning with the ill-ventilated ideals of the day. "As for *Gondibert*," says Lord Macaulay, "those may criticize it who can read it"; [45] and unless we remember how readily Macaulay's sense of propriety was outraged, we fail to account for this asper-ity. With him, the moral lapses of the Restoration justified the blanket condemnation of its literature, and the moral lapses of an individual could evoke a similar judgment. The more detached critic, Henry Hallam, writing at about the same time as Macaulay, not only could read *Gondibert* but could find much to say for it—among other things (and his intention was not satirical) that it was better worth reading than Phineas Fletcher's *Purple Island*.[46] However, Macaulay's attitude was more representative of the age. During the middle of the century one after another of Shakespeare's contemporaries and successors was rehabilitated by the critics, and it is impossible to explain why Davenant failed

---

[44] *Memoirs of the Court of King Charles the First*, II, 36.
[45] "Dryden," 1828; cf. Library of Literary Criticism, II, 218.
[46] *Introduction to the Literature of Europe* (1837–39), III, 37.

to share some of this attention except by the fact that he was considered the pattern of a seventeenth-century debauchee.

One phase of his literary activity was remembered as a result of the efflorescence of Shakespearean scholarship and criticism. In 1869 Karl Elze wrote an essay upon his works incidental to an analysis of his adaptation of two of Shakespeare's plays,[47] and a number of similar essays, usually Teutonic in authorship, followed. For altering Shakespeare Davenant had been taken to task in his own day[48] and in the eighteenth century,[49] but while it had been apparent then that he had erred, it was apparent now that he had sinned. Elze was not so hard on him as some others have been, but his laurels were not watered by this exposure of his "vandalism." Another natural result of the tremendous activity in Shakespearean scholarship was a revived interest in the story of illegitimacy. The rumor, although deprecated, was constantly alluded to, and in 1879 it reached its apotheosis. During a tour of England, the Comédie Française presented J. Aicard's *Davenant,* a short play originally designed to feature Sarah Bernhardt and devoted exclusively to the subject of the supposed Shakespeare parentage.[50] In St. Martin's Church, Oxford, the bones of Jane Davenant and her pious husband had long rested—one wonders if the sexton heard any rattling in the charnel house. In 1884 Halliwell-Phillipps published his *Outlines of the Life of Shakespeare,* and traced the old legend to its inconsequential sources.

In 1872 Davenant's dramatic works were finally republished, as an item in a series of Restoration playwrights. Unfortunately the collaborators in this work had no prestige as critics and little skill as editors, a statement that can be made with less ungraciousness in view of the fact that they themselves were very severe on old Henry Herringman, the publisher of the Davenant folio. A long and quaintly digressive prefatory memoir was laudatory in

---

[47] *Jahrbuch der Deutschen Shakespeare-Gesellschaft,* IV, 121–159.
[48] See the rimed epistle quoted by L. Hotson, *op. cit.,* p. 247.
[49] Thomas Davies, *Dramatic Miscellanies,* II, 115 ff.
[50] A. W. Ward, *History of English Dramatic Literature,* III, 166n.

tone but little calculated to carry conviction. However, the plays were made accessible, and in a text based upon the quarto editions. A few years later A. W. Ward published his *History of English Dramatic Literature,* in which he devoted considerable space to our dramatist and his works.[51] Although stinting in his praise of the individual plays, Ward conceded Davenant an earnestness of purpose, and a very great historical importance— not only as the chief link between Elizabethan and Restoration drama, but as the one who gave the latter period "the best and truest part of its vitality." It is true that he called Davenant "a limb of Fletcher" and perpetuated the familiar tone of patronage. One sentence will serve as illustration:

Devoid of all higher original genius D'Avenant applied himself, in no vulgar spirit nor without taking full advantage of such lights as were vouchsafed him, to the task of satisfying what to him was the supreme criterion of merit, viz., the most cultivated taste (or what appeared to him such) of his age.

There is an Olympian condescension about this, happily not characteristic of A. W. Ward; Davenant seems to inspire this sort of thing. To about this same period also belongs the comment of David Masson and Mr. George Saintsbury. While Masson was inclined to grow humorous about *Gondibert,* which he described as inducing a "gentle stupefaction," he ranked the author's plays above those of Shirley and next to those of Massinger and Ford; he accredited them with "undoubted power, both humorous and poetical with a remarkable inheritance of that language of light, elevated, profuse, and careless ideality which we recognize as Elizabethan." [52] Mr. Saintsbury also ranked Davenant's plays with those of Massinger, Shirley, and Ford, but he was rather cavalier in his description of the dramatist's versification, quoting for illustration one especially atrocious passage.[53]

[51] *Ibid.,* III, 167 *et passim.*
[52] *Life of Milton,* VI (1880), 276 *et passim.*
[53] *History of Elizabethan Literature,* pp. 419–20.

While these last two critics, like Ward, patronized Davenant, like Ward they expressed reasoned opinions. Such was not the case with one of their distinguished contemporaries. The remarks of Edmund Gosse, the last nineteenth-century critic who need be cited, belong in the category of notorious literary attacks:

There is not a more hopelessly faded laurel on the slopes of the English Parnassus than that which once flourished so bravely around the grotesque head of Davenant. . . . His is the most deplorable collection of verses anywhere to be found, dead and dusty. . . . He is not merely a ponderous, he is a nonsensical writer . . .[54]

Why all this heat? one must ask; and the answer, I believe, lurks in the insinuations of the phrase *the grotesque head of Davenant.* A more elaborated explanation would involve a character analysis of this admirable but not infallible critic. Elsewhere in his works [55] Gosse has an extended and astonishingly fluent discussion of Davenant as one of that quartet (including Waller, Denham, and Cowley) which effected the seventeenth-century classical reaction.

During the last few decades there has been a tendency in comprehensive works on English literature to repeat what had previously been said about Davenant. He has become one of those authors whom it seems safe to condemn, and who serve as a convenient foil when other playwrights are discussed; after comparing certain remarks about Davenant's plays with the plays themselves, one must often pass the lamentable verdict—commented upon but not read. Of course there are exceptions to this rule; Professor F. E. Schelling's *Elizabethan Drama,*[56] 1908, is the first comprehensive work in which Davenant's historical importance is discussed without prejudice to the intrinsic merit of his plays, and without any note of patronage. Professor Schelling's opinion that Davenant should be reëvaluated has inspired

[54] *English Poets,* T. H. Ward, Ed., Vol. II (1892).
[55] *From Shakespeare to Pope,* pp. 117–46.
[56] II, 299–302, 342–48.

the writing of the present book. Several quite recent critics and historians have given the poet fair although very brief consideration.

Twentieth-century comment on Davenant in other than comprehensive works on Caroline and Restoration literature has reflected the scientific trend of modern scholarship. Much attention has been given to his adaptations of Shakespeare, to his part in the development of the heroic plays, to his effect upon the evolution of the theatre building. Very little attention has been given him as an individual playwright. An occasional German dissertation is wrested from his works, usually having to do with the sources of this or that plot, but these, no more than the other variety of studies, lead us to the man himself. Today we are apt to plot the contours of forests or to anatomize single leaves— we are not so apt to look at the trees.

4

It would be ludicrous for a defender of Davenant to approve all that has been said in his favor and to condemn the rest. There is as much distortion in the encomiums of Aiken and Barbauld as in the aspersions of Edmund Gosse. If it were possible to form a homogeneous compound from the several centuries of Davenant criticism, it would be found, once the stain of patronage and the sediment of prejudice were removed, that this composite estimate would be perfectly just. Unfortunately, criticism does not function in this way. Some critics have more reverberant voices than others, and the quiet tone of Henry Hallam does not reëcho like the clarion of Lord Macaulay. Many have failed to read Davenant because they have heard the opinions only of those who have thought him not worth reading. Others, as has been pointed out, have allowed the historical importance of some of his work to obscure the interest of the rest; unlike Massinger, Shirley, and the others, Davenant has never been fully evaluated for his own sake.

The professional literary critic and scholar, however, has not been the sole agency in our poet's obscuration. Owing partly to the effect of biographical anecdotes and partly, I suppose, to the impression given by his unfortunate physiognomy, Davenant, unlike such contemporaries as Suckling and Lovelace, has been utterly lacking in personal prestige. The absence of this protective dignity has given free rein to the impressionistic judgments of the casual reader, and the poet has been a peculiar sufferer from the natural self-satisfaction of each successive generation with its own modes and ideals. The world, their own contemporary world, is so much with most readers that they are intolerant of everything foreign to it. An eighteenth-century reader has just fingered the neat calfskin bindings of the sermons of Doctor Ogden; a nineteenth-century reader has just glanced at the latest ethical dictum of Lady Gough; a twentieth-century reader has just heard his radio sound the long musical note marking exactly one and three-quarter minutes past seven o'clock: Inevitably, as each turns to Davenant, he misses harmony with the things he knows. Davenant was of the mid-seventeenth century and his age gave much of his work a coloration intolerably strange to subsequent ages. Everywhere appear the literary arabesques of the day—florid figures of speech, ill-restrained sentiments, occasional outrageous conceits. If we stop to reflect, however, we must concede that these are simply the creatures of another, perhaps more tropically situated, land, and should provoke no animus. A man might reasonably be shocked to find kangaroos, ostriches, and dingoes cavorting about in his own suburb; yet he should have a certain tolerance for these beasts as part of the fauna of Australia. If a present-day poet were to break out in some of the mannerisms common in Davenant and indigenous to his period, we should be justified in viewing them with some sense of dissatisfaction: In up-to-date books it is our inalienable right to demand up-to-date ephemeralities. In a word, Davenant should be, and has not been, read with a sympathy for and understanding of his times.

This is the only proper way to read. To become very austere
in our definition of literature, and to demand of it absolute universality, is not only to limit our reading to a very narrow shelf
but to lose altogether one of the chief joys to be found in books.
The fact that Davenant, like lesser writers in general, was so
much of his times makes him only more engaging. Not only the
mannerisms but the very mind and character of his generation
found expression in his works. I know of few books which can
bring one into intimate contact with an intensely interesting age
as can the Davenant folio. We leaf through its pages, and find
an abiding charm even in such literary ephemera as the occasional poems. Here is one, "To I. C. Robbed by his Man
Andrew"; it contains no great thoughts, no musical harmonies,
but it is interesting; we should be disconcerted to find it simple,
sensuous, and passionate. We turn a few pages and come upon
an "Elegie on B. Haselrick, slain in's youth, in a Duell."
B. Haselrick? Who was this chivalrous but futile youth? A
few pages on is another elegy, written "When Collonel Goring
was believ'd to be slain at Breda." We do know who Goring
was, and we regret that he was *not* slain at Breda. In 1637 Davenant was calling this man the Philip Sidney of the age! We
read on. Here is a poem on "The Countess of Anglesea lead
Captive by the Rebels at the disforresting of Pewsam." What if
this "fair and spicy Daughter of the Morne" is described as ruin-
ing the national woodlands by causing trees to dance to the tune
of her lilting voice? It is an extravagance to make strong critics
shudder—but the Countess was indubitably a charming woman.
The interest of these things as social history is a legitimate claim
upon our attention. Davenant's works as a whole have other
claims, but the poet's merits as an artist have been discussed in
previous chapters and the present point is made because the degree to which his times are reflected in his works has militated so
strongly against him. The genuine reader, the true lover of
books, has an elastic standard. To Isaac Disraeli no more than
to Edmund Gosse did *Gondibert* seem to have a thrilling plot, or

the power to kindle the emotions; yet these qualities failing, Disraeli found a substitute for them: "The book falls from our hands!" said he. "Yet is there none of which we wish to retain so many single verses."

A tolerance for and an interest in a past age fails to make one type of author tolerable. This is the insincere or uniformly uninspired literary hack whose works are laden not only with the mannerisms of his times but also with the marks of his own trivial personality. Davenant is farther removed from this type than from the true literary genius. As a man and as a writer he deserves respect, and since he has rarely received it, we may conclude upon this note.

Concerning his character, little can be added which is not implicit in the biographical chapters. The more one discovers about his life the more admirable qualities one becomes conscious of. His sociability, his loyal friendliness, his enthusiasm, and his old-fashioned chivalry made him "well affected" in his own day, even among those inclined to look askance at a poet setting up as a man of action. Theophilus Cibber wrote with insight when he called Davenant "an inoffensive, good-natured man" even though the phrase tells but half the story. At times his almost irresponsible aptitude for getting into scrapes, financial and otherwise, in conjunction with his humorousness, his adaptability, and his triumphant amiability, reminds us of a type fairly constant among English men of letters. One thinks of Thomas Dekker, of Richard Steele, of Oliver Goldsmith, of Leigh Hunt. But there was another and more strenuous side to Davenant. His hardihood in action, his tenacity of purpose, his resourcefulness and ingenuity, his fidelity to the arts on one hand and to the King on the other, all speak for a certain resilience of underlying fiber. His proneness to alternate the rôles of poet and adventurer, of moralist and wit, of philosopher and business man, is almost comic; yet it bespeaks a true magnanimity of spirit. He would have made an excellent Elizabethan.

Davenant the writer, like Davenant the man, deserves respect.

He was not, like Milton, a plant strong enough to thrive in any soil, and that he wrote during a period of spiritual and artistic exhaustion is apparent in his works. But as we read, we are never far from evidence of his true artistic talent. A fine thought, a beautiful line, a telling transcript from life often rewards our reading of the most rococo dramatic scene or the most fulsome complimentary epistle. His attitude toward his craft is a reassurance of his worth, and it is on this point that John Dryden has enlightened us:

In the time I writ with him, I had the opportunity to observe somewhat more nearly of him, than I had formerly done, when I had only a bare acquaintance with him: I found him then of so quick a fancy, that nothing was proposed to him, on which he could not suddenly produce a thought extremely pleasant and surprising: and those first thoughts of his, contrary to the old Latin proverb, were not always the least happy. And as his fancy was quick, so likewise was the products of it remote and new. He borrowed not of any; and his imaginations were such as could not easily enter into any other man. His corrections were sober and judicious, and he corrected his own writings much more severely than those of another man, bestowing twice the time and labour in polishing, which he used in invention.[57]

Had Davenant been born a generation earlier, this industrious ardor, together with his "wit and fancy" might have enriched the finest portion of our literature. As it is, he succeeded in his devoted effort to please his contemporaries, and, albeit to a lesser degree, in his desire to leave something that posterity would preserve. Why should he be patronized or despised? The *desire of Fame* made him an author. As critics, we should always remember that those who write from *desire of Fame* are of larger soul than we who write from *officiousness of Conscience*.

[57] Preface to *The Tempest*.

BIBLIOGRAPHY

I

DAVENANT'S WORKS

Collections

The Works of Sr William D'avenant K^t Consisting of Those which were formerly Printed, and Those which he design'd for the Press: Now Published Out of the Authors Originall Copies. London: Printed by T. N. for Henry Herringman, at the Sign of the Blew Anchor in the Lower Walk of the New Exchange. 1673. *folio.* (There are separate title-pages to the various parts, dated 1672. The volume includes Carew's *Cœlum Britannicum,* and omits *Britannia Triumphans, Luminalia, Salmacida Spolia, To the Honourable Knights, etc., The Prologue to His Majesty, Macbeth, The Rivals, The Tempest,* and the works listed in the Addenda.)

The Works of the British Poets, R. Anderson, Ed., London, Vol. IV (1795), pp. 765–874. (Contains *Gondibert, Madagascar,* and selections from the non-dramatic verse.)

The Works of the English Poets, A. Chalmers, Ed., London, Vol. VI (1810), pp. 347–435. (Contains *Gondibert, Madagascar,* and selections from the other non-dramatic poems.)

The Works of the British Poets, E. Sanford, Ed., Philadelphia, 1819–23, V, 125–61. (Contains selections from *Gondibert* and the other non-dramatic poems.)

Select Works of the British Poets, R. Southey, Ed., London, 1831. (Contains *Gondibert,* omitting the preface; and selections from the other non-dramatic poems.)

The Dramatic Works of Sir William D'Avenant, with prefatory

Memoir and Notes, J. Maidment and W. H. Logan, Eds., 5
vols., Edinburgh and London, 1872–74. (Omits *Luminalia,*
and substitutes Shadwell's version of *The Tempest* for the
Davenant-Dryden version.)

Editions of Individual Works

(The dates in brackets indicate approximate time of composition)
[1627] The Crvell Brother. A Tragedy. Imprinted by A. M. for
Iohn Waterson. 1630. 4°.
[c. 1628] The Tragedy of Albovine, King of the Lombards: Printed
for R. M. 1629. 4°.
[1629] The Siege. (Originally The Colonel.) First printed in the
folio.
[1629] The Iust Italian. Printed by Thomas Harper for Iohn
Waterson. 1630. 4°.
[1633–34] 1. The Witts. A Comedie. Printed for Richard Meighen. 1636. 4°.
2. Two Excellent Plays: The Wits, a Comedie: The Platonick
Lovers, a Tragi-Comedie. Printed for G. Bedel, and
T. Collins, 1665. 8°.
3. The Wits. Dodsley's Collection of Old Plays, 1780, Vol.
VIII.
4. The Wits. Scott's Ancient British Drama, 1810, Vol. I.
5. The Wits. Dodsley's Collection of Old Plays, 1825–27, Vol.
VIII.
[1634] 1. Love and Honovr. Printed for Hum. Robinson . . .
and Hum: Moseley. 1649. 4°.
2. Love and Honour, and The Siege of Rhodes, J. W. Tupper,
Ed., *Belles-Lettres Series,* 1909.
[1635] The Temple of Love. A Masque. Printed for Thomas
Walkeley. 1634 [1635]. 4°.
[1635] News from Plymouth. First printed in the folio.
[1635] 1. The Platonick Lovers. A Tragæ comedy. Printed for
Richard Meighen. 1636. 4°.
2. Two Excellent Plays: The Wits, a Comedie: The Platonick
Lovers, a Tragi-Comedie. Printed for G. Bedel, and T. Collins. 1665. 8°.

[1636] The Triumphs of the Prince D'Amovr. A masque Presented by His Highnesse at His Pallace in the Middle Temple, the 24th of Februarie 1635 [1636]. Printed for Richard Meighen. 1635 [1636]. 4°.

[1616?–1637] 1. Madagascar, with Other Poems. Printed by John Haviland for Thomas Walkley. 1638. 12°. Imprimature, 26 Feb., 1637 [1638].

  2. Madagascar, with Other Poems. Printed for Humphrey Mosely. 1648. 12°.

[1638] Britannia Trivmphans: A Masque, Presented at White Hall by the Kings Majestie and his Lords, on the Sunday after Twelfth-night, 1637 [1638]. Printed by Iohn Haviland for Thomas Walkley. 1637 [1638]. 4°. (With Inigo Jones.)

[1638] 1. Luminalia or the Festivall of Light, Personated in a masque at Court By the Queenes Majestie and her Ladies On Shrovetuesday Night 1637 [1638]. Printed by John Haviland for Thomas Walkley. 1637 [1638]. 4°. (With Inigo Jones.)

  2. Luminalia. *Miscellanies of the Fuller Worthies Library,* A. B. Grosart, Ed., 4 vols., 1872, IV, 613–630.

[1638] 1. The Vnfortunate Lovers: a Tragedie. Printed by R. H. and are to be sold by Francis Coles. 1643. 4°.

  2. The Vnfortunate Lovers. Printed for Humphrey Mosely. 1649. 4°.

[1638] The Fair Favorite. First printed in the folio.

[1639] The Distresses. (Originally The Spanish Lovers.) First printed in the folio.

[1640] 1. Salmacida Spolia. A Masque Presented by the King and Queenes Majesties, at White-hall, On Tuesday the 21. day of January 1639 [1640]. Printed by T. H. for Thomas Walkley. 1639 [1640]. 4°. (With Inigo Jones.)

  2. Salmacida Spolia, a Masque. Printed by W. R. Chetwood, Dublin, 1750. 12°. (One of a "Select Collection of Old Plays.")

  3. Salmacida Spolia. *English Masques,* H. A. Evans, Ed., London, 1897. Reprint 1906.

[1641] 1. To the Honovrale Knights, Citizens and Burgesses, Of the Court of Commons assembled in Parliament, 1641. The

humble Petition of William Davenant. London printed,
1641. Single sheet folio.

2. To the Honorable Knights, Citizens, and Burgesses of the
House of Commons, Assembled in Parliament. The
humble Remonstrance of William Davenant, Anno 1641.
Single sheet folio.

[c. 1648–1650] 1. The Preface to Gondibert, An Heroick Poem
Written by Sir William D'Avenant; With An Answer to
the Preface by Mr Hobbes. A Paris, chez Matthiev Gvillemot. M.DC.L. 8° (Prints only a few verses of Poem.
It is the same work as the following.)

2. A Discourse upon Gondibert. An Heroick Poem written by
Sr William D'Avenant. With an answer to it by Mr.
Hobbs. A Paris, chez Matthiev Gvillemot. M.D.C.L.
12°. (Prints only a few verses of poem. Entered in Stationers Register for English distribution, 8 Feb., 1649
[i. e. 1650].

3. Gondibert: an Heroick Poem. Printed for John Holden.
1651. 8°. Title-Page sometimes lacks printer's name and
bears date in roman numerals.

4. Gondibert: an Heroick Poem. Printed by Tho. Newcomb
for John Holden. 1651. 4°. (This is described by the
Huth Catalogue and most bibliographies as the first edition.
However, I have seen a presentation copy sent to Charles
Cotton and inscribed in Davenant's hand, December 1651,
a date so far removed from that of licensing (Nov. 7, 1650)
and that of issue (December, 1650, cf. *Mercurius Politicus,*
Dec. 19–26, 1650, and *Perfect Diurnall,* Dec. 16–23, 1650)
that it suggests the possibility that the octavo appeared
first.

5. The Preface to Gondibert. *Critical Essays of the Seventeenth
Century,* J. E. Spingarn, Ed., Oxford, 1908. Vol. II.

[1656] The First Days Entertainment at Rutland House, by Declamations and Musick: After the Manner of the Ancients.
Printed by J. M. for Henry Herringman. 1657. 16°.
(Copies of this work are variously designated in catalogues
as quartos, octavos, and duodecimos, and there may have
been several issues. The date on the British Museum copy

is altered in a coeval hand to November 22, 1656. Cf.
N. & Q. IV, 8, 495.)

[1656–59?] 1. The Siege of Rhodes. Made a Representation by the
Art of Prospective in Scenes. And the Story sung in Recitative Musick. Printed by J. M. for Henry Herringman.
1656. 4°.

2. Reprint of above. 1659. 4°.

3. The Siege of Rhodes: The First and Second Part. The First
Part being lately Enlarg'd. Printed for Henry Herringman.
1663. 4°.

4. Reprint of above. 1670. 4°.

5. Love and Honour, and The Siege of Rhodes, J. W. Tupper,
Ed., *Belles Lettres Series,* 1909.

[c. 1658] The Cruelty of the Spaniards in Peru. Exprest by Instrumentall and Vocall Musick, and by Art of Perspective in
Scenes, &c. Printed for Henry Herringman. 1658. 4°.

[1658] The History of Sir Francis Drake. Exprest by Instrumentall
and Vocall Musick, and by Art of Perspective in Scenes.
The first part. Printed for Henry Herringman. 1659.
4°. (No second part is extant, unless The Cruelty of the
Spaniards in Peru be so referred to.)

[1659] A Panegyrick to his Excellency the Lord Generall Monck.
Printed for Henry Herringman. 1659. Single sheet folio.

[1660] Poem, upon His Sacred Majesties Most Happy Return to his
Dominions. Printed for Henry Herringman. 1660. 4°.

[1660] The Prologue to his Majesty at the first Play presented at the
Cock-pit in Whitehall. Printed for G. Bedell and T. Collins. 1660. Single sheet folio.

[1661] The Law against Lovers. First printed in the folio.

[1663] Playhouse to be Let. First printed in the folio.

[1663] Poem, to the King's Most Sacred Majesty. Printed for
Henry Herringman. 1663. 4°.

[c. 1663] Macbeth, A Tragedy. Printed for P. Chetwin. 1674.
4°. (Subsequent editions may be found in Shakespeare
bibliographies.)

[1664] The Rivals. A comedy. Printed for William Cademan.
1668. 4°.

[1667] 1. The Tempest, or the Enchanted Island. A comedy.

Printed by J. M. for Henry Herringman. MDCLXX. 4°.
(With John Dryden.)

2. The Tempest or the Enchanted Island. *Shakespeare Adaptations,* M. Summers, Ed., 192.

[1668] 1. The Man's the Master: a Comedy. Printed for Henry
Herringman. 1669. 4°.

2. The Man's the Master. Printed for T. Evans. 1775. 8°.
(With slight alterations by Woodward.)

[c. 1635–1668] Poems on Several Occasions never before Printed.
First printed in the folio.

Addenda

London, King Charles his Augusta, or, City Royal, of the Founders,
the Names and Oldest Honours of that City. 1648. 4° (Ascribed to Davenant in printer's epistle to the reader. This ascription is apparently a fraud.)

Wit and Drollery, Jovial Poems, never before printed. By Sir
J[ohn] M[ennis], Ja[mes] S[mith], Sir W. D., J. D., and other
admirable Wits. 1656. 4° (Second edition 1661. The present
writer has seen only the second edition, which seems to him to
contain no verse by Davenant.)

The English Parnassus. London. 1657. (An anthology including
poems by Davenant.)

The Tragedy of Hamlet Prince of Denmark. Printed by Andr.
Clark, for J. Martyn, and H. Herringman. 1676. 4°. An adaptation attributed to Davenant by H. Spencer.)

The Tempest, or the Enchanted Island. 1674. (This is Shadwell's
operatic version, though it is the one that has been reprinted in
the works of Dryden and of Davenant. See M. Summers,
Shakespearian Adaptations, London, 1922.)

The Seventh and Last Canto of the Third Book of Gondibert.
1685. 8°. (Gondibert continued by Another Hand.)

The New Academy of Compliments, etc. Compiled by L[ord]
B[uckhurst], Sir C[harles] S[edley], Sir W[illiam] D[avenant],
and others, the most refined Wits of the Age. London. 1695.
(Term Catalogues, II, 542. Extant?)

Julius Caesar: A Tragedy. London. 1719. 12°. (An adaptation

spuriously attributed on the title-page to Davenant and Dryden.)
The Half Pay Officers. London. 1720. 12°. (Incorrectly described as an adaptation of Davenant's *Love and Honour*. Actually a farce by C. Molloy, with intercalated scenes from
Davenant's underplot.)

II

MATERIALS: BIOGRAPHICAL, CRITICAL, ETC.

(The following list of books is made up mainly of the sources of
information, other than manuscript, referred to in the footnotes, with
the editions more fully indicated.)

Acheson, A. *Shakespeare's Sonnet Story*, London, 1922.

*Act for The Tryal of Sir Iohn Stowel Knight of the Bath, David
Ienkins Esq; Walter Slingsby Esq; Brown Bushel, William
Davenant, otherwise called Sir William Davenant, and Colonel
Gerrard*, London, 1650. (British Museum: 506.d.9.–102.)

Adams, J. Q. *A Life of William Shakespeare*, New York, 1923.

———. *Shakespearean Playhouses*, New York, 1917.

Aikin, J. and A. L. *Miscellaneous Pieces in Prose*, London, 1773.

Aikin, L. *Memoirs of the Court of King Charles the First*, 2 vols.,
London, 1833.

*Allegations for Marriage Licenses issued by the Faculty Office of the
Archbishop of Canterbury at London, 1543–1869*, J. L. Chester
and G. J. Armytage, Eds., Harleian Society, 1886.

Aubrey, John. *'Brief Lives,' chiefly of Contemporaries, set down
by John Aubrey, between the years 1669 & 1696*, A. Clark, Ed.,
2 vols., Oxford, 1898.

Alumni Cantabrigienses, J. & J. A. Venn, Eds., 4 vols., Cambridge,
1922–27.

Alumni Oxonienses, Early Series, J. Foster, Ed., 4 vols., Oxford,
1891.

Belleforest, François de. *Histoires Tragiques*, Vol. IV, Lyon, 1578.

Benlowes, Edward. *Theophila, or Loves Sacrifice*, London, 1652.

Biographia Britannica, Andrew Kippis et al., Eds., 5 vols., London,
1778–93.

Biographia Dramatica, T. E. Baker et al., Eds., 4 vols., London, 1812.

Blackwell, T. *Enquiry into the Life and Writings of Homer,* London, 1735.

Broadus, E. K. *The Laureateship,* Oxford, 1921.

Brotanek, R. *Die englischen Maskenspiele,* Wien, 1902.

———. "Ein Unerkanntes Werk Sir Will Davenants, *"Anglia Beiblatt,* XI (1900).

Browne, W. H. *George Calvert and Cecilius Calvert, Barons Baltimore,* New York, 1890.

Calendar of the Clarendon State Papers preserved in the Bodleian Library, H. O. Coxe, Gen. Ed., 3 vols., Oxford, 1869–76.

Calendar of Treasury Books, 1669–72.

Calendar of State Papers Colonial, 1574–1660.

Calendar of State Papers Domestic, 1619–23, 1623–25, 1627–28, 1628–29, 1634–35, 1636–37, 1637–39, 1639, 1640, 1640–41, 1641–33, 1644–45, 1645–47, 1650, 1651, 1651–52, 1654, 1655, 1659–60, 1661–62.

Calendar of State Papers Venetian, 1640–42.

Calvert, Cecil. *The Lord Baltamore's Case concerning the Province of Maryland. . . . Unto which is also annexed, a true copy of a Commission from the late King's eldest son to Mr. W. Davenant, to dispossess the Lord Baltamore of the said Province, because of his adherence to this Common-wealth,* London, 1653.

Camden Society Publications.

The Hamilton Papers, S. R. Gardiner, Ed., 1880.

The Nicholas Papers, G. F. Warner, Ed., 4 vols., 1886–1920.

A Selection from the Wills of Eminent Persons, J. G. Nichols & J. Bruce, Eds., 1863.

Verney's Notes of the Long Parliament, J. Bruce, Ed., 1845.

Campbell, K. "Notes on D'Avenant's Life," *Modern Language Notes,* XVIII (1903).

———. "The Source of Davenant's Alboivine," *Journal of Germanic Philology,* IV (1902).

———. "The Source of the Siege of Rhodes," *Modern Language Notes,* XIII (1898).

Cavendish, Margaret, Duchess of Newcastle. *The Life of William Cavendish Duke of Newcastle,* C. H. Firth, Ed., London, 1886.

Certain Verses Written By severall of the Authors Friends; To Be Re-Printed with the Second Edition of Gondibert, London, 1653.

Chester, A. G. *Thomas May: Man of Letters,* U. of Penna. diss., 1931.

Child, C. G. "The Rise of the Heroic Play," *Modern Language Notes,* XIX (1904).

Cibber, T., and Other Hands. *The Lives of the Poets of Great Britain and Ireland,* 5 vols., London, 1753.

Clark, W. S. "The Sources of the Restoration Heroic Play," *Review of English Studies,* IV (1928).

Collections of State Papers.

State Papers of John Thurloe Esq; Secretary, First, to the Council of State, and afterwards to the Two Protectors, Oliver and Richard Cromwell, Thomas Birch, Ed., 7 vols., London, 1742.

State Papers collected by Edward, Earl of Clarendon, 3 vols., Oxford, 1767–86.

John Nalson. *An Impartial Collection of the Great Affairs of State,* London, 1683.

Rushworth's Historical Collections, London, 1721.

Collier, J. P. *History of Dramatic Poetry and Annals of the Stage,* 3 vols., London, 1831.

Corser, T. *Collectanea Anglo-Poetica,* XI Parts, *Chetham Society,* 1860–83.

Cotton, Charles. *The Poems of* ———, J. Beresford, Ed., London, 1923.

Curll, E. *The History of the English Stage . . . by Thomas Betterton,* London, 1741.

Davies, T. *Dramatic Miscellanies,* 3 vols., London, 1785.

Delius, N. "Shakespeare's Macbeth and Davenant's Macbeth," *Jahrbuch der Deutschen Shakespeare-gesellschaft,* XX (1885).

Denham, Sir John. *The Poetical Works of* ———, T. Banks, Ed., Yale University Press, 1928.

Designs by Inigo Jones for Masques and Plays at Court, P. Simpson & C. F. Bell, Eds., Oxford, 1924.

"Designs for the First Movable Scenery on the English Public Stage," *Burlington Magazine,* XXV (1914).

Dictionary of National Biography, L. Stephen & S. Lee, Gen. Eds., 64 vols., 1885–1901. The notice of Davenant, Vol XIV, pp. 101–108, is by Joseph Knight.

Dibdin, C. *Complete History of the Stage,* 5 vols., London, 1800.

Disraeli, Isaac. "D'Avenant and a Club of Wits," *The Calamities and Quarrels of Authors,* 2 vols., New York, 1881.

Dowlin, Cornell. *Sir William Davenant's Gondibert,* U. of Pa., diss., 1934.

Downes, John. *Roscius Anglicanus, or an historical review of the Stage,* M. Summers, Ed., London, no date.

Thorn-Drury, G. *A Little Ark,* 1921.

Dryden, John. *The Works of* ———, Sir W. Scott & G. E. B. Saintsbury, Eds., 18 vols., Edinburgh & London, 1882.

———. *Essays of* ———, W. P. Ker, Ed., 2 vols., Oxford, 1900.

Ehrle, K. *Studien zu Sir Wm. Davenants Tragödien und Tragikomödien,* MS Dissertation, München, 1922; Summary, München, 1922.

Elze, K. "Sir William Davenant," *Jahrbuch der Deutschen Shakespeare-Gesellschaft,* IV (1869).

English Literary Autographs, W. W. Greg, Ed., Oxford, 1925.

Evelyn, John. *Diary and Correspondence,* W. Bray, Ed., 4 vols., London, 1870.

Firth, C. H. "Sir William Davenant and the Revival of Drama during the Protectorate," *English Historical Review,* XVIII (1903).

Fleay, F. G. *A Biographical Chronicle of the English Drama,* 2 vols., London, 1891.

Flecknoe, Richard. *Sir William D'Avenant's Voyage to the other World,* London, 1668. Reprinted in Malone's *Shakespeare,* III, 340–44.

Flemings in Oxford, being Documents selected from the Rydal Papers, 1650–1700, J. R. Magrath, Ed., Oxford, Vol. I, 1904.

Fletcher, J. B. "Précieuses at the Court of Charles I," *Journal of Comparative Literature,* I (1903).

Fuller, M. *The Life, Letters, and Writings of John Davenant, D.D., 1572–1641, Lord Bishop of Salisbury,* London, 1897.

Gardiner, S. R. *History of England from the Accession of James I to the Outbreak of the Civil War,* 10 vols., London, 1894.

———. *History of the Great Civil War,* 4 vols., London, 1886.

———. *History of the Commonwealth and Protectorate,* 3 vols., London, 1897.

Genest, J. *Some Account of the English Stage 1660–1830,* 10 vols., Bath, 1832.

Gentleman's Magazine, 1745, 1850.

Gosse, E. *From Shakespeare to Pope,* New York, 1885.

Grammont, Count. *Memoirs of Count Grammont, by Count Anthony Hamilton,* G. Goodwin, Ed., 2 vols., Edinburgh, 1908.

Granger, J. *Biographical History of England,* London, 1769–74.

Great Assises Holden in Parnassus by Apollo and his Assessours, London, 1645; reprinted in *Publications of the Spenser Society,* XL (1885).

Greville, Fulke, Lord Brooke. *The Works of* ———, 4 vols., Fuller Worthies Library, 1870.

Grimm, H. "Shakespeare's Sturm in der Bearbeitung von Dryden und Davenant," *Fünfzehn Essays,* Berlin, 1875.

Gronauer, G. *Sir William Davenant's Gondibert. Eine literarhistorische Untersuchung,* München, 1911.

Grove's Dictionary of Music and Musicians, H. C. Colles, Ed., 5 vols., New York, 1927.

Hallam, Henry. *Introduction to the Literature of Europe,* Boston, 1854.

Halliwell-Phillipps, J. O. *Outlines of the Life of Shakespeare,* 2 vols., London, 1898.

Harbage, A. *Thomas Killigrew Cavalier Dramatist,* University of Pennsylvania Press, 1930.

Hazlitt, W. C. *Biographical Collections and Notes,* London, 1876–92.

———. *Hand-Book to the . . . Literature of Great Britain,* London, 1867.

———. *General Index,* C. J. Gray, Ed., London, 1893.

Headley, Henry. *Select Beauties of Ancient English Poetry,* 2 vols., London, 1787.

Hearne, T. *Remarks and Collections of* ———, E. E. Doble & D. W. Rannie, Eds., Oxford, 1885, etc.

Henrietta Maria, Queen. *Letters of* ———, M. A. E. Green, Ed., London, 1857.

Herbert, Sir Henry. *The Dramatic Records of* ———, J. Q. Adams, Ed., Yale Press, 1917.

Historical Manuscripts Commission.

(II) Third Report, 1872, Calendar of House of Lords MSS, etc.

(III) Fourth Report, 1873, Calendar of House of Lords MSS, etc.

(IV) Fifth Report, 1876, Calendar of House of Lords MSS, etc.

(VI) Seventh Report, 1879, MSS of Sir H. Verney, etc.

(XV) Tenth Report, 1887, MSS of the Marquis of Abergavenny, etc.

(XXIX) Thirteenth Report, 1891, MSS of the Duke of Portland, Vol. I.

(XXXI) Thirteenth Report, 1892, MSS of the Corporation of Rye, etc.

(XXXVI) Fourteenth Report, 1895, Ormond, MSS.

(XLIII) Fifteenth Report, 1898, MSS of the Duke of Somerset, etc.

(XLV) Fifteenth Report, 1903, MSS of the Duke of Buccleuch, etc.

(LXIII) Sixteenth Report, 1905, MSS of the Earl of Egmont, Vol. I, part I.

(LXX) Seventeenth Report, 1911, Pepys MSS.

(XXIII) Twelfth Report, 1888–89, Coke MSS.

Hoare, Sir Richard Colt. *The History of Modern Wiltshire,* 6 vols., London, 1822–44.

Hooper, E. S. "The Authorship of Luminalia and Notes on some other poems of Sir William D'Avenant," *Modern Language Review,* VIII (1913).

Hotson, L. *The Commonwealth and Restoration Stage,* Harvard Press, 1928.

———. Sir William Davenant, and the Commonwealth Stage, MS diss., Harvard, 1923.

Howell, James. *Epistolæ Ho-Elianæ,* J. Jacobs, Ed., London, 1892.

Hurd, Richard. *The Works of* ———, 8 vols., London, 1811.

Hyde, Edward, Earl of Clarendon. *The History of the Rebellion and Civil Wars in England,* 7 vols., Oxford, 1849.

———. *The Life of* ——— *Written by Himself,* 2 vols., Oxford, 1857.

Illies, G. *Das Verhaeltniss von Davenant's 'The Law against Lovers' zu Shakespeare's 'Measure for Measure' und 'Much Ado about Nothing,'* Halle, 1900.

Incomparable Poem Gondibert vindicated from the Witt Combats of

Four Esquires, Clinias, Dametas, Sancho, and Jack Pudding, The, London, 1655.

Johnson, Samuel. *Lives of the Poets,* A. Napier, Ed., 3 vols., London, 1909.

Jonson Allusion Book, J. F. Bradley & J. Q. Adams, Eds., Yale University Press, 1922.

Journals of the House of Commons.

Journals of the House of Lords.

Knox, Vicesimus. *Essays Moral and Literary,* 3 vols., London, 1787.

Krusenbaum, A. *Das Verhaeltniss von Davenant's Drama The Rivals zu The Two Noble Kinsmen,* Halle, 1895.

Langbaine, Gerard, *An Account of the English Dramatick Poets,* Oxford, 1691.

Lawrence, W. J. *The Elizabethan Playhouse and other Studies,* 2 vols., Stratford-upon-Avon, 1912–13.

Leeds, E. Thurlow. *The Crosse Inn and The Tavern at Oxford,* appended to A. Acheson, *Shakespeare's Sonnet Story.*

Library of Literary Criticism, The, C. W. Moulton, Ed., 8 vols., New York, 1901–1905.

Luttrel, N. *Brief Historical Narration,* 6 vols., Oxford, 1857.

Lynch, K. "Conventions of the Platonic Drama in the Heroic Plays of Orrery and Dryden," *Publications Modern Language Association,* 1929.

Malone, E. *Historical Account of the Rise and Progress of the English Stage,* in *Shakespeare: Plays and Poems,* III (1803).

Masson, D. *The Life of John Milton,* 7 vols., London, 1871–94.

Memorials of the Guild of Merchant Taylors, C. M. Clode, Ed., London, 1875.

Meyers, C. "Opera in England from 1656–1728," *Western Reserve Bulletin,* IX (1906).

Minutes of Parliament of the Middle Temple, C. T. Martin, Ed., 4 vols., London, 1904.

Miscellanea Aulica, T. Brown, Ed., London, 1702.

Morgan, A. "William Shakespeare's Literary Executor," *Magazine of American History,* XVI (1886).

Morgenroth, H. *Quellenstudien zu William Davenants Albovine,* München, 1911.

Musarum Deliciae, or The Muses Recreation, by Sir J. M. and Jas. S., London, 2nd ed., 1656; reprinted in 2 vols., London, 1874.

Musgrave's Obituary, 6 vols., *Harleian Society,* 1899–1901.

Nicoll, A. *A History of Restoration Drama: 1660–1700,* Cambridge, 1923, 2nd. ed., 1928.

———. "The Rights of Beeston and D'Avenant in Elizabethan Plays," *Review of English Studies,* I.

Notes and Queries, Fourth Series, Vols. V & IX.

Odell, G. C. D. *Shakespeare from Betterton to Irving,* 2 vols., New York, 1920.

Ogilby, John. *Fables of Æsop Paraphrased in Verse,* London, 1651.

Oldys, William. "Choice Notes," *Notes and Queries,* Second Series, Vol. XI.

Paulus Diaconus. *History of the Langobards, by Paul the Deacon,* W. D. Foulke, Tr., New York, 1907.

Pecke, Thomas. *Parnassi Puerperium,* London, 1659.

Pepys, Samuel. *The Diary of ———,* H. B. Wheatley, Ed., 10 vols., London, 1893–99.

Phillips, Edward. *Theatrum Poetarum Anglicanorum,* Geneva, 3rd. ed., 1824.

Poems on State Affairs, London, 6th ed., 1716.

Register of Admissions to Gray's Inn, 1521–1889, J. Foster, Ed., London, 1889.

Register of All Hallows Bread Street, Ed. W. B. Bannerman, *Harl. Soc.,* 1913.

Register of St. James Clerkenwell, Ed. R. Hovenden, *Harl. Soc.,* 6 vols., 1884–94.

Register of the scholars admitted into Merchant Taylors School, from A.D. 1562 to 1874, 2 vols., London, 1882–83, C. J. Robinson, Ed.

Registers, Marriage, Baptismal and Burial, of the Collegiate Church or Abbey of St. Peter, Westminster, J. L. Chester, Ed., London, 1876.

Retrospective Review, Vol. II (1820).

Reyher, P. *Les Masques Anglais,* Paris, 1909.

Richardson, W. R. "Sir William Davenant as American Colonizer," *E L H, A Journal of English Literary History,* I, 1934.

Rollins, H. "A Contribution to the History of the English Commonwealth Drama," *Studies in Philology in North Carolina,* Vol. XVIII (1921), and Vol. XX (1923).

Rosbund, M. *Dryden als Shakespeare-Bearbeiter,* Halle, 1882.

Rymer, Thomas. *Fœdera,* 20 vols., London, 1704–32.

Saintsbury, G. *A History of Elizabethan Literature,* London, 1891.

Scarron, Paul. *Les Œuvres de monsieur Scarron,* 2 vols., Paris, 1719.

Schelling, F. E. *Elizabethan Drama,* 2 vols., Boston and New York, 1908.

Schmerback, M. *Verhaltnis von Davenant's "The Man's the Master" zu Scarron's "Jodelet, ou Le Maître valet,"* Halle, 1899.

Selections from the English Poets, T. H. Ward, Ed., London, Vol. II (1892).

Spencer, H. *Shakespeare Improved,* Harvard Press, 1927.

Spingarn, J. E. *Critical Essays of the Seventeenth Century,* 2 vols., Oxford, 1908.

Sprague, A. C. *Beaumont and Fletcher on the Restoration Stage,* Harvard Press, 1926.

Stationers' Register, Transcript of, by Edw. Arber, London, 1875–94. (Continuation by Eyre and Rivington, London, 1913.)

Steele, M. S. *Plays and Masques at Court during the Reigns of Elizabeth, James, and Charles,* New Haven, 1926.

Strafford Papers. See Thomas Wentworth.

Stroup, T. B. "Promos and Cassandra and The Law Against Lovers," *Review of English Studies,* VIII.

Suckling, Sir John. *The Poems, Plays, and other Remains of ——,* W. C. Hazlitt, Ed., 2 vols., London, 1892.

Term Catalogues: 1668–1709 A.D., Edw. Arber, Ed., London, 1903.

Thaler, A. "Thomas Heywood, D'Avenant, and The Siege of Rhodes," *Publications Modern Language Association,* XXXIX (1924).

Three Poems Upon the Death of his late Highnesse Oliver Lord Protector of England, Scotland, and Ireland. Written by Mr. Edm. Waller, Mr. Jo. Dryden, Mr. Sprat, of Oxford, London, 1659.

Townshend, D. *Life and Letters of Endymion Porter,* London, 1897.

Vaughan, Henry. *The Works of* ———, L. C. Martin, Ed., 2 vols., Oxford, 1914.

Villiers, George, Duke of Buckingham. *The Rehearsal,* M. Summers, Ed., Sratford-upon-Avon, 1914.

Visitation of London in 1568, Ed. J. Howard, 1869; *Ibid. in 1634-36,* Ed. J. Howard, 1880.

Walmsley, D. M. "The Influence of Foreign Opera on English Operatic Plays of the Restoration," *Anglia Zeitschrift,* LII (1928).

Ward, A. W. *A History of English Dramatic Literature,* 3 vols., London, 1875.

Warwick, Sir Philip. *Memoirs of the reigne of King Charles I with a Continuation to the Happy Restauration of King Charles II,* London, 1710.

Weber, G. *Davenant's Macbeth im Verhaeltniss zu Shakespeare's gleichnaminger Tragoedie,* Rostack, 1903.

Welsford, E. *The Court Masque,* Cambridge, 1927.

Wentworth, Thomas Earl of Strafford. *Letters and Dispatches,* W. Knowles, Ed., 2 vols., London, 1739.

Whitelocke, Sir Bulstrode. *The History of England or Memorials of the English Affairs,* London, 1713.

———. *Memorials of the English Affairs . . . from the Beginning of the Reign of King Charles the First to King Charles the Second His Happy Restauration,* London, 1732.

Williams, J. D. E. *Sir William Davenant's Relation to Shakespeare,* Strassburg dissertation, 1905.

Winstanley, William. *The Lives of the Most Famous Poets, or the Honour of Parnassus,* London, 1687.

Witt, O. *The Tempest, or The Enchanted Island, a Comedy by John Dryden,* Rostock, 1899.

Wood, Anthony à. *Athenae Oxonienses,* P. Bliss, Ed., 4 vols., London, 1813-20.

———. *Fasti Oxonienses,* P. Bliss, Ed., London, 1815.

———. *"Survey of the Antiquities of the City of Oxford,"* composed in 1661-66 by Anthony Wood, A. Clark, Ed., 3 vols., Oxford, 1889-99.

Wright, James. *Historia histrionica,* in *Dodsley's Old English Plays,* 1874-76, Vol. XV.

———. *Country Conversations,* London, 1694.

INDEX